WATCHING THE WORLD

A Da Capo Press Reprint Series

FRANKLIN D. ROOSEVELT AND THE ERA OF THE NEW DEAL

GENERAL EDITOR: FRANK FREIDEL
Harvard University

WATCHING THE WORLD

By Raymond Clapper

Edited and with a biographical sketch by

MRS. RAYMOND CLAPPER

Introduction by

ERNIE PYLE

DA CAPO PRESS · NEW YORK · 1976

Library of Congress Cataloging in Publication Data

Clapper, Raymond, 1892-1944.
Watching the world.

(Franklin D. Roosevelt and the era of the New Deal)
Reprint of the ed. published by Whittlesey House, London, New York.
Selections from the author's newspaper columns, radio broadcasts, and magazine writings from 1933 to 1944.
1. United States–Politics and government–1933-1945–Addresses, essays, lectures. 2. World War, 1939-1945–United States–Addresses, essays, lectures. I. Clapper, Olive Ewing, 1896-1968. II. Title. III. Series.
E806.C56 1975 320.9'73'0917 75-31817
ISBN 0-306-70730-6

This Da Capo Press edition of *Watching the World* is an unabridged republication of the first edition published in London and New York in 1944.

Published by Da Capo Press, Inc.
A Subsidiary of Plenum Publishing Corporation
227 West 17th Street, New York, N. Y. 10011

Manufactured in the United States of America

Raymond Clapper

WATCHING THE WORLD

Photograph by Life Magazine Photographer Thomas D. M

Raymond Clapper resting on his rock in woods near his home after a walk with his dog "Pepper."

Raymond Clapper

WATCHING the WORLD

Edited and with a biographical sketch by

MRS. RAYMOND CLAPPER

Introduction by

ERNIE PYLE

Whittlesey House

McGRAW-HILL BOOK COMPANY, INC.

London *New York*

WATCHING THE WORLD

This book is produced in full compliance with the government's regulations for conserving paper and other essential materials.

PUBLISHED BY WHITTLESEY HOUSE

A division of the McGraw-Hill Book Company, Inc.

Printed in the United States of America

THIS BOOK IS DEDICATED

to the friends and colleagues
who have formed
the Raymond Clapper Memorial Association;
and who will bestow an annual award
on the Washington newspaper correspondent
whose writings in the previous year
have most perfectly embodied
the ideals of fair and painstaking reporting
and sound craftsmanship
that marked Mr. Clapper's work,
and have contributed most to public enlightenment
and a sound democracy

The editor has taken the liberty of arranging the material in such a way that the chronological order is maintained as far as possible within each chapter. Small liberties have been taken here and there in the wording to effect a more flexible transition. Extreme precaution has been taken throughout not to change the meaning or philosophy.

Ten years of Raymond Clapper's columns, broadcasts, and magazine writings have been combed to supply the material. The effort has been to choose the articles that portrayed his best thought and style yet contributed to a continuous picture of the history of the decade from 1934 to 1944.

INTRODUCTION

There were long faces among the correspondents on the morning we learned that Ray Clapper went to his death in the Pacific. We have all been moved and hurt by the loss of friends many times in this war. We never get calloused to it, but after a while we build up an acceptance of it and cease to be surprised. When the word came of Ray Clapper's death, however, I had to take the day off. I tried to do my regular writing but nothing would come out. My mind was not in Italy.

We had known each other for twenty years. He was always generous and thoughtful of me. Time and again he went out of his way to do little things that would help me and to say nice things about me in his column, and I cannot remember that I ever did one thing for him. Those accusing regrets come when it is too late.

There was nothing flashy nor eccentric nor glittering about Ray. He was a sound man who worked like a dog, was intelligent and honest, and used for the foundation of his writings two things—vast experience and good common sense.

I had known Ray Clapper in his home at Washington and known him bunking down at night under an olive tree in Sicily; known him in London and in the flat spaces of the Middle West. There was something in him so normal, so like other people who live in houses and have families and dogs and fireplaces, that when he came to the wars somehow it always seemed impossible that anything could ever happen to him.

He was in no sense an adventurer. When he flew over the hump to China, went along on the Rome raid, took a close look at the fighting in Sicily or made himself a part of the Marshalls invasion, it wasn't because he yearned for exciting things. He did it because he thought it his duty to inform himself about world events and the viewpoint of our men in the actual combat areas. I know that to be true, because he told me so more than once.

Ray Clapper was blessed with the good things that come to people who are successful. He was accepted by the great; courted by the near-great. And yet he kept on working at terrific tempo, stayed personally just as he always was, and remained cognizant of the little things.

Ray believed in himself, and he avoided that state of mind which might have made it impossible for him to understand the views of others. Over the years he changed from one political viewpoint to another. Occasionally he would state bluntly in print that he had been wrong. But his work was so fully based on hard, factual reporting, and so little on ivory-tower dreaming, that it was bound to be almost always right. His mind was pliable, but his integrity was unshakable. I doubt that he ever wrote a line out of opportunism; I am sure he never wrote a line he didn't believe.

More than anything else he was a crusader for the right of people to think things out for themselves and make their own decisions, and he spent his life giving them information that would help them. People believed what he said because they could sense the honesty in his writing.

This collection of Ray Clapper's work is not only a monument to him. It is an investment in sound thinking. And to newspapermen it should be a perpetual challenge to keep on doing the best we can.

ERNIE PYLE.

In Italy, April 1944.

Contents

Acknowledgments

The contents of this book have been compiled from the published manuscripts of the last ten years of Raymond Clapper's work. The editor wishes to express thanks and make grateful acknowledgment of reprint privileges to the following:

Scripps-Howard Newspaper Alliance
The Washington Post
Life Magazine
Look Magazine
Liberty Magazine
The Reader's Digest
The Forum
The Yale Review
The Crowell-Collier Publishing Co.
Henry Holt and Company, Inc.
Cosmopolitan Magazine
McCall's Magazine
J. Walter Thompson Co.

Raymond Clapper

WATCHING THE WORLD

Biography

MY MOTHER stood at the kitchen window looking down Armourdale's Twelfth Street in Kansas City, Kan. It was an upstairs window because we lived over my father's grocery store. Mother said, "Look at that boy go on that bicycle! That's Ray Clapper. Mark my words, of all the boys in Armourdale he'll probably go fartherest in this world." I was twelve years old at the time, quite uninterested in boys.

A few days later my father treated several of my playmates to a grab in the candy grab bag. Each piece of candy was wrapped in a "fortune." Mine read, "You will marry"—and below that phrase was a picture of a boy on a bicycle.

Ray Clapper had worked hard for the bicycle. His parents were poor; his father at the peak of his earning in a soap factory never made over $18 a week. They lived in a tiny frame house which Will Clapper had built with his own hands on a little piece of land on Scott Avenue that backed up against the railroad tracks. The roundhouse was less than a block away.

Pa Clapper's house was doll-like in size and spotless in cleanliness. The black train engines belched dirt; the factory fires smoked out the sun; a stench of meat killing and packing hung over every rosebush; but inside the Clapper house the curtains were washed weekly and soap was abundantly used. A cherry tree bloomed behind the white fence and a grape arbor hid the chicken run. All this was in marked contrast to the rest of the neighborhood.

Born on a farm in La Cygne (The Swan), Kan., on Memorial Day in 1892, Ray was of the plain people. Dad Clapper was small, stocky, bald-headed, thick of chest and arms. Of Pennsylvania Dutch ancestry, he came from Pennsylvania and Indiana to a small Kansas farm. From there after Ray was born he migrated to Kansas

City to work in factories because he could not earn enough on the farm to raise his only son.

His wife, Julia, was a nice-looking woman with a good mind and a fine sense of humor. She was deafened in early life from neglected ear abscesses. A hard worker, she seldom read even the daily papers.

Every Sunday they went to the Baptist Church. Religion was their whole emotional life and its severest tenets were their way of life. Outside of prayers, sermons, rereading the Bible time and again, they offered little intellectual stimulation to their son but much fundamental advice about honesty and the straight and narrow virtues. Kindly but bigoted, ignorant because of lack of opportunity and education, they feared the outer world. Suspicious of neighbors, they had few friends. They ate simple food; a ten-cent piece of round steak with mashed potatoes and gravy made a meal. They arose before dawn and worked hard.

Dad Clapper died when his son was in Russia. The old man probably didn't even know where Russia was. It is doubtful if he had ever looked inside a geography. But he quoted Bible passages by the hour and devoutly believed a Christian life led straight to a heavenly life "safe in the arms of Jesus."

The little Ray in overalls studied arithmetic in old Morse School, walking 3 miles back and forth. Although there were no books in his home he developed a library of clippings from *The Kansas City Star* Sunday supplement that supplied all the neighborhood students with material for English themes throughout their high-school years. These clippings covered every subject from baseball to geometry, from famous suicides to politics, from actresses to symphonic music. A brilliant student in history, geography, and English, Ray hated languages, mathematics, and science. And no faculty adviser ever persuaded him he needed any truck with Latin.

Ray earned the bicycle in the good old American way—up before daylight delivering newspapers and in summer vacations working in my dad's grocery store. Barefoot he stood before my father asking for a job. He was only eleven, little but strong, with a pallid face under a mass of black, wavy hair. His enormously beautiful gray eyes urgently pleaded for a job. A wagonload of watermelons had been emptied on the sidewalk. "Let's see if you can tote these melons inside," my father said. Young Clapper went at it full steam ahead. But Dad discovered later that probably half of them were ruined by the young man's energy in tossing them about.

Years later, in the first bombing mission over Rome, Italy, Ray recalled the fragile quality of watermelon insides. He wrote, "As soon as we were out of enemy area an amazing quiet settled over the ship. Our copilot, Colonel R. H. Smith of Nashville, asked the waist gunner on the interphone how the watermelons were that the colonel had placed in the ship for cooling (in the stratosphere). The melons were nicely chilled, but when the colonel cut them, back at the field, they had spoiled inside from the jouncing of the plane."

In his adolescent years Ray read everything he could find about his hero, William Allen White, the Emporia, Kan., editor and sage. When he was seventeen he made a pilgrimage to Emporia to see Mr. White and came home fired with the ambition to own a small-town newspaper and wield great influence. He figured out his own method of attainment—to learn to print the paper first. So he got a job as a printer's devil in a small printing establishment owned by the Kellogg sisters. These two cultured businesswomen had great influence over the boy. They lent him books and urged him to go to see the good plays that came to the Orpheum. Through them he began to be interested in the larger world. He became first a printer's devil, then an apprentice, and finally a journeyman with a union card in his pocket.

Two decades later Emil Hurja gave our ten-year-old son a fine printing press and type to set him up in the printing business. He gave it to the boy but, like fathers with electric trains, it was Ray who got the real kick out of the gift. He taught son Peter how to set type and helped him print many dollar boxes of stationery and hundreds of school program folders. Peter pocketed the money from these activities and profited from the training in setting type, spelling, selling, and bookkeeping, but his father had the fun of printer's ink on his hands and the clank of a press in his ears.

After grade-school graduation Ray worked three years before

going to high school at seventeen, when most boys were finishing. He never gave up his printing job; he'd go to classes in the morning, ride the rattling trolley after school to the print shop where he'd work until 6 or 8 P.M., then home to study for next day's classes.

Maybe it sounds dull for an adolescent boy, but the fire within him drove relentlessly. He had fun. He learned to swim with a gang of Armourdale boys in an old creek that fed the Kansas River. He played a little tennis on municipal courts; he tossed a baseball about. But mostly for recreation he walked with a friend, arguing, gossiping, thinking aloud about life, sex, religion, the world.

At the old Central Presbyterian Church we belonged to a progressive group of Christian Endeavorers, vibrant, alive, full of fun and earnestness. We had grand picnics and a few hilarious hayrack rides.

When I was sixteen I fell in love with him at a Sunday evening Christian Endeavor meeting. As the leader for the evening, he sat alone on the little platform, announced the hymns, read the lesson, and opened the discussion. I don't remember the lesson or what he said; I saw only his great eyes looking out of the dark circles of skin that always surrounded them. Afterward he asked if he might walk home with me. I had never walked blocks alone with a boy. Each of us clung to opposite sides of the pavement. He did kid me a little by asking if I still practiced "The Flower Song" on the piano, and said, "The worst part of working in your dad's store was having to listen to you practicing upstairs on that piano every day. It took you a long time to learn to play that piece."

He had learned to play the violin a little so we organized a church orchestra. That gave us a good excuse to spend evenings practicing. What an awful mess we made out of "Onward, Christian Soldiers" and "In the Gloaming"!

We saw each other daily at school, three times at church on Sundays, and at picnics and parties. My parents began to make formidable noises, saying I was too young to be going steady with anyone. Ray knew what he wanted and was persistent for a year, making a nuisance of himself at our house. The more they objected the

Photograph by D. P. Thomson, Kansas City, Mo.

Olive and Raymond Clapper shortly after their marriage in 1913.

firmer grew his determination. They forbade me to see him or to walk home from church with him.

One Monday morning they threatened to send me to visit relatives far away because he had walked home with me on Sunday night. On the streetcar going to high school Ray said, "Well, let's get married." It was a sunny spring day in March, 1913. I don't think either of us really believed we could get married. Right after our 9 o'clock class we went to the courthouse, three blocks away. I had schoolbooks in my arm but we dashed into the city library and left them on a secluded shelf. We were sure someone would stop us. "Your age?" "Twenty-one," Ray said. "Eighteen," I said. "Do you want to be married by the judge or a minister?" Scared to death, Ray answered, "The judge, I guess." No one questioned our lies about our ages. Ray was actually within two months of twenty-one; I only a little past seventeen. In three minutes we were man and wife, gingerly clutching a marriage license festooned with doves and red roses.

We walked out into the spring sunshine, frightened and shy, and took a streetcar to the big adjoining Kansas City, Mo., where Ray bought a wedding band of gold for me and a tiny diamond engagement ring. He was quite a plutocrat, as he had saved $450 from his printer's earnings.

The tip-off to me, however, about this boy I had married was when he purchased a noon edition of *The Star* with screaming headlines "J. P. Morgan Dies." He forgot all about his trembling bride to read every word about the great financial colossus. We were en route on our honeymoon trip to Excelsior Springs, Mo., a summer resort near Kansas City. As I sat in the interurban train I got mad at his neglect. When he finished his reading he turned to me and said, "Honey, the passing of J. P. Morgan marks the end of an epoch in America. These ruthless fortune makers won't have things all their way much longer. What a story J. P. Morgan made."

After three days we returned to Kansas City and took furnished rooms. Ray started working full time as a printer. Three weeks later we paid $200 of his precious $450 as down payment on a tiny house.

We never lived in that house. Ray came home one night seemingly very angry. I wondered, as I often did over the years, what I could have done to make him so angry. But he wasn't mad at me. Pacing the floor, he finally announced, "We are going back to school. We can never get any place without an education."

The early September days found us walking with knapsacks on our backs to Lawrence, Kan., to attend Kansas University. We had a difficult time matriculating because we had no high-school diplomas. Much work had to be made up. We worked so hard; we had so little. However, Ray was happy, soaking up information, reading, working day and night. We lived in two rooms and did all our own work—cooking, laundry, housework, arising early enough to make the half-hour walk up Mt. Oread to 8 o'clock classes.

We used to be hungry, too, at times. Each Saturday morning we rose at 4 A.M. and walked to the railroad station, sometimes even through snow and sleet, where I caught a train to Kansas City to give music lessons all day to supplement our finances. The second year fortune began to smile upon us when Ray became correspondent for *The Kansas City Star,* which used much university news. Too, he became managing editor of *The Kansan,* the daily paper of the university.

Merle Thorpe, later famous editor of *Nation's Business,* was head of Kansas University's School of Journalism in those days. He recalls, "One time Ray got the president of the university out of bed in the middle of the night to query him on a last-minute news break. The president commented at length, and then politely asked the identity of the metropolitan editor." Ray was taken aback but confessed he was just a journalism student. The president was a kind man but he was a little sour over the interruption to his night's sleep, even as Ray came to be in later years when the telephone never seemed to stop ringing day or night.

During the three years we attended Kansas University we were socially "unacceptable" because we were married and living in a community of four thousand unmarried boys and girls. We did not go to dances, seldom could afford a football game, and were too busy to loaf around the college hot spots. For relaxation we walked and we talked and we played silly games while we worked. When we got mad at each other we wrote indignant notes for our little bulletin board that hung on a screen.

As vacation approached in 1916 Ray corralled a job with *The Kansas City Star*. By autumn Blanchard Michel of the United Press had hired him to go to Chicago to begin his long and valuable press-association apprenticeship.

Chicago, how far away it seemed to our Kansas feet, how wicked, interesting, and glamorous to our Kansas hearts! We had never seen a huge lake of water, a ship, or a skyscraper. We thought we knew about packing plants, foreign populations, slums, and heart-aches. We didn't know about the effete East, as Chicago seemed to us. For a year we soaked up manifold impressions. While Ray worked, I studied social work at Chicago School of Civics and Philanthropy. We lived at Graham Taylor's Chicago Commons. At night we liked to walk along the lake front, talking of famous people who came to the Commons—Jane Addams, Julia Lathrop, Clarence Darrow, Raymond Robins.

We went to art galleries, to concerts (especially if Ray could wangle free seats), to lectures by red socialists, to hear speakers urging United States' participation in the war or against it, to relief rallies for starving Belgians. The war in Europe seemed quite unreal, like a Greek tragedy. We were too concerned with Chicago's poor. We dreamed of finding a cure for poverty. We believed universal education could remedy most evils. We wanted cleanliness of body and soul for all God's children. Carl Sandburg's Chicago poems were meat to our souls.

Child of the Romans

The dago shovelman sits by the railroad tracks
Eating a noon meal of bread and bologna.
A train whirls by, and men and women at tables
Alive with red roses and yellow jonquils,
Eat steak running with brown gravy,
Strawberries and cream, eclairs and coffee.
The dago shovelman finishes the bread and bologna,

Washes it down with a dipper from the water-boy,
And goes back to the second half of a ten-hour day's work
Keeping the road-bed so the roses and jonquils
Shake hardly at all in the cut glass vases
Standing slender on the tables in the dining cars.

Yes, even though "Chicago, the Hog Butcher for the World" taught us how callous and cruel mankind can be, it gave us the first taste of man's relentless upward surge toward the four freedoms. It invigorated.

"Ray, can the world ever be filled with clean, free people?" I would ask.

"Well, I suppose it is a long evolutionary haul. But if it ever happens it will start here in the good old United States. The only chance is here. The only form of government that can do it is a democracy."

The United Press shifted Ray to Milwaukee, then to St. Paul. After a year he begged to be sent East. When they refused he wangled a job promoting a Christmas-seal campaign in New York State for the sole purpose of getting within geographical range of his ambition's goal—the nation's capital. The autumn of 1917 found him in Washington, the political reporter's heaven.

I would get a job as a social worker in one town where he was only to find in a few weeks that he would move on, ever closer to this goal of Washington. I grew restive under the changes; we were separated so much and I was so young. I would see bright and enticing bypaths; Ray saw only one—he was going to be the best political writer in the country.

He worked, he studied, he worked; always he worked.

During the years he wrote for the United Press he measured his own merit by complaints that came from Democratic editors: "Clapper copy slanted too much toward Republicans," and from Republican editors: "Clapper copy slanted too much toward Democrats." If a story succeeded in arousing both these reactions he felt he was doing a good, unbiased job.

In the house of our dreams which we built in 1940 is a pair of andirons for the library fireplace designed by our architect, Alfred Kastner. One is a donkey, the other an elephant "for the unbiased political commentator," Mr. Kastner said.

In the draft of the First World War Ray was classified as a married man and was not called up. He felt a terrible urge to enlist but worried about leaving me. He never served, never saw the dreadful trench warfare, never participated with his contemporaries in the greatest experience of that era. Through the years he became more and more self-conscious and unhappy about this, sensing he had somehow not lived up to his own ideals. Had the war lasted I'm sure he would have gone in, but it ended quickly for our armed forces. I think he felt it was the greatest mistake he ever made, and it certainly was a contributing factor to his ceaseless efforts to be in the Second World War as completely as it was possible to be. He wanted everlastingly to be in North Africa, in India, in China, in the Pacific, in the thick of the fighting among the young soldiers toiling against the cumulative foes of mankind's freedom.

"What does Ralph or Van or Newman say about the kind of world they want after this war?" he continually questioned our young daughter about her beaus. He desperately wanted these sheltered youngsters, so young, so unprepared, to understand why they had to fight. At every battle front it was they he wanted to question, and he earnestly listened to their answers.

Working for the United Press, his first journalistic scoop came when Warren Harding was nominated for the presidency by the Republican Party leaders in that famous smoke-filled room of George Harvey's in Chicago in 1920. About 3 o'clock in the morning Charles Curtis, of Kansas, came out of that room, found Ray hanging about in the corridor, and told him, "They're going to try to put over Senator Harding." It was a clean beat and as Ray always explained it, "Kansans stick together." I remember how nice it was to receive a dividend of $100 from the U.P. for that work in the early hours.

Until the Harding period I had always believed that, like the tired businessman, a newspaperman liked to forget his work when he came home. For years I deliberately disdained an interest in national politics, but I found my associations with it inevitably absorbing as I came to know the personalities. As we spent all our leisure time with other newspaper people, I learned that newspapermen are a race apart. They know so much, they are so keenly alive to all the nuances of life, that they never desire to get away from their work.

Then the quiet Coolidge was sworn into the presidency by his father on a Vermont farm and prosperity became the normal way of life. The nation's wealthy became wealthier, and new millionaires were made daily on the stock exchange. Newspapermen, however, were not prosperous; $100 a week was good pay.

During the "roaring" twenties Ray wrote occasionally for *The Nation* and read it and *The New Republic* avidly. His bent in these years was definitely toward labor, critical of capitalism and its grip on the nation's resources and wealth. You will see from his writings how severely he later criticized labor and its leadership in the war years, but he never doubted the workingman's ability, given education and a free system, to attain his rightful share and his rightful part in governing the country.

During these years he served apprenticeship on Capitol Hill in the press galleries of both the House and the Senate. He collected much data on grafting and racketeering in small and great things by the senators, representatives, and executives in public departments, which he later published in his first and only book, *Racketeering in Washington.* It showed neglect and inefficiency in the conduct of the public's business, nepotism, flagrant abuses of franking privileges, congressional "wild life" trips at taxpayers' expense, soft jobs for political appointees, and all kinds of spending de luxe.

After we had been married ten years we decided to start our family. Janet was born in 1923 and Peter in 1927, the year Lindbergh flew across the Atlantic. When in January, 1923, we brought our infant daughter home to our apartment Woodrow Wilson lay dying one block away. My first day home from the hospital we walked to his house on S Street to stand with bowed heads amidst the little crowd holding vigil there.

Janet thrived and we bought a little house on Thirteenth Street in Washington. It was hard going financially. We sold our model-T Ford to meet the expenses of settlement. I had one new dress that year, a light blue wool, but Ray had no new suit. Mornings he toiled in the little garden over our first rosebushes and spirea. He wasn't a good gardener; he plucked the buds off the iris thinking they were the dead flowers. He did the marketing to help me. He fed the baby, proud as all fathers are, making extravagant claims of her cleverness. At four months of age, according to him, she would point to the four stars on the late edition of a newspaper, proving I've forgotten what.

We had our first real Christmas tree. Strenuously Ray built a base to hold and steady it. On Christmas Eve we awakened Janet and brought her downstairs to see the gaily lighted tree. He put her down on the floor to fix something, and before we knew it she had had her fill of the bright lights and had crawled quietly to the kitchen to play with his hammer and saw under the kitchen table.

Throughout the twenties Ray worked, worked, always worked. Meals were always late, playtimes limited. He read voraciously. He began to try to earn more money selling occasional pieces to magazines. In 1925 *The American Mercury* bought "Happy Days," a rollicking story of how prohibition abolished the sale of liquor in the House and Senate restaurants. He used the money to buy a typewriter so he could write magazine pieces at home.

In 1929 Ray came in off the White House and Congressional beats to become Washington manager of the U.P. The new office was swank, the staff of reporters excellent, but he didn't like executive work; he was unhappy bossing other men. In 1931, when businesses were crashing everywhere, the U.P. decided to retrench. Ray had been depressed generally for several weeks. I thought he was not well. Driving him to the bus one morning, I asked him what the trouble was. He sobbed, "Oh, God, I've got to fire six men. I can't do it. They all have families; they are good men. I can't do it." But he did. It added some bitterness to his soul.

The working newspaperman never makes enough to tide over unemployment; he usually has no resources beyond strong legs and an active mind.

At 7:30 one summer evening during Hoover's administration, four of our friends—Tom and Hannah Stokes, Lyle and Connie Wilson—drove up to our house in Chevy Chase, asking if Ray had come home. I answered that I was still keeping his dinner hot. Was something wrong? They said they had come as friends to help me pack up to leave for Canada. Amid hilarious laughter they told me they thought that Ray had, that afternoon after a White House press conference, talked roughly and rudely to the President by telephone, disagreeing over the release time of a story from the conference. In those days Hoover was highly unpopular with the press; he didn't have the light touch and he was very sensitive to everything written about him. The situation was just tense enough for me to be genuinely alarmed. When Ray got really angry he was violent in language. The reporters in the office had heard him yelling into the telephone, "You know where you can go. I will release this story in time for the morning papers." Of course the President was not on the other end of the line, only a poor defenseless secretary, but Ray's colleagues liked his courage and his force.

Bath-tub gin days, lush Wall Street prosperity, speeding automobiles, infant aviation, homemade radios, and jazz bands passed into the depression days when banks closed and able-bodied men sold apples on the streets. We had seen the bonus marchers, veterans of the First World War, chased by troops down Pennsylvania Avenue, Douglas MacArthur at their head. We saw their shacks burned. Businessmen committed suicide by the hundreds and in every heart lurked fear of the tomorrows. Newspapermen knew the tragic signs in the air. I remember Ray went to the bank and drew out in cash sufficient funds to pay the United Press staff. He tried to protect his men and his family, but everyone lost in those dreadful days. My milkman came to the door asking me to pay my bill ahead of time. His other customers had no cash and his family could not buy food. Everyone feared robbery, riots, bloodshed.

A cold rain chilled us that inauguration day in March, 1933. The sky was as dark as our hearts. Warmth came in the thrilling words of the new President, "We have nothing to fear but fear itself."

Confidence and assurance radiated in that great acceptance speech.

Even more reassuring was a conference the President called late that night with the managers of the three press associations. He explained to them in simple words the immediate steps he intended to take to stabilize the banks, why it was necessary to close all of them for a short time, the moves he hoped Congress would take to regularize the nation's shattered financial nerves. In this first act of careful explanation to the press Roosevelt displayed his aptness at public relations. Those three press-association managers were prepared to guide the writing of their staffs which supplied the news to the whole nation. This first contact of F. D. R. with the press tremendously impressed Ray Clapper. It was the method he had long advocated for public men—candidly put all your cards, all the facts, on the table with newspapermen, tell them exactly what you intend to do and the reasons. Then trust to their sense of responsibility to the country and to their profession to handle the story sanely and reasonably.

In 1929 we bought a larger house in Chevy Chase, Md., a suburb of Washington, D.C. That made us citizens of Maryland. I registered as a Democrat and became an active participant in state and national politics. I wanted Ray to become a voter. I believed every citizen ought to vote. Ray believed it too, but he refused to register and vote, fearful that he might be tempted to think and to write as a vindication of his own vote. He explained this decision as follows:

"I was free to criticize either party without having the precinct chairman call and ask me why I was being disloyal to my party. Once some time ago I was told by a Republican friend of mine that it had been found that I had registered as a Republican in Kansas back in 1920. I had completely forgotten the matter and still do not remember it although I am inclined to take my friend's word for it. I have never bothered to check up on it. To some this may seem like indifference about my responsibilities as a citizen and perhaps there is some basis for that complaint. If so I'll just let it stand. To me it seems more important to keep free from entangling alliances in this particular kind of work—somewhat as a judge retires from active politics when he goes on the bench. I have followed the same rule with regard to propaganda organizations and have refused to join any of the numerous committees. I make the same reply to all of them. Often I am in complete accord with the purposes but I do not wish to become affiliated and be bound by a policy that might interfere with freedom of comment in my column. I have no objection to crusading by those who wish to do it. I am not the crusading type and prefer to be free to criticize or praise, to analyze and interpret as the day's news seems to require without having to sustain a position or policy of my own."

Ernie Pyle once asked me, "What is it that makes Ray tick, what makes him slam or praise first one side, then the other? What makes his writing reflect his own honesty?" I answered, "He is not selling anything."

Those who knew Ray Clapper best also knew that his largeness of spirit was coupled with impatience and temper. Ray was irritable about little things. It hurt him to hear a motorcar engine raced needlessly; the crunching of an apple or a piece of ice in the mouth sent him into shivers of annoyance. I never really learned how to keep his daily temper smooth. He couldn't endure tardiness. Whenever we had to catch a train Ray would be at the station half an hour ahead of time. Once when I was in an ill humor he started scolding me for lateness in bringing the car to meet him. Suddenly, to our joint astonishments, I started talking back. I yelled, "Who do you think you are to get so angry over a ten-minute wait? I've had a sick child to care for, phone calls, marketing, dishes to wash. I won't stand for it." Ray looked at me a moment, then let out a mighty roar of laughter. "Why, honey, that's wonderful. Why don't you always lash back at me? I know I'm hard to live with. I'm unreasonable. Just talk back to me. You are so good-natured all the time it makes me feel like a boor."

If I got sick he was frantic. "Why don't you take care of yourself? Get the doctor quickly." He was helpless and furiously angry with fear.

When the contractor building our house in 1940 said the house could not be ready for us until a month after the promised date,

Clapper rounded up the architect, contractor and workmen and stormed so furiously they worked day and night. The job was finished on schedule.

The burst of anger the family remembers best came at breakfast Feb. 6, 1942. I was still in the bedroom dressing and the rest of the family was asleep. Ray was eating breakfast, reading the morning paper. Suddenly he let out a blast that literally shook the house. "God damn it!" I dashed out to him, expecting to find him scalded in steaming coffee; both children leaped from their beds frightened and trembling. "What is it, what's happened?" Still yelling, he banged on the paper. "Look at this scandal in Civilian Defense. Mrs. Roosevelt's protégée Mayris Cheney is going to teach rhythmic dancing to children. This is a war. We can be bombed. Is this civilian defense, is it? Why does the President allow Mrs. Roosevelt to clutter up Civilian Defense with her pets?" He wrote a supercharged column on it that day: "I hope Westbrook Pegler will come down here and do one of his justly celebrated scalping jobs on the Office of Civilian Defense. I mean on Mrs. Roosevelt, too, because half the trouble around there could be got rid of if the President would haul her out of the place."

In spite of this he admired Mrs. Roosevelt tremendously and often said history might accord more space to her than to the President because she fearlessly championed causes that are unpopular today but that would be routinely accepted two hundred years from now. Future citizens will wonder why we fought them, as we wonder why our predecessors fought vaccination.

In a letter to me from the South Pacific in 1944 he wrote glowingly of the many marines, soldiers, and sailors who tenderly bragged they had seen Mrs. Roosevelt when she went into their forsaken jungles to bring a touch of home and America to them. When the marines fought bitterly to take Hill 660 at Cape Gloucester the Japs advanced with eerie Banzai screams, "Marines, prepare to die. Blood for the Emperor." The marines charged ahead, yelling, "Japs, you prepare to die. Blood for Eleanor."

In the early thirties Ray Clapper began to do some platform speaking. He had a quality in personal appearances very like Will

Rogers, a down-to-earth humor. Looking like a Middle Western farmer, he would plant both feet firmly on the floor, stick out his beaklike nose, poke out his head from between his shoulders, and say, "The trouble with newspapermen is they know too much about both political parties. A magazine writer the other day was struggling to get a label for me. I'm glad not to be pegged Republican or Democrat but I could have shown him a recent pan letter which said, 'You are a damned rabbit-footed, feather-legged, yellow-bellied liar. Is that clear?' "

His first trip to Europe was to cover the London Naval Conference in January, 1930. The United States delegation was headed by Secretary of State Stimson. They sailed on the historic *S.S. George Washington* which carried Woodrow Wilson to the Paris Peace Conference. It was the third effort of the United States within a decade to reduce the heavy burden of naval competition. The King of England opened the conference. The British, the French, the Italians, the Japanese gave great banquets and receptions. Prime Minister MacDonald entertained at Chequers. Nevertheless, the conference "skirted close to tragedy," Ray said upon his return. "There are many who believe the powers met at London without sufficient confidence in each other's good intentions." Speaking Mar. 14, 1930, before Life's Underwriters in New York upon his return, he said, "The failure of the present conference might ultimately lead to another world conflict. They are acting more like duelists choosing their weapons than a group of governments which solemnly have adopted a treaty not to resort to war. If they could step back and view the spectacle they make, flourishing the Kellogg Pact in one hand and reaching with the other for as many 8-inch guns as they can gather up, faster progress might be made."

In a letter to me written from London, he said, "Listen—don't tell anybody but I had to get a silk hat for last night. It cost $7.50. Over here everybody wears silk hats at night. Most of the parties are at hotels so I could sort of sneak in and get away with a soft hat but I just couldn't go to Lady Astor's and the French Embassy in that old soft one so I went and done it. I won't wear it in Washington." He never did, either, although the family tried repeatedly on great occasions to make him up as a big shot in a silk hat.

Karl Bickel of U.P. sent Ray on to Paris and Berlin—a postgraduate course in higher journalism, Ray called it. He loved Berlin. "It's more like cities at home, clean and beautiful."

For years he had refused foreign assignments. He never acquired a taste for living abroad. He missed orange juice, American cigarettes, and, most intensely, the whole American way of life.

In 1937 he took me along on an extended tour of Europe. We wined and dined in gay, irresponsible Paris; we lingered in Geneva watching the dying League of Nations; we tramped through Moscow's rubble-strewn streets sensing that Russia was staggering into a mechanical age amid bloody purges of her people. We felt at home in London where the only worries were Wally Simpson and the Spanish civil war. In Germany we shuddered at the efficient iron thumb of the Gestapo and the factory chimneys belching smoke day and night to manufacture the instruments of war. We idled in Austria where an aged flower girl grotesquely symbolized Vienna's romantic past. I can never forget the peasants of Poland digging barefoot in the potato fields nor the Hungarians forever drinking coffee on the open terraces, dreaming dreams of their wars, mouthing words about freedom but eyeing the Nazis with ill-concealed envy.

Anyone with half an eye could see that war was inevitable. We were scared to death. When Ray returned to report in his columns and in speaking trips how certain war was, people eyed us with sad shaking of the head as though to say, "The poor Clappers are seeing things under the bed."

We saw and heard Hitler address 40,000 frenzied Germans. Our taxi from the Adlon Hotel on Unter den Linden drove through miles of soldiers with drawn bayonets on guard along the streets through which Hitler was to pass to the Sportspalast. We passed through tight battalions of guards to enter. The aisles inside the building were lined with still more armed soldiers. Military bands played stirring martial music as only the Germans can play it. We sat in press seats in the balcony very near the stage. All of Nazidom's big shots were there—Goering, Goebbels, Himmler, Hess. The excited audience seethed with heiling and guttural noises. A crimson carpet down the great center aisle threw a red glow upon the faces of Hitler's own elite guard standing shoulder to shoulder in ankle-length black greatcoats and black steel helmets. Every man stood over 6 feet tall. They resembled giants from Hades with their crimson faces and unsheathed bayonets.

Suddenly a solid roar arose; everyone was on his feet, men yelling, women hysterical. We saw a funny little man in a raincoat run down the aisle and leap upon the platform. He truly resembled Charlie Chaplin to American eyes. He threw off his hat and coat (someone must have caught them) and leaped upon the stage. He began to speak at once without introduction as soon as the cheering audience quieted. Words poured from his lips; the famous lock of hair kept falling over his eyes and being pushed back by a jerk of the ever-tossing head; hands flayed about; mad hysteria filled the air. Thousands listened as one man; the lusty shouts seemed to come from one great mass throat and belly. He raved, he ranted. Were we to be caught in Berlin at the outbreak of war? My poor children! Surely he was declaring war—nothing short of that could account for the vehemence. I knew little German, so I couldn't follow for an instant this wild rave. I leaned over to an English newspaperman industriously taking notes. "Please, what is he saying?" "Oh, he is only telling them to give to the poor." The occasion was the opening of the winter relief drive like our Community Chest drives. I sighed gratefully and leaned back to watch Hitler's great act through to the end.

In London we made a pilgrimage to Kensington Gardens to see the statue of Peter Pan. We had an especial reason. When our son, officially named William Raymond, was born, his three-year-old sister named him Peter Pan. In her brief life she had already had James Barrie's *Peter Pan* read to her three times. The copper-haired baby looked like the reincarnation of the little boy who could fly to the "never-never land." Peter Pan he was for three years, but the Pan was dropped along with baby ways.

Again, during the London blitz in 1941, Ray made a pilgrimage to the Peter Pan statue. Sandbags covered it securely, completely obscuring the fairies and the tiny mice and rabbits. He peeked through the crisscrossed bags to see cobwebs and dust covering the little bronze animals which in peacetime are polished by loving strokes and petting from myriad children's hands. He told of this pilgrimage in a broadcast to the United States from London, saying, "I think I know now what it is the people of Britain are fighting for. They are fighting so that their children may come back to Kensington Gardens to stroke the tiny animals on Peter Pan's statue in peace and safety."

Ray Clapper left the United Press in 1933 to join the staff of *The Washington Post,* owned and published by Eugene Meyer, a rich man who never "lost the common touch," a Republican who was never blind to the changing world. This change meant more money, and Ray was writing again instead of directing reporters. He could see his future and he liked it; yet he approached the change with fear and misgiving, for his was a loyal soul and he disliked change of any kind. Just as he was a one-woman man so he was a one-organization man.

When Eugene Meyer and his assistant general manager, Mark Ethridge, suggested a year later that Ray try to write a daily column, we discussed it pro and con far into the night. I was opposed to it because in 1934 the place of the columnist in journalism was uncertain. It seemed to me that editorial comment was more potent from the mouths of editors; I doubted Ray's appeal to the reader who wanted a glamorous personality. But Ray said, "I want to try it. In a straight news story you have to leave out so much background, so much meat, or else bury it at the end of the story. I want a chance to feature it so that people will see and understand what really goes on in the government. I'll probably fail because, as you say, I have no glamour for the public, but it's a temptation to try to write lots of the kind of thing you and I talk about that other people might like to read too. I'd make it like a news story right on the nose of the news but put into it what I'd like someone to tell me if I was living out in Kansas about day-to-day background in Washington."

On Sept. 28, 1934, *The Washington Post* in a box announced, "What causes news? What peculiar circumstances—outside influences—personal motives, make up the forces which create headlines yet never appear in the conventional news story? In an authoritative and absorbing new daily feature called 'Between You and Me,' Raymond Clapper takes readers backstage in the day's news. He reveals how and why things happen as they do."

Ray honored Eugene Meyer. They disagreed frequently, but never did Mr. Meyer by argument or executive order attempt to sway his columnists' opinions or writing. I have heard Meyer and Clapper ferociously disagree and argue at a dinner party until I feared the next morning's mail would bring Ray a dismissal card. But Eugene Meyer can truly say, "I wholly disagree with what you have to say but I will defend to the death your right to say it."

To my surprise "Between You and Me" became a success and I read it as avidly as did everyone else in Washington.

In late December, 1934, old ties called Ray back to the Scripps-Howard fold when Lowell Mellett and Deac (George) Parker offered him the chance to appear in Roy Howard's string of papers throughout the nation. Ray wanted particularly a New York outlet as well as a Washington one. Again it meant more money. Ray never received from Scripps-Howard a salary commensurate with Pegler, Broun, or Hugh Johnson but he made up for it when George Carlin, manager of United Feature Syndicate, started syndication of his column to newspapers all over the nation. George Carlin's faith, loyalty, and friendship to Ray were a high light in his life as were those of Karl Bickel.

Ray believed his success would be slow and hard. He preferred a slower climb to the spectacular one-night success, believing it built a firmer reader habit and thus assured a continued success instead of a flash in the pan. Walking in our woods one cold November day in 1943, he shyly said, "Carlin says I am syndicated in 176 papers with ten million readers. I think that is remarkable. My slow but steady increase is due to the patience of the editors of this country who were willing to string along printing my heavy serious stuff, plugging it when more exciting gossip columns might have brought more readers. They deserve the credit, not me."

Toward Roy Howard, Ray acted like the schoolboy with his teacher, the teacher whose judgment he respected but whose methods he deplored. They seldom agreed about presidential candidates, the war, the peace, or anything else—not even about what made interesting copy. But their principal disagreements came about through Clapper's continual branching out into magazine writing and radio broadcasting. Roy Howard liked his trained seals to produce for Papa Scripps-Howard and no one else. He constantly resented extracurricular activities. To Ray these other activities meant more money for the family, for schooling and "the memories we can buy" with it. They meant terrible, heartbreaking work at breakneck speed day and night and week ends. They meant no vacation the last two years. They meant bushels of fan mail and pan mail, the ever-ringing relentless telephone, going without meals, the unlimited drain upon body and mind.

The radio sponsors paid five times what Scripps-Howard paid, but it took Roy Howard to reduce Ray to the little boy whenever his success got very big. The day after Otto Fuerbringer's splendid article on "The Average Man's Columnist" appeared in *The Saturday Evening Post* (Nov. 6, 1943), Ray's pride and joy were dashed to the ground. It had meant so much to him to be written up in the *Post,* but Roy Howard "kept him in" after an editorial conference to say, "The column is moving too much into the 'I think' class and hasn't enough of the news and reporting in it. You better pep it up, it's getting dull."

When Ray came home and told me this I was furious. Ray said, "No, that's good for me; Roy is right, but if I ever got a swelled head you can trust Roy to take it down."

In justice to Ray Clapper I must emphatically say he was ardently loyal and devoted to Roy. He would never allow anyone to say a derogatory word about him. Once he ordered that never again should I invite a certain man to our house who had derided the "little dynamo."

What did Ray Clapper look like? *Time* magazine Oct. 21, 1940, described him as follows:

"Ray Clapper is a middle-sized man with wise eyes, stooped shoulders, and a burning conviction that journalism is the most important profession in the world. In themselves, these attributes would not make him unique. The quality that long ago lifted Scripps-Howard's Clapper out of the ruck of columnists is his knack of translating some event into sound sense on the very day that people want to hear about it. Somehow he manages to move a half step faster than the mass mind."

Otto Fuerbringer in *The Saturday Evening Post* said that:

". . . at fifty-one, Clapper is slightly paunchy, slightly stoop-shouldered. . . . He has a large head and thick tousled hair, which, together with his sloping shoulders, give him the appearance of a bear. Pictures taken with a flash bulb, which accentuate the dark circles under his eyes, give him somewhat of a panda look."

Ray was always voicing a desire to dress like an *Esquire* gentleman, but his conservative blue business suits or gray tweeds took on the contours of his "panda" form and his trouser legs bagged fore and aft from his double-jointed knees. A dress shirt rode up his chest, at the end of the evening looking like a tired sheet around his neck. Dirty old sweaters and slap-happy slacks made him happiest. These he wore on our many walks or to chop wood at the sawhorse he made. We christened that sawhorse with a bottle of water and a poem composed and read by Donald Richberg in fitting ceremonies to inaugurate Ray's plans to reduce his waistline. He weighed 179 pounds, too heavy for his 5 feet 9 inches.

He bewailed his inability to play games. He had never had time to learn, hence his great pride in Peter's football, basketball, and track achievements.

He read voraciously. He read and reread Emerson's *Essays* throughout his life and kept a copy by his bed. He moaned over lack of time to keep up on all the wonderful new books, the new plays, the radio. He exhorted the children to tell him about new personalities such as Frank Sinatra. He never had time to see, hear, or read all that enticed him. His hunger for music was satisfied in recent years with sitting alone in our living room listening to *Porgy and Bess,* Beethoven's "Fifth Symphony" and *Oklahoma.* Over and over he would play "Bess, You Is My Woman Now," "I Got Plenty of Nothing and Nothing's Plenty for Me," and "Everything's Up to Date in Kansas City."

I have inquired of ladies who were his dinner partners, "What did he say at dinner?" They would invariably answer, startled, "Why, I did all the talking. He listened." Yes, he listened, with head thrust forward jutting from his chest as though he had no neck, earnest gray eyes searching your face in an attitude as though all you said was the most fascinating and interesting dope he had ever heard. He led you on, made you feel you were spouting words of great wisdom. In a group he seldom spoke unless goaded by overwhelming conviction in argument. Then he would hurl straight to the point a biting comment that left his adversary stuttering.

He never rose to the social-lion bait. When he returned from a thrilling trip I always hoped he would shine at dinner parties by relating the exciting interviews with prime ministers and generals or give the low-down on a foreign situation as he did to me. But I was forever disappointed. He would be flustered when we returned home. "These people don't really want to hear. They ask questions but before I can answer they have answered their own questions with what they think, and they dash on to a new question which they then answer to their own satisfaction."

He loved to go to Mrs. J. Borden Harriman's Sunday suppers where the great lights of the world were teased by this magnificent hostess into discussing their views. Mrs. Evelyn McLean fascinated him with her daring mixtures of men and women of violently opposed views. There you would see Republicans and Democrats, New Dealers and Old, isolationists and interventionists dining in guarded cordiality. Ray knew the great leaders of this period but to him they were all most respectfully just another guy named Joe.

The places in nature's beautiful world Ray Clapper loved included Minnesota's lakes, Canada's mountains, Bermuda's beaches, and New York's Finger Lakes, but the dearest place of all was

Delaware's Rehoboth Beach. His passion for its salty surf bathing and its hot summer sand was an abiding one. Many summer vacations we spent there in a rented cottage by the sea among beloved friends—the Donald Richbergs, the Ed Goodriches, Sam Clyde's family, Paul Leach's, the Spakemans, the Tooey Spaatzes, and the Henry Berliners. A four-hour auto trip from the nation's capital, Rehoboth was a million miles from the stress of producing a daily column.

Head under a gay-colored umbrella after repeated plunges into the booming sea, Ray would lie with legs, chest, and arms exposed to a burning sun that changed his skin from beige to almost chocolate. He tried not to talk politics or world affairs. Luxuriating in leisure, he nevertheless read the papers and magazines avidly and made notes, but never phoned the office. Sometimes he would go on a fishing trip at early dawn; frequently he played a badminton game. At night and on rainy days he read for long hours. Each meal was digested well after gay banter with Janet and her friends and he would fall into deep sleep, a very happy man.

We had many song fests. Ed Goodrich, Henry Berliner, and Tooey Spaatz played guitars. Over Scotch highballs they sang hours on end. Crouched near by Ray would listen, seldom singing but blissfully happy. Several of his favorites were "The West Virginia Hills," "Don't Strike Your Mother," "We Never Mention Aunt Clara," and "On a Bicycle Built for Two."

The rule against discussion was strictly enforced on his last vacation—one whole July in 1942 at Rehoboth. He read Tolstoy's *War and Peace,* which depressed him mightily because Napoleon's period of conquest so closely patterned Hitler's. He tried to concentrate one day upon his reading as we sat on the screened-in porch. Janet, her friend Betty Frost, and I kept talking, laughing. I was teasing Ray. He got angry and looked up to hurl a command that became a classic in the family, "Oh, go read a book."

That was the summer Betty and Janet invited some boys down for the week end. Saturday afternoon five enormous and handsome Georgetown University boys arrived. They piled into the tiny cottage. Only Ray was on hand to greet them. He came upstairs to tell the girls of the arrival, his eyes big as saucers. "The whole Georgetown football team is downstairs. Jesus, they're big. Somebody come down and help me."

He always instructed me to be sure to rent a cottage without a telephone. But I missed up that July. It turned out to be good luck because it was that little party-line phone that brought him the big radio contract to take Raymond Gram Swing's place under White Owl Cigars sponsorship.

The nondiscussion rule was broken late one night toward the end of that July. It had been a hot blistering day and we sat rocking on the porch in the cool darkness, quietly talking with my sister about family affairs. Finally we were silent for a long time. To our astonishment Ray suddenly burst out, "I've got to talk. I can't stand it any longer. Tonight outside Stalingrad the whole future of civilization is being fought out by the Russians and the Germans. No matter what we do, no matter how much or how little the United States has sent to that battlefield, our whole future depends on the Russians holding. The lives of men born a hundred years from now will be deeply affected. And we cannot do one thing about it, not one thing. If they don't hold now, no force we can ever bring to bear will stop the Germans and the Japs. Oh, God, we are losing—every day our situation grows worse. Defeats, defeats—our Navy reduced to ashes, the bungling at Washington, an Army training with wooden guns, what can we do? It's too late, too late unless the Russians hold."

He talked on for two hours while shivers went up and down our spines as he outlined in detail our pitiful lack of preparedness. It was a great and beautiful experience to hear this man who really knew all aspects of our country's plight cry out of his heart for help to save his dearly beloved land and its precious democracy.

Ray had come back from war-anticipating Europe more isolationist than ever. After Munich he began to change, recognizing that the balance of power in Europe was shifting, that this change made necessary strong defense and pressure to check the aggressors. He recognized that British sea power must be kept in friendly hands. Explaining his change, he wrote, "I try to learn from events. Events are not consistent; therefore why should I be consistent?"

After Hitler's swift gulp of France and the Low Countries Ray became frantically alarmed, fearful that Britain could not hold alone, visualizing a Nazi-ruled world that even our great strength could not long withstand. He felt our free institutions would have to be scrapped to make a wall of actual military security. Our free system of enterprise would be sacrificed to a stern military regime geared to the task of fighting off massive German divisions brought over in the captured British fleet to storm our ports and bomb our cities.

Everyone who lived through 1940 to Pearl Harbor in December, 1941, will remember the bitterness of the isolationist fight. Columnists, editors, as well as men in public life, were deluged with abuse. Ray's life was threatened; his mail was fearful and frightening. One day I received a small package wrapped as a gift. When I opened it I found a miniature black coffin with a paper skeleton inside marked "Your husband."

Declarations of war stopped most of these threats, but some vicious die-hards continued sending abuse. The most consistent of these was a penny-postcard writer who knew our home address. Almost daily throughout the war this anonymous panner, often treasonable and always insulting, wrote open postcards, addressing Ray as "Dear Stupid." The family looked forward to these. When a day or a week passed without receipt of one we would say, "Poor dear stupid has been picked up by the F.B.I. at last." However, I'm afraid "dear stupid" is still at large. At least the cards were still coming to Ray when he went out into the Pacific.

The "Senator Wheeler incident" really hurt Ray in his heart as much as any trouble he ever had. Wheeler in his early days gave promise of fine statesmanship. He was a Western liberal, an honest, forthright leader. We even thought he might be President someday. So it was with pain that Ray watched bitterness grow in this man of great promise.

On Oct. 28, 1941, Senator Wheeler on the floor of the United States Senate attacked Ray, saying he was registered as a British agent with the State Department and that after his registration as such the tenor of his articles completely changed. Senator O'Mahoney jumped to Ray's defense.

Ray went at once to see Senator Wheeler and also wrote to him as follows:

"I am sure that you do not wish to make an unfounded charge against my integrity as a newspaperman.

"Reference to the facts will show that both of your statements are incorrect.

"Last December, at the request of the United Feature Syndicate, which distributes my daily column, I agreed to write twelve weekly articles for the *London Daily Mail.* Upon inquiry at the State Department I was informed that this contract should be registered under the law, which was done. The articles were completed on schedule and that was the end of the arrangement. I have had no other arrangement of any kind before or since with any foreign newspaper or any other foreign agency or government.

"As to the statement that my views were affected by this arrangement, you have only to read what I wrote at the time of the fall of France in the summer of 1940 and on many other occasions over the last two years to see that there is no truth in that."

Most people would not have bothered to register a private contract with a foreign newspaper but Ray, in his leaning-over-backward attitude always to do the honest, proper thing, did register with the State Department under the Act of June 8, 1938, just to be sure he was acting correctly. It was his undoing—Mr. Milquetoast took the law too literally and it bit him; at least it opened up a crack in his armor where an attack could be made.

Congressman William P. Lambertson referred to Ray on the floor of the House of Representatives as an agent of the British government. Ray wrote to him, "I think you have done me a great injustice. This statement is not true as you could have found out by checking with me or the State Department. Please be fair enough to correct this."

Of course the attackers never looked up the contents of the

London Daily Mail articles. They dealt entirely with political and economic conditions in the United States, a straight reporting job of news here, and did not express attitudes or opinions about the United States entering the war.

"Senator Wheeler never made a straightforward correction. He twisted his explanation although he knew better," Ray wrote on Nov. 1, 1941. Bitterest pill of all to Ray was to receive an avalanche of mail calling him "un-American."

Broadcasting was difficult for Ray. He had what is called in radio "a white voice," meaning that its tones lacked resonance and color. He took lessons in diction; he hummed continually and sang lustily in the shower bath because his teacher thought it might help to lower his Middle Western twang. He gave up smoking to keep a clear throat.

His voice and diction he knew were bad. He worried lots about it. When he reached home late at night after a broadcast he would announce his arrival by calling "Boo." I always ran out to hear him asking coyly and anxiously, "How was it?" "You were fine tonight. You only made one fluff and you are getting into a more conversational manner which is good." Or—"Ray, I hate to tell you but we think the broadcast stank tonight." These comments were all concerned with his voice and delivery, never with the contents of the broadcasts which, like his columns, were universally good.

Frankly, I never felt I truly knew what was going on in the world or what any event meant unless I read what he had to say about it or heard him explain it. His was a gift of simplicity. I was the ordinary person—his "milkman of Omaha."

Broadcasting was hard on him also because on broadcast days he could not find time to eat a nourishing dinner. He would have to write the broadcast from 5 P.M. to 9 P.M. after a hard day's work that would crush any ordinary person. A fifteen-minute broadcast, 1,500 words, is equivalent to writing a magazine piece. It is done under high pressure with a ticker reeling off the latest news. I always fed him warm food when he got home at 11 P.M.

A song-fest at home in Washington. Left to right: Peter, Janet, Mrs. Clapper and Raymond Clapper.

His utter weariness distressed me deeply. Could nothing be done to ease the strain? We talked a lot about it. He would say, "If I just didn't have to see so many people, if the telephone didn't interrupt. But, Jesus, I have to see these people, I have to go to these luncheons, these dinners. I learn so much from them. You can't tell an out-of-town editor who buys your column that you haven't time to see him, nor a senator or general who wants to know what you think about our situation in North Africa. I don't know. Mrs. Shamel (his secretary) is wonderful and she shields me from cranks and busybodies, but there just aren't enough hours in the day."

He wouldn't delegate work to assistants because he had to see things and people himself. He was constitutionally a leg man, his own reporter, and he always got his news the hard way.

When Ray went into the Pacific war area he lost his White Owl radio sponsorship. It was the only job in his whole life he ever lost. His sponsors wanted continuity of the program, but broadcasting from war zones cannot be continuous. When the U.S. Government urges a newspaperman to go into a war theater in order to write so the folks back home will understand the war and what their fighting men are doing, loss of income and the wishes of a radio sponsor become relatively unimportant.

He went to the Pacific. He did not come home. I like to think the pressure would have eased; that Ray could have had some restful peace; perhaps he would, at long last, have ceased working so dreadfully hard. Yet I know he wanted to go right back to London this spring in time for the opening of the second front. I know he would have jumped from one end of the United States to the other during the political campaign this summer.

He had a book he wanted to write and a crusade to wage. He never crusaded for anything in his life, but he dreamed of helping in the mighty effort to bring about a peaceful world in our tomorrows.

Ray Clapper was of the earth of America. Democracy was an instinct with him. He knew without thinking what would be good or bad for this country. He lived long enough to know that freedom's victory was sure. If only he might have participated in what we hope to make out of that victory!

The morning of Feb. 3, 1944, the Navy Department issued the following announcement:

"The commander in chief of the Pacific Fleet has reported that a plane in which Mr. Raymond Clapper was a passenger engaged in covering the Marshalls invasion collided with another plane while forming up. Mr. Clapper was in the plane with the squadron commander. Both planes crashed in the lagoon. There were no survivors."

For fifteen days afterward his newspapers were able to print his daily column posthumously. In a Scripps-Howard editorial this was explained as follows:

"It was no matter of chance which enabled us to continue his column daily without interruption. Whereas some of us might have considered the arduous journey to Australia and the South Pacific islands job enough in itself, he managed not only to keep his column coming daily, but to build up a 'cushion' of advance copy against the day when he would go to sea with a task force and be unable because of radio silence to send us anything for days or perhaps weeks.

"And when the task force did set out, and he could no longer deliver his copy to us, he kept on turning out columns so that he would be ready when transmission was available. After his death the Navy delivered these articles to us."

When his worn brief case likewise was returned by the Navy to his home it contained hundreds of illegible notes taken while talking to soldiers, fliers, officers, and Navy men manning battle stations. Curiously, however, there was one highly legible note written in the past tense which was concerned with the bombing mission which caused his death. It read:

"Went out in torpedo bomber plane to see finish of Eniwetok. Went with squadron commander. Purpose to burn island, strategy could be used other islands. Contrast this bombing with that of bombing of Rome. Squadron called 'Bunker Hill Hotfoot.' Back in time for lunch."

It seemed uncanny and slightly eerie, but he was only preparing ahead of time to write for the folks back home his description of the flight that ended his life. He intended to write it after lunch.

Unto death he worked, always the reporter.

Journalism

5/23/42

TWICE within our generation we have had pointed out to us that events in foreign countries thousands of miles away eventually reach out and take men out of their homes and jobs and put them behind a gun in some foreign country. If the American people are going to be smart enough to get along in this kind of a world they will have to take an active part in dealing with these affairs, which, although far away, bounce back into our faces.

That means a new task for the American press. It means that foreign affairs no longer remain in a separate compartment. They must be covered and discussed with the same firsthand knowledge and firsthand background that we have always applied to American politics, industrial news, and sports.

An editorial writer can sit in his office and read for a week about a new British budget. But he could go to England, talk to officials firsthand, really learn something about it, and be back in New York in no longer time. Furthermore, he would also have a store of material on which he would be able to draw for a long time afterward.

Full use of this new opportunity by the American press would not only be a most desirable enterprise but I think it is going to be imperative if we are fully to discharge our responsibility to the reading public.

After this war it will take a nation of fast and clear thinkers and extremely well-informed people to stay on top of the heap. We were poorly informed after the last war, and it has cost us dearly. We cannot afford another such disaster.

If we are going to exercise the leadership which I think we must exercise, it means that we shall have to revise some of our economic conceptions. Questions of international trade will assume complicated forms far more difficult to deal with than ever before. And American public sentiment which does not fully understand what must be done may, through its ignorance, bring pressure on Congress to frustrate our best interests as we did after the last war in pushing up our tariffs at the time when our own interests required that they should go down.

Flying reporters, flying editorial writers, flying columnists, the eyes and ears of the American people, have a job ahead of them which can be one of the great adventures of American journalism. Never in all time has any private institution had the opportunity to render a service compared with that which the American press can give by taking advantage of this new means of getting around.

We have put wings on the printed word by utilizing the telegraph and radio. I think the next move will be to put wings on our own feet so that when we reach the telegraph office we will have something more authoritative to say. I think it will be one of the greatest privileges that can come to any man to be a newspaper worker during the next decade when we shall have all of these mechanical facilities made to order for our particular work.

3/36

It is curious, when you think of it, that in our government which rests upon a foundation of public opinion, we never have developed any technique for measuring accurately what that opinion was except by the broad generalized verdicts at election time and such information as senators, representatives, and other public officials could gather haphazardly through correspondence and personal contacts.

The press is a public institution with a responsibility to the public. That responsibility, most newspapermen agree, is essentially to present a fair and accurate account of the news and, in addition to that, to throw such light upon the meaning of that news as it can through its editorial columns and its special commentators.

Discussion is the breath of a democracy's life. The constant challenge of one opinion against another is essential. Without it democracy becomes a fragile hothouse growth liable to snap under the first gust of opposition wind. The editorial page is—or should be—America's town hall.

The type of debate and the type of newspaper writing that must make a thing either black or white, that must distort it out of all proportion, that take a set of facts or circumstances and are impelled to throw in a dash of sensational overstatement, are an imposition on the public.

In recent years a new element has been introduced into the editorial picture. That is the syndicated comment column. One or more of these is found in most of the newspapers throughout the country.

As one of the lesser of these commentators, I venture to suggest that these comment columns are a mixed blessing to the editor.

They do provide him with national political comment written on the scene of action, where there is more complete access to the situation and a better opportunity to study it closely than is afforded to the editor sitting in his sanctum two or three thousand miles away. Usually these commentators are men of considerable experience in analyzing public affairs and can contribute something toward the clarification of them. In that respect they make a valuable contribution to the thrashing-out process which is involved in the development of public opinion.

Yet there is some danger that these commentators will sap the strength of the editorial page. On a recent trip into the country, particularly in certain sections where Roosevelt is rated strong, I thought I detected a tendency in some newspapers to let the syndicated comment columns carry the hod, as if the editor felt that discretion was the better part of valor and, instead of lashing out against the New Deal, preferred to keep his editorials mild and tactful while allowing his real convictions to be presented by syndicated columnists.

I would not make this as a charge, for when the subject was touched on it was explained that editors desired to present both sides. Whether that was a bit of rationalization or not I, of course, do not know. In any case I believe it would be a serious loss if the newspaper editor should develop any tendency to leave discussion of national affairs entirely to his paid contributors in the East. Sound opinion is built up from the grass roots and not from the observations of writers in Washington. Washington, for the moment, is the newspaperman's paradise, with a page 1 story around every corner.

And paradoxically, though newspapermen never worked harder, they never had so much help and cooperation from the government. Not only is the Administration making big news every hour on the hour but it has recruited through the entire government an exceptionally able corps of press-relations men. These functionaries are of infinite help in reporting the day's news out of Washington. And I think it is infinitely better for each newspaper to hit out in its own way, with the indigenous flavor of its own community, than to lean upon the most erudite observations from Washington or New York. Let these outside writers be a stimulus to editorial thought, not a substitute for it.

12/39

A responsible newspaperman with questions of general importance has little difficulty in clearing with a Cabinet officer either directly or through an assistant. That is true too with senators and representatives, and with state and local politicians. They are never too busy to explain the background of a situation to a responsible newspaperman. They know through long experience that they can trust reporters and editors, and that it is better to give a full picture even though part of what they say is confidential, than to risk an editorial or a news story written through lack of information and understanding.

This working relationship between the politician and the press could well be emulated in many other fields of activity. Business would have been much better off long ago had it adopted a similar policy. Businesses alert enough to do so have found it greatly to their advantage. The medical profession has been negligent in this regard. Every working newspaper reporter has his own personal stories to tell about the difficulties of obtaining accurate information from hospitals—information which the patient usually would be perfectly willing to have given out. Here I know it will be said that reporters are prying into private affairs which are none of their business. Yet as a matter of fact the reporter in most cases is seeking simply the details which friends of patients are anxious to learn about, and which he finally obtains by word of mouth, correctly or otherwise—often otherwise.

The majority of successful politicians get as much out of newspapermen as newspapermen get out of them. Practically every politician has his friends among newspapermen and editors upon whom he tries out ideas and gets their reaction. He lets them punch holes in his case, and gathers from them advice as to timing, always of great importance. In fact one of the pitfalls in our business is the constant temptation of a newspaperman to "go statesman." After a reporter or editor is asked a few times for advice, he begins to think of himself as a statesman, and if he doesn't watch out that is the end of a good newspaperman.

5/20/39

Personal memo on the newspaper business:

The chief reason that demagogues thrive is that the newspapers—and the radio—pretend to take them seriously. Not editorially perhaps, but in the news columns, which is what really counts.

If you asked newspapermen here or elsewhere what they really thought of this latest blast out of the Dies investigating committee, I suspect that most of them would say it was 90 per cent hogwash, played up out of all proportion to its real importance. Any skilled newspaperman, knowing nothing about the story, could read it in the newspapers and be certain that it was flimsy "headline" stuff.

The offense of the newspapers is that, making a fetish of "objectivity," they present this kind of dubious material exactly as if they actually took it seriously. I find in the latest editions of Washington newspapers [May, 1939], the most recent blast out of the Dies committee describing an "anti-Jew crusade" covering several columns, played in the lead position, with headlines giving it additional importance.

High up in the accounts in headlines, or in blackface type, is the word that John D. M. Hamilton, chairman of the Republican National Committee, is to be called before the Dies committee because, according to a witness, he "gave the names of Republican committeemen to participants in the (anti-Semitic) campaign."

Every newspaperman in Washington knows that anybody, by writing to the Republican National Committee, can obtain a printed list of the committee members. He can get the Democratic names by writing to Jim Farley. There is no secret about that. The lists are printed in the World Almanac, as John Hamilton pointed out when, for later editions, he had an opportunity to set the matter in its proper perspective.

But the news accounts kick off with the plain, flat, unexplained statement of a witness that Mr. Hamilton sent a committee list to the anti-Semitic agitators, leaving the inference to be drawn by the average reader that in some way Mr. Hamilton was mixed up in the activity. It was Mr. Hamilton who spoke out last fall against the Jew-baiting senatorial primary campaign in Kansas of Rev. Gerald Winrod, a Republican.

When some of us months ago said the Dies testimony "exposing" red activity was trivial, unverified stuff blown up with hot air, we were regarded suspiciously as secret radical sympathizers. I hope that it is permissible to similarly point out the weaknesses in the present smearing treatment of John Hamilton without being regarded as a secret sympathizer with the Republican National Committee.

Those outside the newspaper business complain that the press "distorts" the news, meaning that it is twisted and given an editorial slant. That is not the trouble.

Newspapers have made a fetish of "factual objectivity" and have carried it to such extremes that, as is seen in this instance, a "deadpan" straightaway statement, all literally correct, leaves a completely erroneous impression with the reader. And if the reader is left with an incorrect impression, the reporting, no matter how "factual" it may be in the literal sense, is misleading. Is such misleading of the reader to be justified on the ground that "Dies said it and therefore it is news"? To say that Mr. Hamilton, according to a witness, gave the names of Republican committeemen to participants in the anti-Semitic campaign leaves the impression that this was something unusual, a special favor to the group, when as every Washington newspaperman knows it was nothing of the kind. Is it good journalism to let that insinuation go through unexplained to trusting readers under the excuse of being "objective"?

It is this kind of "objectivity" that builds up demagogues. Newspapers don't do it intentionally. The cry that they deliberately "distort" news is itself a gross distortion. The distortion comes about, in such instances as this one, through a technical, literal accuracy which unconsciously leaves a distorted impression on the reader. The trouble arises because a demagogue hands a half-truth to the reporter who thereupon, trying to be accurate, relays the half-truth to the reader in exactly the same literal manner that he would relay a whole truth.

8/25/39

Those who think newspapers are warmongers, and that they look forward with relish to war news because it sells newspapers, may be surprised to know that in this particular group of newspapermen who foresee the likelihood of our being drawn into war if it continues long, several said that they dreaded the prospect. One said that the thought of it made him want to get into some other activity, because of the things he would have to do under pressure of violent public war hysteria.

Some recalled experiences during the last war when, under similar pressure, men were subjected to suspicions because they had German names. City councilmen who opposed changing the names of German streets were hounded. Trustees of a hospital bearing a German name were publicly censured until they were forced to change the name.

In wartime, public sentiment becomes so inflamed that all fairness, reason, and sense of proportion are submerged. To these newspapermen, and no doubt to most of my craft, these are the things which make war abhorrent in prospect—the temporary debasing of human nature that is inevitable under such stress. There are few newspapermen, or newspaper publishers, who want war just because it sells newspapers. Most of them are more reluctant about it than the average person who is less conscious of the devastating effects of war fever upon the communities in which they live.

8/30/37

It has been said that dictators regard a free press as a nuisance and abolish it, and that believers in democracy also regard a free press as a nuisance but thank God for it. Roosevelt undoubtedly goes into the second category.

Even broader than this problem of the free press is the whole relationship of a people to its government. Dictators insist upon blind, unquestioning adherence. The leader, once given authority, is to be handed a blank check and thereafter no questions are to be asked.

The opposite attitude is that expressed by Baldwin just before he retired as Prime Minister. He had been saying that democracy was the most difficult form of government and that autocracy was an easy form because all do as they are told and are saved the trouble of thinking.

He said that he received letters, some telling him he was a fool and some saying he was a great man.

"But," he added, "one letter that really makes me feel rather a fool is when people write and say that they trust me so much that they would follow me anywhere. I should not like to be followed that way by anyone."

But just last week Postmaster General Farley was saying proudly that this was exactly the way the American people were following President Roosevelt. They didn't know much about the Supreme Court proposal, perhaps, but if Roosevelt wanted it they were for it. That makes a rather hollow foundation for democracy and it should give the President more concern than the hostile press.

Surely, after the last election, he doesn't lie awake nights worrying about the hostile press, does he?

9/17/41

Free speech and free criticism present a problem to a nation at war or in the midst of intense preparation as we are.

In his press conference [September, 1941], President Roosevelt criticized political discussion in connection with the defense effort. He saw no reason why party questions should come into the situation in a time of danger such as this. General George C. Marshall, Chief of Staff of the Army, mentioned to the American Legion the difficulties of creating an efficient army in the midst of continuous investigation, cross-examination, debate, ridicule, and public discussion. In several instances, Army officers while acting to enforce discipline have been subjected to public criticism and ridicule.

Those who consider that we do face dangers will sympathize with the President and General Marshall in their respective points.

The best control in these matters is that which comes out of a sense of responsibility on the part of the public—particularly on the part of Congress and writers and speakers. They all have an enormous effect upon public morale and it seems to me they have a responsibility to the nation in that respect. It is just as inexcusable for a man to throw a verbal stink bomb into a crowd as it would be to sabotage machinery in a defense plant. There is sabotage to public opinion just as there is sabotage to machinery.

It is not necessary to curtail free speech and free criticism. They can be a blessing or a curse, depending upon how they are used.

By exercise of a sense of responsibility, the people of England have retained freedom of debate after 2 years of war. Soapbox speakers still draw crowds in Hyde Park. While I was in England several newspapers were campaigning to throw out one of Churchill's Cabinet ministers, the minister of aircraft production. Some in the government wanted to strong-arm the press into silence. Others in the government refused to permit such tactics and the press went its own way, demanding the Cabinet resignation. I read one editorial which criticized Churchill for not paying enough attention to administration and to production, and which remarked that he couldn't take criticism and that he insisted upon surrounding himself with weak yes men. If Roosevelt's name had been substituted for Churchill's the attack would have read like one of General Johnson's columns.

Mr. Roosevelt may not like criticism any more than Mr. Churchill does. But after weeks of criticism he has just now, by a simple stroke of his pen, slashed the red tape which has caused a scandalous delay in lend-lease orders. Some weeks ago I was called on the carpet here by a high official for criticizing O.P.M. as having missed the boat, as being muscle-bound in red tape, and as having misjudged the need of converting industry to war work. Others have made the same criticisms with forceful detail. Mr. Roosevelt did not like some of this. But in the end he was compelled to recognize that the criticisms were well founded and finally was driven to reorganize the whole show.

It would be a dangerous day when we abandoned free speech and criticism. Second only to that danger is the reckless perversion of this precious weapon of democracy. The only safety is in a people sufficiently grown up and responsible to handle this weapon to strengthen the nation and not to wreck it.

10/3/41

Yes, about Secretary Hull. His seventieth birthday sneaked up on him, but the newspaper correspondents who cover the State Department knew about it and gave him a birthday cake, just to show what they think of him. He has been in public life almost 50 years. Secretary Hull told the newspapermen that one of the most important lessons he had learned during that time was that statesmen and peoples must recognize the strong responsibility of meeting those requirements which liberty imposes on those who enjoy it.

When you learn that, you learn the secret of democratic government. Democratic government is nothing but the daily business of respecting the responsibilities that liberty imposes. Liberty is not a negative thing. It is not an absence of control. That is anarchy. Liberty is achieved through the control which rests within oneself and not in somebody else. The judgment with which this self-control is exercised determines whether you have liberty or mere confusion or anarchy. That is the responsibility that liberty imposes upon those who enjoy it, as Secretary Hull put it. If they disregard that responsibility, then liberty is lost and you have either anarchy or control imposed by someone else, by any Hitler who is strong enough to seize control and exercise it.

Now I remember. It was about newspapers. All the editors are busy this week doing editorials about the newspapers and freedom of the press. What Secretary Hull said about statesmen and peoples having to meet the requirements that liberty imposes upon them goes for newspapers, too.

But so long as newspapers exercise that sense of responsibility, they are entitled to their freedom and will undoubtedly retain it. Free politics and free discussion go hand in hand, and the press is a vehicle for them.

Democracy needs all of this in times of emergency as much as in normal times. The only difference is that the times impose greater responsibilities upon the exercise of these liberties. The cost of recklessness is too great to be tolerated as long as it would be in normal times.

9/16/42

Newspaper Week is coming along soon but I see something about an American war correspondent being captured by the Axis during a British raid on Tobruk, so this is a good time to talk about a reporter's work.

The captured war correspondent is unidentified as I write, but circumstances indicate he may be Larry Allen of the Associated Press. In any case, evidently an American war correspondent was going about his daily work, which in this case took him out on a British attack at Tobruk.

Larry Allen has been shot up and shot down during this war, as have a number of other correspondents. A score of them went across in the Dieppe attack and had men shot down all around them.

Never before has individual freedom hung so precariously as it does now. Correspondents are trying to report this desperate struggle blow by blow because every blow counts.

In addition to the war correspondents who are risking their lives by going into the thick of battles are some who have paid the price in another kind of work. I am thinking of J. B. Powell, who served as an American journalist in China for so many years. The Japs had him marked for years and they finally caught him in Shanghai. They tortured him and left him broken and maimed for life. The National Press Club of Washington is raising a fund for him. Newspapermen all over the country are joining in because they recognize J. B. Powell as a man who has courageously and at fearful cost to himself stood his ground for freedom.

Those are the lives that make newspapers something more than a 6 per cent investment, as William Allen White once put it. Those are the lives that give their inspiration to a whole army of newspapermen and women who would rather devote themselves to trying to find and report the truth than do anything else in the world.

You can make your criticism of newspapers. Any working newspaperman can make more of them than anyone outside the business can make. A newspaperman scarcely ever reads over his piece in print without seeing that he could have improved it with a little more work. Most newspapermen feel that the speed at which they must work is sometimes a handicap and prevents them from digging as deeply as they would like to do. We are often puzzled, the more we look into something, to know what the truth is. Try it sometime around Washington. The more people you talk to, the more confused you will become. You get tangled up in a cross pull of wires as one official pulls against another.

Particularly in wartime your working newspaperman struggles always against indecision and conflicting decisions. Some officials think it is better to suppress differences and put up to the public a smooth plaster front that looks solid but which underneath may be as phony as a World's Fair pavilion.

For instance, some officials here see no harm in public discussion of India. We are sending troops and lend-lease aid there. If it is that important, then aren't we within bounds when we take exception to London's bullnecked course which is the same one that brought such disaster in Burma and Malaya? But some British correspondents here, attempting to inform their papers in London of American sentiment, find their dispatches heavily censored on this side before being sent across. This while London censors permit British criticisms of the Churchill policy to be sent to American newspapers.

Everywhere in the world, newspapermen trying to tell the truth must filter through censorship. No newspaperman questions the necessity for tight military censorship, though he may argue over incidental details. But political censorship is spreading also among the free nations under the guise of not giving the Axis anything that it might make use of.

The press of the democratic world is the only free forum left. I believe that on the whole the free press has exercised a sense of responsibility and restraint called for by the times. Therefore, it is not comforting to see some nameless employee sitting at the cable head deciding with a whack of his pencil the kind of political news about the United States that British correspondents can send back to their papers in London.

11/29/39

This dispatch is written to keep the record straight. Or if you don't like it, just call it a political writer's alibi.

This is no message for posterity. It is a personal memo addressed to those who can't read a political column for what it says but must discover some hidden significance behind it.

Over several months I have frequently written about Paul McNutt. He looked like good copy to me because he seemed to be a coming figure in the Democratic presidential group—and the subsequent amount of newspaper space given to him vindicates that judgment. Yet friends are indicating to me that they regard me as a "McNutt man." When Thomas E. Dewey was running for governor of New York, he seemed to be a figure destined to be much discussed and I wrote quite frequently about him. Then I was a "Dewey man." In 1935 I thought Alf Landon most likely to obtain the Republican presidential nomination in 1936 and I wrote

Raymond Clapper (left) with famous foreign correspondent Webb Miller sprinting down New York street in October, 1932.

a great deal about him. Then I was a "Landon man." Throughout all of this time I have written much about President Roosevelt, so I am—whenever that label serves some purpose—described as a "New Deal journalist."

It's all hogwash.

Like all political writers I gather favorable and unfavorable impressions of political figures who are in the news or who are about to appear in the news. These impressions color what is written. The assumption is that readers want to know what a writer thinks of the man about whom he is writing—at least that's the first question asked whenever reader and writer meet face to face. So these impressions go into the copy, directly or indirectly.

No writer can be completely objective. There is no reason why he should be. The attempt to be so results in some curious newspaper copy, often causing the real substance to be killed out of a dispatch as a sacrifice to a kind of superficial factualness.

Some time ago a reporter, obliged to write "factual" copy, was handling a Supreme Court decision. He first wrote that the "Supreme Court had rebuked Secretary of Agriculture Wallace." Then he decided that was a bit of interpretation which was forbidden under the rules of his office. Yet he knew that was the import of the decision. So he consulted a more ingenious colleague who changed the sentence to read, "The Supreme Court's decision was generally regarded as a rebuke to Secretary Wallace." By inserting the phrase "generally regarded" the rule of factual reporting was technically complied with.

If a writer cannot be completely objective, he can be independent. I know of newspapers which exhibit the most unreasonable likes and dislikes, and yet are independent and are so recognized. But every political columnist has a label pasted on him—he is either New Deal or anti-New Deal. Newspapers considered independent are in some cases pro-New Deal and in other cases anti-New Deal. Can't it be so with a columnist? Does he have to be suspected of trying to be a typewriter Warwick?

I expect to go on spilling out copy for many years to come, God and my editors willing, and to see many faces come and go. So for the record, put me down as an independent, enjoying a number of likes and dislikes, some of which, I hope, are justified, and some of which no doubt are cockeyed, and all subject to change for real or fancied reasons. That's that.

12/5/38

Hey, Elmer! Mister Andrews, what are you trying to do to us with your wage-and-hour law?

On my desk is a formal office notice concerning your wage-and-hour law, to wit:

"All persons on the pay roll are asked to place themselves on working schedules of 40 hours a week, and are hereby notified that no one must work in excess of 44 hours per week without express permission. Whenever permission is granted and an employee does work in excess of 44 hours, he must report to Mrs. Jeffries the extent of such work, not later than Monday following the week in which he worked overtime."

So instead of writing a column, I must write up last week's report for Mrs. Jeffries, our efficient office manager.

Sunday. Came in late. On way to office got idea for a column about the divided Republicans. Easy subject. Made a mental note to use some of material obtained from Kenneth Simpson in New York several weeks ago, also something Editor Harold Johnson of Watertown, N.Y., said in a letter, and a slant from a conversation with Tom Dewey before election. Snatches of something I heard recently in Kansas and Minnesota came back to mind and fitted in, along with several odds and ends from conversations with various politicians here and in other cities during last few weeks. By the time I reached the office I had the column fairly well worked out in my head, and it took me a little more than an hour to write it. Then I was through.

Monday. Decided last night to write another column about politics but today a congressman came in and talked for an hour about the defense problem and the public attitude toward it. So I scrapped the political idea to write about defense. I remembered something Representative Louis Ludlow had said about his war referendum, and some questions which had occurred to me while reading *The Ramparts We Watch* on an airplane from Chicago to Washington 2 weeks ago. Dictated on mail, went to lunch, returned, and knocked out column in about an hour. But after looking it over thought it was clumsy and rewrote part of it. Total writing time about 2 hours.

Tuesday. Planned some time ago to write on Republican National Committee meeting today. Arrived at office 9:30 A.M. Dictated mail, then to Carlton Hotel for Republican meeting. Stayed for luncheon (free on Republican National Committee), listened to speeches, hung around all afternoon talking with politicians. Took 15 minutes out to interview some of them on radio. Had material and outline all in mind on returning to office at 4:30 P.M. Through writing at 5:45. Went to cocktail party and listened to two Supreme Court justices, John L. Lewis, and conservative Publisher Eugene Meyer in free-for-all argument about where capitalist system is headed. Discovered they didn't know any more about it than the rest of us, which is going to help me in my work, I hope. Then to buffet supper for new Philippine delegate, who is the John D. Rockefeller of the islands, and he talked informatively on Philippine and Pacific questions. Background and ideas there for several future columns. Home shortly before midnight. Writing time 1 hour 15 minutes.

That's half of my week. Wednesday a friend of Justice Brandeis came to office indignant about pressure to get him off bench so Frankfurter could go on. After checking by long distance and several local calls, had material for a column about that. Thursday attended monopoly hearings but wrote about free congressional sugar junket to Florida on basis of several telephone conversations. Friday wrote about patent question which O'Mahoney committee is about to investigate, drawing material from following: (1) File which I have been accumulating for several years; (2) conversation with a businessman friend on beach at Rehoboth, Del., during last summer's vacation; (3) discussion with a businessman whose firm is being investigated by the monopoly committee; (4) data from O'Mahoney committee investigation. Writing time 2 hours.

For the week, that adds up to 10 or 12 hours' writing time. As for the rest, I can't figure how much is work and how much is play. They are much the same in this business. We get some of our best material over highballs, and when I'm in the office, I'm practically loafing.

So, Mrs. Jeffries, if it's all right with you, it's all right with me just to put me down for 40 hours flat. We won't count thinking time, so-called, and ideas that come out of the shower bath. And if one of Elmer's investigators comes around to paste a $10,000 fine on you with 6 months in jail for the second offense, I'll lie like hell to get you out of it. After all, much as I like the wage-and-hour law, I have a family to support and I can't afford to give up newspaper work to become a timekeeper.

11/21/38

I have just come from the funeral of an old friend and colleague, Rodney Dutcher. We first worked together more than 15 years ago on the United Press. He richly deserved the tribute which President Roosevelt paid to him as a reporter who was "fearless and objective."

That is as complete an epitaph as any working newspaperman wants when he goes to press for the last time.

To be fearless and objective. In our business those are the trademarks of quality. With them a newspaperman has everything. Without them, he can't have much. Writing? That is only putting it down on paper.

To be fearless and objective is an achievement in our business. It is an achievement for a human being, beset as we all are with countless little half-hidden fears, to take the cold facts and lay them on the line. A thousand little inhibitions stare up at us from our typewriters. They say don't use this and don't use that. The facts are in hand but sometimes it takes a muster of cool determination to put them down in print.

To be objective also is an achievement. We are born with emotions and we easily acquire prejudices. It is natural to coddle, pamper, and nurse them until they turn on us and boss us, and lash us into a daily shriek. To see the facts through this haze of emotion, to let them filter through, to keep still and let the facts do the talking—that, if you've never tried it, is an achievement.

Most newspapermen in America try to develop these qualities because they are, within the business, the marks of the good craftsman. And newspapermen, above everything else, want to be good craftsmen, and because they are thinking of that more intensely than about money, they have been taken advantage of and in many instances have been poorly paid for work which is of the highest importance in a democracy. We are, or should be, the eyes and ears of democracy and most newspapermen, as was Rodney Dutcher, are conscious of the obligation.

In only a few countries, besides our own, are newspapermen given this responsibility. Few countries now have any use for newspapermen who are fearless and objective. Those qualities are not wanted. Governments, politicians in power, tell newspapermen what to write in many countries. To be objective and fearless in Germany today is the quickest way to land in a concentration camp. An American kind of newspaperman would be, under some governments today, an ideal target for the firing squad.

In introducing President Roosevelt at the thirtieth anniversary dinner of the National Press Club here, Harold Brayman, correspondent of *The Philadelphia Evening Public Ledger* and president of the club, praised Roosevelt as a "newspaperman's President."

"The news sources here," said Brayman, "have remained open, the most open of them all being the White House press conference, where questions are still welcome, whether pertinent, impertinent, or too pertinent, and where the free press reaches its highest degree of freedom."

Some people think Roosevelt is too dictatorial. But Roosevelt and his most indefatigable critic, Mark Sullivan, still exchange pleasantries at press conferences. And at a press conference a few days after the recent election, Pete Brandt, of *The St. Louis Post-Dispatch,* asked Roosevelt if he wasn't facing a conservative coalition in Congress that would cause him trouble. Roosevelt said he didn't think so.

"I do," Pete Brandt shot back. Nothing happened except that Roosevelt and everybody else laughed.

Roosevelt can dish it out. He also can take it.

Because our public men are like that, because we have always protected the free press in America, it is possible for newspaper reporters to try, as Rodney Dutcher did, to be fearless and objective.

11/7/38

Somebody who wants to do his country a good turn should start a society to drive the ghost writer out of politics. Ghost writing has become such a commonplace in politics that it is taken for granted. A politician is assumed not to have bothered to prepare his own written speeches. Ninety per cent of the political speeches which you have listened to in this campaign [November, 1938], were not written by the candidates who delivered them, but by some press agent, or some anonymous hired hand slaving secretly in the back room.

This practice has existed from the days of George Washington, whose Farewell Address was ghostwritten for him by Alexander Hamilton. When you hear a political speaker, you are almost safe in assuming that somebody else wrote his speech for him. This practice goes from Roosevelt down in both parties. It has turned political speaking into a synthetic, artificial, somewhat phony form of ballyhoo.

The public's only means of sizing up a candidate is by what he says. Yet most candidates spend their time shaking hands and listening to delegations, and parading, and then just as they mount the speaking platform a secretary shoves up the text of that night's speech which has been ground out by the ghost writer.

Postmaster General Farley, chairman of the Democratic National Committee, doesn't write the speeches he delivers. They are written by Eddie Roddan, who is assistant to Charley Michelson at Democratic National Committee headquarters. Republican Chairman John Hamilton's speeches are written by his publicity director, Franklyn Waltman. Both of these ghost writers are former Washington newspapermen. Each maintains a party headquarters speech factory, in which political speeches on any subject are ground out for any political candidate who wants literary help. Once I thought I detected a conflict of policy between two leading party figures, but I was promptly assured by the party ghost writer that I could not be correct because he had written both speeches and he knew there was no conflict between them. He had tried to say the same thing in different words, in the two speeches.

Harding and Coolidge had the same White House ghost writer for a time. He was Judson C. Welliver, once a Washington correspondent, and hired by Harding to write speeches. Welliver studied the florid Harding style and imitated it perfectly. When Harding died, he continued for Coolidge in the same capacity, imitating Coolidge's more abrupt style. He took great delight in editorials which commented on the contrast in literary style between Harding's speeches and those of Coolidge, he having written both.

In the current Ohio senatorial campaign, Robert Taft, the Republican candidate, is a changed man. Once he was an outspoken, hard-shell reactionary. Now he calls himself a liberal. Once he was a dull sour puss who couldn't unbend. Now he is a lively, jolly handshaker, the soul of affability. They tell me in Ohio that the change was wrought by a squad of brain trusters, advisers, ghost writers, physical trainers, and what not, who took the crown prince of the Taft family in hand and streamlined him. The job was so well done that if he has good luck in the Tuesday election he is ready now to be placed in the show window as a 1940 model.

The backstage ghosters are powerful fellows. Smart writers can pull the mouthpiece candidates around by the nose. Soon after the 1936 election Republican Chairman Hamilton began saying in his speeches that the Republicans must begin to think about the people "across the railroad tracks." It was a new line for John and inquiry developed that he had a new press agent. The chap was something of a liberal. But he didn't hit it off at Republican headquarters here and eventually left. He is now with Tom Dewey in New York, and Chairman Hamilton's speeches long ago resumed their tone of sturdy conservatism.

If a political candidate can't get up and make a speech of his own, if he has to hire a press agent to write it for him, then why not let the press agent be the candidate? Voters are entitled to know what a candidate thinks and what he knows. If a candidate or a politician can't stand up and talk for 30 minutes or an hour about issues of the day in his own words and with his own thought, then he ought not to fake it by shoving out a speech which some ghost writer ground out for him.

Democratic government is, to a considerable extent, government by discussion. It is not enough to have good ideas. In a democracy it is important to be able to sell them to the public. If a political candidate is so inarticulate that he cannot rise to his feet and express himself with reasonable clarity, force, and sincerity, he is miscast—because he will need those very talents to advance his program in the public mind and in legislative debate. He had better give way and allow the ghost writer to be the candidate and himself seek some appointive office which does not require platform ability.

This ghost writing has developed into a considerable political fraud on the electorate. Every politician's speech, like his income-tax return, ought to bear a sworn affidavit stating whether or not the speaker has had the assistance of others in the preparation of the text. We would get worse speeches but genuine ones.

9/3/40

This one will be about reaching an understanding between you and me, on the business of writing a newspaper column.

Ordinarily I don't discuss the tricks of the trade, but just now perhaps they are a matter of legitimate concern to at least some readers and some editors. I note one gossip columnist remarking that he was aghast the other night to hear one of America's most gifted and eminent columnists (that excuses me) say ruefully, "I don't dare write anything really critical of Willkie. Not if I want to remain in this business."

I don't know who he heard say that, if anybody. It sounds screwy to me.

We get pressure both ways. Several days ago I had a letter from an editor demanding to know whether I intended to support

Willkie, because if I did, then he would have to look for another column. It's all in a day's work. But if anyone else is interested I'll repeat here what I said in reply, because readers are as much entitled as editors are to know it.

The reply was as follows:

"You ask whether I will definitely support Mr. Willkie and add that, if so, you probably will be obliged to run another column that is supporting Mr. Roosevelt.

"If I could give you a definite reply I should be glad to do so. I am an independent writer and chain myself to no candidate or party. From day to day I try to report, add up, analyze, and interpret developments from an independent point of view. Such opinion as finds its way into the column arises from the same point of view. Sometimes this is favorable to Mr. Roosevelt and sometimes not. Sometimes it is favorable to Mr. Willkie and sometimes not. How it will add up toward the end of the campaign I don't know, any more than I knew in 1936. For several weeks I was favorable to Gov. Landon. As his campaign developed I lost my enthusiasm for it and favored the reelection of Mr. Roosevelt.

"At the moment I lean toward Mr. Willkie for reasons which have been touched upon in various columns. But the campaign is young and I want to see more of it before I close my mind.

"One thing is definite: I have never been nor do I intend to be a propagandist for either party. Any editor who wants a journalistic mouthpiece for one side or the other will be disappointed in this column.

"I believe there is a place for a truly independent column. I believe there is greater need than ever for a column which plays the game, not of some party or candidate, but of the independent newspaper reader who is trying to think his way along.

"Columns of varying points of view are now such an established feature in practically every newspaper that readers do not associate them with a newspaper's own editorial policy. In fact, many editors have told me that they are deliberately trying to present a variety of viewpoints as a matter of reader service. I have noticed that many of them, as you have done, frequently write editorials taking issue with columns in their own papers. This has always impressed me as excellent journalism. The reader feels that his newspaper is fair and willing to give all sides a hearing.

"While I cannot answer your question in one sense, I can in another. If you want a column which will be 100 per cent for Mr. Roosevelt every day, my column will not meet your requirements; because, even should I lean to Mr. Roosevelt on balance, there will still be days when the column is likely to be critical."

Sometimes I envy those who are hell bent 100 per cent for or against their man. One can then pack a real punch into his copy. When a writer stays so much in the gray his copy seems weak and timid and indecisive beside that of a hard hitter who sees it all black or white. Also, it must leave readers uncertain at times, and with a feeling that there is nothing fixed that they can tie to. I regret that. But in this business you don't last unless you are yourself.

11/21/40

I have often thought that one of my shortcomings as a newspaper columnist is that there are many days when I come down to the office without an opinion all white-hot and ready to burn its way through the typewriter and to the printed page. Everyone, especially a newspaper columnist, is expected to have an opinion on any subject in the day's news. It may be a good opinion, or a poor one, but strong or weak, an opinion he must have.

I go out among my friends. They fix me with a sharp eye and demand to know what I think. What do I think about the aircraft strike? Will Britain hold out? What about Joe Kennedy? The Greeks? John L. Lewis? Everybody else has an opinion. You're a columnist. What do you think?

Then comes my feeble contribution. More than half the time I let them down. They have caught me cold without an opinion, with nothing but a vague, stammering, evasive reply. They look at me accusingly and think I am holding out on them, saving it up for a column. Half the time I let it go at that rather than make the shameful confession that I haven't any very definite opinion.

It must be great never to be in doubt, always to know what you think, to know right off whether the great man whose name has been on every tongue is a saint or a skunk for what he said in a political speech the other night.

In writing a column one feels he is letting his readers down unless he has a hard-hitting opinion to serve up six days a week on the regular deadline. The writer who appears in print these days without clubbing his readers over the head with an opinion is put down as an odd fellow, with something missing, as if he had walked down the street without a necktie. All of this has made me very unhappy, especially during the political campaign. It wasn't a crime in that campaign to have the most vicious, unwarranted, insupportable opinion but it was a crime not to have an opinion. Better a poor one than none at all. Readers wrote in protesting. Why didn't I have the guts to say what I thought? That's what they wanted me to answer them. No beating around the bush that way, Clapper.

Someone kindly directed me to an old book of essays, first published 30 years ago by H. W. Fowler, and the one for my case was entitled, "If I Had Opinions."

I had thought all this business was of recent origin, but 30 years ago this author found that it was hardly permitted to anyone to have no opinions at all. He observed that whenever he raised a question among his friends, someone was always certain to reel off a systematic lecture about it which showed a thorough consideration of the subject in all its bearings. He concluded that they gave all their leisure time to forming opinions and to organizing their thoughts neatly so that at a moment's notice they could put their hands on a set of opinions about any subject in earth or heaven.

Having no opinions of his own, he was reduced to borrowing them from others and found that it worked very well.

Not a bad idea. When one sets about to inform himself so that he may reach an intelligent opinion, he finds so much on both sides that it is obvious one side is not all wrong and the other all right. He becomes one of those colorless, uninteresting, and universally scorned "yes—but" persons. That's all he gets for his trouble. But if he skips all the study and inquiry, snatches up the first opinion that he comes across and thrusts it aloft as his opinion which he will defend to the death, he becomes a strong, decisive man who knows his own mind. He may become a great leader of men. The multitudes bow before such self-confident wisdom. The first thing you know you may have a dictator. Then you can't have any opinions of your own.

But now we're going around in a circle, so let's forget it.

10/3/40

American newspapers have designated this as a National Newspaper Week in order to emphasize anew the importance of a free press.

As a writer I am one of the journeymen in the business, one of the hired hands, as distinguished from the management. I have noted what critics have said about the press, about distortion and suppression of news, and about business-office control. The critics have not always been wrong. Everyone in the business knows that there are times when the press is its own worst enemy.

Throughout my life, beginning with my school days, I have made my living in journalism, and as long as my legs hold out I expect to do so. Journalism has given me rewards, both spiritual and material, far beyond my early expectations. For that I am and always shall be humbly grateful.

I look about and discover that I have much more freedom than most people in other lines of work. How many, many instances have occurred in the daily observation of all of us when we see that people in other walks of life are subjected to pressure which prevents them from saying what they think and believe. How often must a rising junior executive trim the sails of his own personal convictions on economic and political questions through fear that he will come into disfavor with his superiors. Talk about social lobbies in Washington. Is there any social lobby more powerful than the country-club lobby? Is there any pressure stronger upon the individual than the sentiment around the luncheon-club table? How often does a businessman, a professional man, suppress his own judgment because the group with which he must do business leans so strongly toward another view? Each person can answer that one in the privacy of his own mind out of his own observation. The real dictator in this country, the real foe of free thought and free speech, is that subtle censor which we all know and feel but seldom recognize in public.

Compared with that network of restraints which operate upon people in so many walks of life, the working newspaperman lives in a paradise of freedom. That is why so many men are reluctant to leave journalism for other kinds of work. They know how much freedom they have and they know how much more free they are than those caught in the hierarchy of other walks of life.

I am less concerned about the freedom of the press than I am about the freedom of the reader. Let the reader be tolerant, open-minded, interested in hearing both sides. That's the way to have a free press. You won't keep a free press with a public that only throws cantaloupes at somebody it disagrees with. Democratic discussion cannot be carried on by means of tossing eggs at political candidates. When the public no longer wants free discussion, when it no longer wants to hear what the other fellow has to say and simply throws tomatoes at him, then you are working into a state of mind which points toward the end not only of a free press but of all free institutions. Egg throwers make dictators. The lady who threw the wastebasket at Willkie will get something worse than Roosevelt or Willkie if her state of mind becomes a national state of mind. Those are the kind of people who have quit thinking and want somebody to tell them who to throw eggs at.

4/2/43

This Government is playing with the dangerous idea of carrying the technique of a controlled press far beyond anything we have experienced before in this country.

A United Nations food conference is being arranged to take place within a few weeks. The President has desired to hold it at an isolated location some distance from Washington where the meeting could be easily protected from the public view.

Newspapers have been requested not to attempt to send reporters to cover this conference or to try to talk to the delegates representing the United Nations.

Such arrangements go far beyond the sphere of military censorship. They reach very frankly into political censorship.

Obviously the reasons that prompt the White House to feel that a United Nations conference should be thus isolated from the normal operations of newspaper correspondents will be the same reasons that will be found persuasive by Administration officials when subsequent United Nations conferences are held.

Newspaper editors have been requested to accept this policy. What else will they be asked to accept if this precedent is established?

There could have been no objection if the Government had called in the press, explained some of the considerations, and emphasized that international relations might be done serious injury by irresponsible handling of news or comment.

But the press is being given no opportunity to be either responsible or irresponsible. It is proposed to shut it out flatly.

Anyone will recognize that the United Nations are still in the formative period, that their first meetings may thrive or wither, depending upon how they are carried off. An irresponsible press can do fateful damage to international relations, particularly in a time like this.

But a free press is not necessarily an irresponsible press.

For evidence in behalf of a free press as against the type of control now proposed for the United Nations conference, I go directly to our own Government propaganda service itself.

The Office of War Information is an enormous organization. It employs dozens of excellent newspapermen and magazine writers, men who have made their reputations in competitive private life.

Yet, the skillful propaganda prepared by these expert craftsmen falls short. It doesn't ring true enough. So O.W.I. sends out, for the information of the people in foreign countries, the actual daily columns and editorials of well-known American writers and newspapers.

The Government prefers to send abroad the regular work of these writers, and to give newspapers abroad the opportunity to print current columns of many of the American columnists, because this is the genuine propaganda of truth, the genuine discussion that goes on in America.

Abroad they don't want special propaganda written particularly for them. They don't have confidence in it.

But when they read what Americans themselves are reading in American newspapers, when they are, so to speak, listening in on discussions taking place in the free press here in America, then they believe it.

Hand-tailored propaganda is discounted abroad as it is here at home. Everybody abroad has been propagandized by experts for years. All the tricks are known.

What concerns me about this proposed exclusion of the press from such a nonmilitary affair as an international food conference is that the same reasons will be used to impose a similar blockade on the press after the war. If we are afraid a free press will damage the United Nations now, won't we still be afraid of it after the war?

4/12/43

Some may wonder why the newspapers are concerned over the wish of President Roosevelt to keep the first big United Nations conference closed against the press.

It is a conference concerning food, and a considerable portion of the work will be technical and of comparatively little general interest.

I myself do not expect to report the conference or even be in the country when it is held. Yet I am very much concerned over the attempt President Roosevelt has made to exclude the press from all contact with representatives at this conference.

I am concerned about it because I hope there will be many United Nations conferences and I want the people to know about them and to share in them. I hope that nations will be meeting in this way for generations to come. I hope the people of all countries will have more and more control over their governments. I hope we are to have an increasingly democratic world, and that the nations of this democratic world will solve their problems meeting together in friendly conferences and not ever try to solve them by the method of mass murder that has been resorted to up to now.

If the people of all countries—and I think this applies unquestionably in Germany and Italy and perhaps in Japan—could have had their way there would have been no war this time.

This week we are paying honor to the memory of our patron saint of democracy, Thomas Jefferson. He believed that laws and institutions must go hand in hand with the progress of the human mind. But always the strength of society, in his judgment, rested in the heart of the people, in acceptance of the decisions of the majority, in freedom of religion, the press, freedom of discussion, and in the preservation of civil rights.

In the preservation of all this nothing is more basic than free discussion. And the press is one of the principal agencies of free discussion.

There is no military reason why the press should not have free access to the first United Nations conference, which is to open May 18 at Hot Springs, Va. Yet President Roosevelt by his own personal direction, against the earnest protest of Elmer Davis of O.W.I. and of others in the Government, has persisted in ordering arrangements that will treat newspaper and radio representatives—who after all are merely eyes and ears for the American people—like moral lepers.

They are to be excluded from any contact with delegates. A newspaperman who takes his work seriously considers that he is honor bound to learn as much and report as much about public affairs as is possible. He makes only one reservation and that is that he must be guided at all times by the requirements of national security. Yet newspapermen are to be denied access to the hotel where the delegates will live.

Thomas Jefferson once said that if a people had to be without newspapers or without government they would do better without government.

But a democratic people needs both. Certainly good government needs good newspapers.

What was true in Jefferson's time while the young United States were learning to walk is equally true now when the United Nations are taking their first steps.

Mr. Roosevelt thinks of the press as a nuisance, or as an irritation, or as offering a medium through which mischief might be done during the United Nations food conference.

A totally irresponsible and malicious press could do perhaps fatal damage. But the American press and the British press have shown that they are not as a whole either irresponsible or malicious. On both sides of the Atlantic the press has observed voluntary censorship, and beyond that has contributed energetically toward assisting with the war.

Surely Mr. Roosevelt does not think the press should omit all comment on the work of the United Nations food conference. But such comment must be based on independent newspaper reporting at Hot Springs itself. What confidence can be inspired and what useful comment can be made on the basis of official communiqués alone? The very thought of it is absurd to any newspaperman who knows how communiqués are written and how little is said in them. We know how they are doctored and how they must be devitalized to cover up even healthy and moderate differences of opinion. Only saps believe that official communiqués tell the whole truth.

If the press is to be thrown out into the gutter at the first United Nations conference at Hot Springs, the press may as well prepare to be similarly parked at future United Nations conferences where more difficult questions will be discussed.

9/1/43

Since the Quebec conference ended, White House and State Department discussion of our foreign policy has been largely confined to denunciation of newspaper columnists and especially to calling Drew Pearson a liar.

President Roosevelt cut Pearson's throat from ear to ear in the most savage outburst of temper I can recall at a White House press conference. It is barely possible they are using Pearson to put the fear of God into all of us. Whether that was the purpose or not I will say that so far as I am concerned they have practically succeeded.

Whatever I might think about what goes on in our State Department, and whatever I might think about the attitude and capabilities of some of our people in the State Department, I would not wish to make criticisms that would place me in the White House list of people who, it says, are helping the enemy and are therefore virtual traitors.

It is hard in these times to know what constitutes helping the enemy. Often it is the truth that they say helps the enemy—for instance if you told about some secret military plans in advance, that would be helping the enemy. You have to take the word of the White House and the State Department as to what criticism or discussion will help the enemy. They could be wrong about it but that won't help you when the President tears you apart like an ancient lion devouring a Christian martyr.

If these were normal times one might say that newspaper writers were being taken entirely too seriously around the White House and the State Department. I wouldn't dare think of it now, but it is ridiculous for two big men like Roosevelt and Hull, with so many important things to be done, to allow one newspaper columnist to throw them into a week's hysterics.

I don't mean to be critical. Not at all. But ordinarily a person would say to himself that if Roosevelt and Hull were not so much worried over what a gossip columnist says, and were not so busy thinking up rough things to say about him, taking up two of Hull's press conferences and one of Roosevelt's, then perhaps—well, it mustn't be said in these times, you know.

12/6/43

Roosevelt, Churchill, and Stalin have ended their conference at Teheran. At my elbow is the unpublished advance press material telling about it, with the three-power statement regarding Germany that was prepared by the three great leaders of democracy last Wednesday.

I can't tell you what it says because as this dispatch is written, the material is not yet released for publication. But at a party last Saturday night I heard all about it in detail. It was common talk in Washington. The advance material which I still can't mention in this dispatch was sent out over newspaper cables and wires last Saturday.

However, the so-called secret about the Teheran conference has been dispatched literally all over the world. The Russian people were told about the conference last week through their official news agency. The Axis talks about it. And everybody has been allowed to print the news about these conferences carried by the Axis radio and press.

This is not a mere controversy over the release of press material. It is a flagrant case of mayhem against the democratic freedom of the press. Our voluntary cooperation in censorship has been grossly imposed upon.

The excuse given is that secrecy is necessary for military security. But any half-witted spy, blindfolded, could pick up the information that has been distributed over the last week end through the vast international press systems of the world. Last Thursday, the Axis radio was describing the former Shah's palace in Iran where the three democratic leaders were supposed to be meeting.

If military security was involved, why was the advance material sent across the ocean where thousands would see it a couple of days before publication? No censor in his right mind could possibly find a military reason for not publishing the advance material when it reached our office from the United Press about 2 o'clock Saturday afternoon.

The Cairo conference was even a worse botch. There were American and British correspondents in Cairo, war correspondents whose loyalty had been carefully investigated and many of whom had risked personal danger in covering the Allied side of the war. They were treated like scum at this conference although they are trusted in the highest military headquarters.

We read secondhand gossip how Churchill wore a 10-gallon hat and danced a jig, and how the supply of Scotch ran out at Mena House the night the conference met there, and how the President's son-in-law, Major John Boettiger, turned up there and joked with Chiang. And also how the American war correspondents were barricaded outside the area and were not permitted to send any dispatches about this affair going on in Oriental secrecy while the Axis was helping itself to the ear of the world about it all.

Why were American correspondents kept far away from the barricades under the shadow of the pyramids? Why was not Secretary Stephen E. Early, or Elmer Davis, or somebody who knows about press relations, taken along? They had room for the President's son-in-law and a special jeep which was flown from America with the President. Steve Early would have been more useful freight.

There must be a thrill for such powerful Allied leaders as they go into seclusion behind élite guards and settle the affairs of the world. But they are slipping into a state of Oriental arrogance regarding the interest of the democratic peoples in their activities.

It is not a very good thing politically for Mr. Roosevelt to be doing at this time. He is needed, and all the leaders are needed, and such conferences ought to be held frequently. But democratic leadership cannot afford to cut itself off and become barricaded behind this wall of pseudo secrecy.

The press was given cavalier treatment at the Hot Springs food conference last spring. At the Atlantic City relief conference some correspondents lost interest in going to report that first United Nations meeting because, although they recognized its vital importance, they were notified that they would be treated like lepers.

12/7/43

Reporters are not privileged individuals in themselves. They are the eyes and ears of the people back home. Perhaps the military has spoiled us, but war correspondents are trusted and given cooperation by military and naval headquarters in a way totally lacking at these conferences by our political heads of states. These are strange signs in heads of so-called democracies.

Yet such conferences are necessary and no obstacle and no prejudice should thoughtlessly be raised against them.

Perhaps it is a paradox of this period that in order to win the victory necessary to the democratic way of life, and to organize the postwar security necessary to that life, we must for the time being work through four men who have the personal leadership of the war. It almost amounts to depending on four personal dictators, for in such conferences as these the three or four principals present have the power to make irrevocable decisions. The decisions are irrevocable because the train of events necessary to effectuate the decisions can be put into effect without recourse.

This is almost saying that we are at the mercy of four indispensable men. I cringe from the phrase, yet it is almost that, in the sense that these four men are the best available instruments for the job. They are the best men because they are there. Willkie might have been better than Roosevelt—if he had been put in there in 1940. But so much consists in being there. As Oliver Wendell Holmes once said in commenting on John Marshall, "a great man represents a great ganglion in the nerves of society, or to vary the figure, a strategic point in the campaign of history, and part of his greatness consists of his being there."

To a greater degree by far than ever before we have placed our destiny in the keeping of one man. What Roosevelt has agreed to at Teheran we may not know entirely for a long time to come. He has cast the die for the United States perhaps in decisions from which there can never be any turning back. In that sense we are completely at his mercy.

But when we see votes cast as in New York state last month, and as in Kentucky, and all over the country, I don't believe any of us can seriously feel that the American people are in danger of losing fundamental control of their government. All except one of the big northern industrial states are now Republican. The switch to Republican control in Congress is expected by almost everybody in politics. With that change already in progress, we need not worry about the danger of losing popular control.

JOURNALISM

12/29/43

We whose daily work is to report public affairs and to comment on them will find 1944 a year to test everything we have.

We shall be harder put to it than ever to report with understanding and perspective, and to interpret with balanced judgment the strange torrent of events that roars through these decisive days.

Editorial writers, columnists, and commentators seem to me to be under the same obligations of conscientious loyalty to what they understand and believe that public men are under. We writers freely demand that senators, representatives, Presidents, and office-holders and politicians generally, show moral courage and loyalty to their convictions, even at the risk of being retired to private life. This year we may have to face some of that same kind of testing ourselves.

Highly controversial questions will have to be faced. No matter what one says, he is likely to lose friends. Dale Carnegie will have a market for a new edition of his book after this year is over.

During 1944 people will be taut. Many casualties are coming, and victories, no matter how thrilling, will not erase the anxious lines on the faces of those who wait for news of their loved ones far away. People under stress are less tolerant and are more ready victims for vicious demagoguery.

Not since the Civil War have we had an election in wartime, and it will be a severe trial for our democracy. Never have we had such highly organized pressure groups badgering Congress for special favors. There are severe race tensions. We cannot pretend they don't exist.

Yet democracy is not on trial. Democracy has won its victory. The revolt of Europe against Hitler, the bitter hatred of Fascism and Nazism that seethes all over Europe, the sabotage in Denmark, the unconquerable spirit that waits in Norway, the refusal to accept the New Order, are evidence that self-government has met its test and has won in the affections and longings of people over the brutal system of the Nazis.

Democracy is in danger chiefly in that it is liable to make a bad mess of affairs through poor management. We are in danger of overindulgence, of refusing to put ourselves through the discipline necessary to survive or even to check inflation—as the strike threats on the railroads and in steel, and the fight against price control, suggest.

Democracy is not an efficient form of government, but efficiency is not enough, and this inefficient form of government is more desirable in the end because of the other values which it preserves. But democracy is based on self-discipline, and ours right now is very poor. This won't kill our democracy but it may leave it misshapen and ill and miserable instead of healthy and growing and happy.

If expectations of the top Allied people are fulfilled, Germany will cease to be a military force by fall.

The exploratory discussions between Roosevelt, Churchill, and Stalin leave some of the participants convinced that there is little likelihood of issues arising between them that could be serious enough to threaten future peace. Germany and Japan have been the menaces throughout this century and are potential sources of trouble for the remainder of it. Once they are disarmed we can keep them so, and have two generations, at least, of peace and security.

That opportunity and how to realize it will be the underlying concern of what we write and say in the coming year.

The task of finding our way to that is the great task of public discussion and public opinion in America for 1944.

Democracy

5/5/39

IT IS appropriate for the President of the United States to receive distinguished foreign visitors under strictly civilian auspices. Personally I like to see him take them on at Hyde Park and give them American hot dogs. That's us. Let Hitler and Mussolini put on the war shows.

When an American ambassador goes to his post, from the Court of St. James's on down the list, he appears in simple evening dress. No medals. No trick uniform. No title. Just plain "Mr. Ambassador" dressed exactly as he would go to the annual formal dance of the Elks Lodge. Our President wears no uniform. In his office he wears an ordinary business suit. For formal day appearances he wears a cutaway. For evening appearances he wears a white tie and tails. No decorations. No title. Just plain "Mr. President." You don't even call him excellency.

That is America—so strong that it doesn't need to bolster up its confidence with a lot of grand-opera stage props.

1/21/41

America has been in peril many times. It has been in peril from without and from within. But it has never retreated. Not even when the odds were much against it. There has always been a spirit—greater, as Mr. Roosevelt said, than the sum of the parts—which has come through the shouting and doubting and kept the path of our faith lighted.

8/21/39

The inner core of civilization is found not in esthetics but in the conduct of human beings. Many have said it better, but the idea is that civilization is the art of going after some of the things you want without elbowing your neighbor too roughly while you are about it.

4/6/39

Out of the narrow-minded mixture of red tape and prejudice which has kept Marian Anderson, the great Negro contralto, from the concert stage in this capital of democracy is growing as if with divine justice one of the most notable tributes of recognition ever accorded a member of this long-suffering race.

She wasn't allowed to sing in the D.A.R. hall nor in the public-school auditoriums. But on Easter Sunday she will sing at the foot of the noble statue of the emancipator of her race, on the steps of Lincoln Memorial. Her audience will number millions of high and low. The three radio networks will broadcast her voice.

Thus, through the actions which denied America's own Marian Anderson the ordinary concert stages here, available at fancy prices to a steady procession of foreign artists, her voice will now be heard by millions who otherwise might have lived out their lives without ever having heard of her.

The nice people who found rules to deny her the hearing that Russians, Germans, Italians, Poles, Jews, and all other races of the earth receive on the concert stage in Washington have unwittingly played into the hands of the professional organizations of Negroes. Walter White, Secretary of the National Association for the Advancement of Colored People, the chief lobbyist for the Negro cause, who when in Washington stays at one of the most socially correct hotels, is taking full advantage of this incident to develop race pride. His organization is encouraging Negroes to make the Easter Sunday pilgrimage here.

But the affair has become much larger than Walter White and his organization for the advancement of Negro rights. The Administration here has seized upon the affair to demonstrate the tolerance which it is felt properly belongs in a democratic nation.

The idea for having Marian Anderson sing on the steps of the Lincoln Memorial came from a Southern-born Administration official, Oscar Chapman, Assistant Secretary of the Interior. He sold the idea to his chief, Secretary Ickes. The White House is sympathetic, Mrs. Roosevelt having brought the whole affair to national attention by her resignation of protest from the D.A.R.

Chapman's idea of using the Lincoln Memorial grew out of an incident in his childhood. He was born in Virginia, and as a lad in grade school had a stern lesson in intolerance. His eighth-grade graduating class had a small fund and wished to give a present to the school. He bought a picture of Lincoln. His teacher was tolerant and accepted the gift.

But when the children carried word home to their parents, and the news got around, the school board was in a rage. The picture was ordered taken down. Oscar was suspended, but through the intercession of a Methodist Sunday-school superintendent he was restored to class. Bewildered by the angry feelings aroused in the school board, Oscar began to ask questions. From that time he has taken the side of tolerance in every showdown that has come his way.

What does the color of Marian Anderson's skin have to do with her ability as an artist? What is the difference between the Nazis driving opera singers off the stage because they are Jewish, and Americans in Washington closing their concert halls to a recognized artist because she is of the Negro race? The difference is this: We don't expect anything better in Germany now. But in Washington we have a shrine for Abraham Lincoln. In the long run, we can be proud that this shrine has been made available for this Easter Sunday gesture of race tolerance. It's the principle of the thing, and it won't even matter much if Marian turns up with laryngitis.

12/4/39

The American rule is to find the practical compromise between individual freedom and the requirements of living in close quarters with one another.

You don't need a building code on the farm. But downtown in a big city a man simply can't erect any kind of building he wishes. That might seriously damage his neighbor's property. So you have a building code, a restriction on individual freedom, but a practical restriction.

Where private enterprise proves inadequate, we put the Government, local or Federal, to work—as with T.V.A. and as with countless municipally owned utilities. Yet if our telephone system works satisfactorily—and any American who has traveled abroad will agree that it does—it becomes foolish to switch it to public ownership.

To say that all things should be owned privately or that all things should be owned publicly is doctrinaire. The American way is to use the method that works best. To talk about socialism versus private capitalism in such matters is to fan the air with meaningless words.

Prohibition came and went. It was a most drastic infringement of individual liberty, the excuse being that liquor was a public nuisance. Yet I don't recall anybody saying that prohibition was leading us to fascism, socialism, or anything else. We didn't know about ideologies then. Well-known Republican individualists fought for prohibition. We tried it out. It didn't work. We got rid of it. That's the American way.

3/7/38

It is probably correct that democracy is inefficient. It temporizes and dawdles. Your dictatorship acts, and there is no monkey business.

It is plain that democracy hasn't got sense enough to come in out of the rain. Still we love the old softy.

6/27/36

One must indeed have great faith in popular government if he can maintain it unshaken through a national convention. Democrats, engaged in renominating a great idealist for President, sink to the level of the lowest common denominator, which is plenty low.

They push and yell in a seething, bedraggled, sweating mob. Two fat ladies, dressed in gingham kiddie dresses, carry placards endorsing the more abundant life. Governor Earle of Pennsylvania, who told the convention his ancestors came over on the *Mayflower,* is dragged through the crowd as he clutches the Pennsylvania standard and blows a 25-cent horn.

A buxom gal in white tries to kick off her hat, giving the photographers an extremely candid camera shot, which makes the afternoon newspapers, garters and all. From his roost on the balcony a movie photographer throws out his own shower of torn paper to dress up his shot.

Delegates from Arkansas, where a few days ago a woman social worker was beaten because she attempted to befriend share croppers who live under conditions sometimes worse than slavery, march around the hall shouting for the New Deal and lauding Roosevelt the humanitarian. North Carolina, which in 1928, when Al Smith was something of a liberal, voted against him for fear he would bring the Pope over to run the country, now parades itself 100 per cent for Roosevelt and the New Deal.

In this mass of yelling delegates are hundreds of ragtag, bobtail politicians who haven't the faintest idea what the New Deal is. Furthermore, they don't care. To them, Roosevelt means jobs. Along comes a live donkey, seeming for the moment to be the calmest, most deliberate member of the crowd, gazing about upon his intellectual inferiors.

Governor Bibb Graves of Alabama makes a speech, but 25 feet away you can't tell what language he's talking in. You finally pick up just exactly two familiar words out of the whole speech—"Roosevelt" and "heart." But nobody cares. Everyone knows he won't say anything. None of them do. Grandmothers, who ought to have been put to bed with the children, are shoving, jumping up and down, yelling until you think their teeth are going to drop out. Down among the adults are occasional children, half-smothered, screeching something that Daddy told them to. Tammany, sullen, sore because it has not received enough patronage, shuffles along with the marchers because a city election is coming up next year and Tammany wants to move back into City Hall.

You have here something as primitive as a tribal war dance, egged on by the deep elemental peals of the organ, which roll out stirring instincts no doubt as thunder stirred the savage, goading the crowd on as if with the pulsing beat of a giant mechanical tom-tom.

Speakers likewise sink to the level of the crowd. In hours of oratory there is not a single new thought, and only one laugh—at an ancient story from Governor Davey for which, bad as it is, the crowd seems grateful. All of the stagnant, shopworn, weary words that have fallen from the lips of men throughout the ages are gathered up and hurled at the convention. Just one man stands out, one man in whom the crowd recognizes sincerity, earnestness, unselfishness, ability, and some comprehension of what Roosevelt is trying to do. And he is a member of the class most despised by the New Dealers, a banker—Governor Lehman of New York.

Any man who can take such material as this, who can take Bourbon South with its peonage, its oppression of the share cropper and the Negro, its underpaid textile workers and its child labor, and with it also take the Tammany organization and its little imitators in a number of Northern cities, and out of those elements build such a movement as the New Deal, is a leader of men, a statesman who can make bricks without straw.

But perhaps Roosevelt didn't make the New Deal movement out of such pitiful material. Perhaps his real strength is among others, among the average citizens not represented by the participants in the Philadelphia mob scene. Perhaps these so-called leaders, now just concluding their week's war dance, are merely camp followers who know a good thing when they see it.

At least it makes you feel more hopeful about democracy to think that way about it.

12/2/41

It goes without saying that in a democracy the most intimate relationship should exist between the people and their government. There should be a constant exchange between the two, with the government keeping the people advised as to what it is doing or would like to do and the people telling the government what they think.

4/5/38

Democracy is not a God-given process that can survive anything. We have seen it wiped out in some other countries. It is a human creation, and as we have seen, it can be killed by human hands. Like liberty, it requires eternal vigilance. It requires more than that. It requires intelligence, understanding, mutual confidence, forbearance. There are and always will be deep conflicts of interest.

Under dictatorship the head of the state resolves these conflicts in his own way and you acquiesce or else. Here and in some other adult countries we have tried the enlightened method. We say that if you give light the people will find their own way. An intelligent people like ours will if they are given the chance.

10/40

A strong and free nation comes of strong and free men, just as a great forest is not a mass of weak, starved, and stunted trees, but one in which all of the trees have grown large and strong.

Our method of government assumes continuous, loose-jointed, internal conflict. It assumes even more than that. It assumes that partisan debate works in the long run for the common good.

10/31/40

Democracy is supposed to be the form of government which requires the highest level of public intelligence. When one looks back over political history and sees the trivial issues which have played such an important part in elections, the surprising thing is that we have been able to make such good decisions. They say God works in mysterious ways his wonders to perform. It must be the same with democracy.

9/19/36

In the presence of such an audience as President Roosevelt addressed at the closing of the Harvard Tercentenary, politics seems appallingly backward, the most blind and stupid of human arts.

Here within Harvard's historic Yard were assembled men whose names you have never heard, pioneers in the land of knowledge, heretics who overturned the prevailing ideas of their times, specialists in many fields who have explored our universe, each of them an unfamed Columbus in his own world. Ten of them are Nobel Prize winners.

Here is the man, you probably never heard his name, who discovered vitamins and thus gave every mother a sales talk with which to force unwanted spinach down the little gullets of the coming generation. There, inconspicuous in a row of mortar-boarded professors, is the aged little fellow whose discovery made blood transfusions possible, whose knowledge may have saved the life of your child, or your own.

Over toward the end is a frail little Japanese, the man who discovered the cause of epidemic dysentery.

Honors were awarded for advancement of knowledge in science, history, language, letters, for notable achievement in telling us about the world in which we live, for achievement in exploring the intricacies of the mind, for achievement in correcting the infirmities of the flesh. But no honors were announced for achievement in the equally important art of government, in the business of living together, within the nation and within the world.

In this same Yard, under these same elms, a similar meeting took place 100 years ago yesterday, to commemorate the two hundredth anniversary of Harvard's founding. Those men also were leaders of thought in their time. But how little they knew. Few of them had any suspicion that the world was more than 4,000 years older than Christ, for the idea of evolution had not yet been established.

No fossil remains had been found to tell us that our ancestors went further back than Adam. The bones of the Neanderthal man were still sleeping undisturbed many feet below the soil in Germany. The Piltdown man was still resting in peace. Archeologists had not yet begun to use the spade. Greece and Rome were then pictured on the first pages of the story of mankind, not as the flower of millions of years of human existence.

In the Harvard Yard of 1836 there was no loud-speaker to carry the voice of President Conant to the most remote spectator, no radio to carry the President's words to the whole country.

What would those Harvard men in 1836 have thought if they could have come back here yesterday and heard the chimes from Southward, England, and Stanley Baldwin, speaking from London? What would they have thought of the airplane that flew overhead, or of the air-cooled trains that brought the old grads back? How much has politics, the art of government, progressed since Andrew Jackson's time? We are now arguing whether Jefferson was a New Dealer.

This meeting yesterday adjourned until September 18, 2036, 100 years from now. No one present will be there. No one living today will be there. No one born in the next 10 years is likely to be there. What will the world of 2036 be like? This gathering met in front of the beautiful memorial chapel, erected recently in memory of 11,000 Harvard students who served with the Allied forces in the World War and of three who served in the German service.

Will they meet in 2036 in front of a new memorial chapel, erected to the memory of Harvard men who have died in some other war? Or will this be the last memorial chapel? Will human beings by that time have learned how to live as friends with each other, will they have discovered how to make available to everyone the great blessings of civilization which are now available only to a favored few?

Will politics still be a contest between ignorance and stupidity, fought on the level of the lowest common denominator, or will the intelligence and knowledge which is transforming the physical world around us by that time have penetrated into the field of government, to work there the miracles like those which are commonplace now in every other sphere of human activity?

What a story, for some reporter not yet born, the four hundredth anniversary of Harvard in 2036 will be!

* * *

6/12/37

We cannot safeguard democracy merely by strapping our Government into a strait jacket. Our real safeguards are our biennial elections and our freedom of speech and press through which we can keep the spotlight of criticism active. If, with those powerful weapons, the American people are not intelligent enough to keep control of the situation, it's good-by democracy, no matter what we do or don't do.

10/27/39

Protection for democracy lies not in making the presidential office powerless and sterile, but in retaining in the hands of the people the power to change the occupant.

4/7/37

Dictatorships go on the theory that no one else could do the job —that one man is indispensable. Democracy rests on the theory that public opinion governs. While leaders are important in a democracy, it should not be dependent upon one leader. If a democracy does not have several men in reserve competent to take the helm, it is only kidding itself that it is a democracy. If our form of government ever becomes so intricate that only one man can run it, we are in trouble.

A good executive is one who builds an organization which can carry on whether he is on the job or not. He gives it his spirit and impresses his stamp upon it. He gives it drive and galvanizes a certain latent energy in it. But if he has the future of his institution at heart he tries to build something that will live of itself and produce its own leaders.

2/12/41

Theoretically every little boy in America can grow up to be President. But everyone in politics knows that very few men have that indefinable combination of gifts that makes a real leader in a democracy. Democracy produces many good men but few champs. Only a handful of our Presidents have been anything more than good mediocre men. In our time Wilson and the two Roosevelts have risen above the ordinary run—in the sense of having made great impact upon their times. Mr. Hoover almost made it, and with better luck he might have succeeded. Except for these, one must go far back before our time to find really big men in the White House.

This country sadly needs big men. The fact that there was not another man in the Democratic Party who carried the enormous popular appeal of Mr. Roosevelt was partly responsible for his third-term renomination. Mr. Roosevelt went in partly by default. I don't overlook the inside conniving that pulled off the nomination, but that would not have been so easy had there been a satisfactory figure to offer as an alternative.

Unless we are going to have Mr. Roosevelt forever, real leaders, with national popular strength, must be developed.

7/15/39

Democracy isn't overthrown by a strong man singlehanded. It commits suicide and then a strong man comes in and kicks the body out of the way. That's the ultimate stage, from which we are, thank God, a long way, here in the United States. But there is no reason to think we are automatically immune.

1/3/39

Representative government is, as every believer in democracy must believe, an essential of popular government. But leadership also is an essential of the whole animal world, including humans.

Britain, birthplace of representative government, has developed parliamentary leadership to a point of greater power than exists in our system. The prime minister is all powerful, with no constitution or supreme court to stand in his way so long as he holds his majority in Commons. But he can be overthrown at any time. Leadership is different from dictatorship. Both answer the human need for guidance except that under dictatorship the people lose all right of control, whereas under democratic leadership the people retain their right to make a change by stipulated and peaceful methods.

10/11/39

This war has served to drive home to all of us the conviction that the state should exist for human beings, not human beings for the state. Society and the state grow out of human beings, and when human beings decay, when their morale is wrecked, when they cannot find the means of livelihood, when they are in desperate want, they turn to dictators as did the oppressed and neglected Russian peasants and the frantic, helpless German people.

3/37

Dictators are born when a nation's people are desperate, when self-government breaks down. They are avoided when government meets its responsibilities efficiently.

Roosevelt

1/20/37

In public affairs, greatness is partly in the man, partly in the times.

3/37

Surely you know him, this man who found a nation ridden with fear and brought it through to new confidence;

Who summons courage equal to the hour, either to close the banks or to cross good souls by offering beer to thirsty White House guests; who lashes out at his enemies with hard scorn yet whose heart melts when he sees a lonely young girl at her first East Room party and tells her, by his order, to command the most handsome young man on the adjoining terrace to waltz with her;

Who speaks before throngs with such seeming assurance yet whose hand, we see, trembles while he waits out the long applause; who stands with dignity before the world, yet who as a kindly host draws a familiar, crumpled pack of cigarettes from his pocket and, with apologies, offers them to the lady on his left, even as you and I;

Who lives with human warmth in a thousand flashing moments, on and off the national stage, as scenes come tumbling into memory . . . visiting, on the eve of his first inauguration, an obscure shop in New York to ask an old Negro to come with him to Hyde Park and pack his beloved ship prints for the journey to Washington . . . winding through crowds which press about his slowly moving automobile with their echoing murmur, "I almost touched him" . . . back from a Pacific cruise, leaning, tanned and smiling, on the bridge of the cruiser *Houston* as it warps to dock at Portland, Ore., sighting on shore a Harvard classmate of 30 years ago and calling out as one old grad to another, "Hello, Curtis. Class of 1904" . . . pausing during a speech from the rear platform of his train to explain, "I'll have to wait a minute; there's a grand kid fight going on down here" . . . reluctantly revealing his election guesses in which he grossly underestimates his own popularity . . . laughingly arguing with his staff that he could make a better campaign against himself than his opponent does, because he knows his own weaknesses . . . driving for hours in an open automobile under a drenching rain and dismissing it as a trifle with the remark, "I don't mind having my shoes full of water, but I don't like to sit in a bath tub with my clothes on" . . . solicitous over the poor, careworn fellow on the curb in Philadelphia who, in a gesture of gratitude, tosses his watch into the automobile; imploring the police to find the man and return it . . . moving, day after day, in the East and in the West, in the North and in the South, always through seas of countless, unknown thousands, a living symbol of democracy;

Who, born in luxury, linked by family to ten Presidents, has made himself the champion of forgotten men and women, using his talents as was said of Benjamin Franklin, in an attempt to subdue the ugly facts of society to some more rational scheme of things; at peace with himself and at ease in his job; fixed in purpose, flexible in method; concerned not so much that the rich shall sleep peacefully in their beds but that everyone shall have a bed in which to sleep;

Who, afflicted so that he is unable to move a step without support, is yet a man of action; who has traveled more, been seen and heard by more, been voted for by more free men and women than anyone else before him;

Who wants to bring about in his time a world which shall venture some few paces on into the vistas of hope which science and man's ingenuity have opened to us, to write in the pages of time his small message, as a friend who is with us for a few bright hours before he travels on.

1/27/34

A dozen House Democrats marched into President Roosevelt's office to impress upon him the importance of giving more jobs to deserving Democrats.

The President turned his smile full face on the grumbling representatives and, after letting them talk 50 minutes, told them in substance that it was swell of them to drop in, and wouldn't they get together often and, incidentally, hereafter make their complaints more specific.

That didn't exactly satisfy the hungry delegation, but the President had called them by their first names and had treated them so considerately they had to go outside and announce to the press they were satisfied, but that they would hold further conferences.

Postmaster General Farley, who attended, remarked dryly that the meeting was a "social success."

6/34

It seemed as though no President would be able to please the critical fourth estate, and certainly a good many did not expect that Mr. Roosevelt would be able to. An accurate reflection of the state of mind among the Washington correspondents who were awaiting the arrival of the new President is recorded in a dispatch to *Editor and Publisher* from its Washington representative, carried in the issue of March 4, 1933, the very day Mr. Roosevelt took office. This dispatch, after reporting the Roosevelt plans for franker press relations, added, "In fairness to both Mr. Roosevelt and the press, however, it must be recorded that the new deal in press relations is hoped for rather than actually expected by the correspondents."

Mr. Roosevelt came on to Washington. The correspondents saw him and were conquered. He won them and he has still a larger proportion of them personally sympathetic than any of his recent predecessors. The percentage of dissenters grows slowly with time. But it is still small, relatively. He has the reporters more with him than their publishers are. It is the reverse of the line-up under Coolidge, when the publishers were generally supporting him and their correspondents at Washington had their tongues in their cheeks. Newspapermen in Washington are increasingly dubious about many of the policies of the Roosevelt Administration but this has reacted almost none at all on his own popularity with them. It is impossible to give accurate statistics, but the situation may be roughly suggested by saying that if the reporters are 60 per cent for the New Deal they are close to 90 per cent for Mr. Roosevelt personally.

Newspapermen are constantly amazed at his knowledge of administrative detail, as revealed in his offhand answers to their questions at press conferences. Above all they like his good-humored and smiling spirit, the mark of a man at peace with himself and at ease in his job.

For the vast group of correspondents who are not regularly assigned at the White House but who attend the semiweekly press conferences, he also is pleasant. He is patient in answering their questions, never loses his temper, ducks delicate inquiries not by scowling in disapproval but with a wisecrack. Some of the best bons mots which circulate in Washington originate from the highest authority.

He never sends the reporters away empty-handed.

At his first press conference Mr. Roosevelt announced abolition of the written question and said he would rather have the reporters shoot at him orally.

Mr. Roosevelt threw the press conference wide open. No questions are barred. In the average session twenty or thirty questions will be asked—about Japan, war debts, the housing program, silver, tariff, liquor, whether a Cabinet officer is about to resign, literally any subject that pops up in a reporter's fertile mind. Sometimes the President will merely smile and say, "I will consider that question was not asked." More often he will duck by saying, "Let's wait until the next conference on that; maybe I'll be able to talk to you then." Or he will reply, "I don't know a thing about that, Fred; I wonder if you have it confused with something else which I will describe in this way." Answering another question, he will say, "I can give you a good tip on that if you don't say I said it." Or he will explain a complicated question in great detail as a guide to the reporters. Again he will discuss a situation on the understanding that nothing will be printed at all—his purpose being to give the reporter a glimpse into the presidential mind so that he will not jump to erroneous conclusions.

But most of the time what President Roosevelt says can be outlined as coming from him, though actual quotation marks are not to be used unless specifically authorized—the purpose here being to assume full responsibility for what is said but not for the exact language uttered offhand.

The system is accepted as fair to the President, to the press, and to the public; and no serious violations of confidence or other complications have resulted. Over more than a year it has been demonstrated that the President can talk to 200 men twice a week as frankly as he chooses, with complete assurance that what he says will be reported accurately and his confidences protected.

6/29/36

No one who was at the Philadelphia convention will easily forget the night at Franklin Field, which revealed Roosevelt, not merely the good political showman, but a master ripened into the fullness of his powers. It is not probable that many of us who were there shall experience anything like it again.

After a week of cheap, tinhorn ballyhoo which never rose above the level of a shoddy political war dance, a new spirit of dignity seemed to settle over the convention scene as it moved from the turbulent hall out into the evening calmness under the open sky.

Probably 100,000 persons were there, undoubtedly the largest political audience ever assembled in this country. In nearly 20 years of political reporting, I have never in any political meeting observed quite the atmosphere which dominated this night. The audience was not noisy, wild, nor hysterical, but it was sympathetic—deeply so, I should say. It listened. It seemed to understand.

Undoubtedly the arrangements contributed toward creating this mood. Instead of a brassy band blaring out "Hail, Hail, the Gang's All Here," the Philadelphia Symphony Orchestra played the final movement of a Tschaikowsky symphony. Imagine warming up a political meeting with a symphony concert. At first it seemed a foolish mistake. You can't pep up a political audience on Tschaikowsky.

Then beside the director's stand a small, white, doll-like figure appeared, Lily Pons, the Metropolitan Opera Company's little song-

Raymond Clapper at Democratic Convention, Chicago, 1932, dictating to a teletype operator for thirteen hours straight running when Franklin Roosevelt was nominated Democratic candidate for the Presidency.

bird. She bared her tiny throat to that vast crowd, to whom she must have appeared no larger than a snowflake, and sang the "Song of the Lark." One hundred thousand people sat in breathless enchantment. In that vast ocean of people gathered for a political hurrah, there was not the faintest stirring, not a sound save the muffled clicking of telegraph instruments in the press box. When she finished, dozens of political writers were on their feet joining in the deafening applause. Something had happened to that audience. It had been lifted, not to a cheap political emotional pitch, but to something finer. It was ready for Roosevelt.

He entered the arena, not to some raucous thumping air, but to the symphony orchestra's stately stringing of "Pomp and Circumstance."

Preliminaries were dispatched quickly and then Roosevelt spoke. It was his moment. It was now or never. This was the flood tide of his opportunity.

With a voice never more confident, never more commanding, never warmer in its sympathy, Roosevelt played upon his audience with one of the most skillful political addresses of our time. It was more than a feat of showmanship. It was a work of art which all of the political instincts of the Roosevelt dynasty were summoned to aid.

Economic royalists . . . We have conquered fear. . . . Privileged princes of new economic dynasties . . . The spirit of 1776 . . . The flag and the Constitution stand for democracy, not tyranny; for freedom, not subjection; and against dictatorship by mob rule and the overprivileged alike. . . . The enemy within our gates . . . We cannot afford to accumulate a deficit in the books of human fortitude. . . . Divine justice weighs the sins of the cold-blooded and the sins of the warm-hearted in different scales. . . . This generation of Americans has a rendezvous with destiny. . . . It is a war for the survival of democracy. I am enlisted for the duration.

Each word was loaded with the subtle power of suggestion, designed to sap the force of every attack from his opponents. Like the fathers of 1776, he was fighting not political royalists but economic royalists. Memories of his battle against fear and panic in

March, 1933, were awakened as if to recapture once more the mood in which the nation hailed him as its deliverer. The Republican Party promises to restore the people's liberties. Roosevelt declares war for the survival of democracy. His mistakes are those of a warm heart. They will be judged leniently.

But the master's superb touch was still to come. As he finished, standing there with his mother and family around him, the strains of "Auld Lang Syne" floated out over the audience. There was a pause. "I'd like to hear 'Auld Lang Syne' again," the President said. The audience joined in, these thousands and Roosevelt, as old friends who had fought through the crisis together. Still a third time it was repeated. As a political theme song, it will be a hard one to beat.

In a moment Roosevelt was gone. The audience stood in its tracks for quite some time, as if still under the spell, and then quietly began to leave.

10/1/36

President Roosevelt and Governor Lehman were riding back from the armory to the railroad station in an open automobile. As they arrived at the station, the driveway was blocked by a uniformed men's chorus of the American Legion, which sang several songs. The last one was the President's favorite, "Home on the Range." The White House warbler, Secretary McIntyre, joined in but the rendition would have been superb even without Mac's assistance.

"That's fine," said the President. "I think I'll have some pictures taken."

So he and Governor Lehman got out of the car and took their stance in the front line of the chorus. Legion hats were placed on their heads. Cameras lined up and the chorus began singing the old wartime favorite, "Pack Up Your Troubles in Your Old Kit Bag." Roosevelt sang with them, and at the end, he threw his head over close to the singer next to him and twisted his mouth in a barber-shop-baritone finish.

A trivial incident to you and me because it was all done so simply and naturally, just as you might act at the end of a good party. Yet imagine Hoover doing it, or Coolidge or Wilson. And I don't think Governor Landon sings either, at least his Republican friends insist that he is not a radio crooner. Roosevelt had reason to be tired. He might have been bored at being delayed in reaching his train where rest and isolation awaited. There also was his dignity to consider. Presidents just don't sing in public. He might have politely thanked the Legion chorus for its effort and gone on.

You say it was good politics for him to do what he did. It was. But the reason he is a good politician is that such things come naturally and instinctively to him. You say a duck swims well, but that is because swimming comes naturally to a duck. It doesn't have to take lessons.

The distinguishing thing about Roosevelt as a politician is his acute sixth sense. He needs less prompting, less coaching, less hunching by idea men than the average candidate. His best speeches are not the ones prepared for him but the ones he writes himself, when he dispenses with tiresome facts and swings out gaily with satirical references to angry old gentlemen who have lost their silk hats. He liked that touch in his Syracuse speech.

All of this suggests why Roosevelt functions on the campaign trail with such smooth efficiency, with the natural athlete's work. Roosevelt's whole week has been made merry by a story which he retells to his visitors. A Republican candidate, being driven through crowds in a certain city, heard shouts for Roosevelt. Showing some annoyance, a lady politician riding in his automobile sought to reassure him. "Don't pay any attention to them," she said, "they are only working people."

Roosevelt the candidate passes by no opportunity. He lays a cornerstone of a new medical unit at Syracuse University and remarks pointedly, "I have laid many cornerstones and as far as I know, none of the buildings has tumbled down yet."

This is a P.W.A. project, one of the many for educational purposes, so in a few words Roosevelt seizes this opportunity to say that such expenditures of Federal money have permitted educational facilities to expand during the depression without loading heavier tax burdens on local communities.

Thus everything is grist for Roosevelt's mill. He snatches ideas for his speeches out of casual conversations, out of everything he sees, out of the removal of railroad tracks from the main street of Syracuse, out of what 10,000 years of wear and tear will do to the face of Jefferson carved on the side of Mt. Rushmore, out of the rainbow that appears over his shoulder in North Carolina. When Roosevelt is out campaigning, he "finds tongues in trees, books in the running brooks, sermons in stones," and vote fodder in everything.

Republicans may charge, as Colonel Knox did the other night, that Roosevelt is a waster at Washington. Be that as it may. But when the President puts on his battered dusty-colored campaign hat, when he hooks up the loud-speakers to the rear of the presidential train, when he goes off of the Government official expense account and on the Democratic National Committee account, all boondoggling ceases. Roosevelt the politician wastes nothing, not even—unlike the Chicago packers—the squeal.

11/10/36

Roosevelt defies labeling. Like all dominant personalities, he cannot be pigeonholed. He is himself his own type.

Roosevelt is best described in his own terms—the quarterback. He gave this description of himself at the beginning of his first term. It still remains the best one-word key to him.

6/25/38

Roosevelt frankly regards himself as a politician and the presidency as a political office. He considers himself one of the most skillful politicians who ever sat in the White House. In this he probably would bow only to Andrew Jackson, whose fighting tactics, whose wealthy and powerful enemies, whose ability to keep his popularity afloat through a serious depression, all so closely parallel Roosevelt's own story. Roosevelt thinks the failure of some of our ablest Presidents has been due to the fact that they were poor politicians and did not recognize that the presidency is a political office.

10/17/42

Mr. Roosevelt was a politician before he was a statesman and the love of the game of politics still remains. He turns back to dabble in it at times as a famous engineer might go back to playing with electric trains in his basement on a rainy Sunday.

Only a short time ago, at the New York State Democratic Convention, he attempted to break James A. Farley in a struggle over which should name the Democratic candidate for governor of New York. He soon found himself playing a smalltime political game, the final act of which was to force delegates who were against him to go through a personal roll call, something that had not been done in a New York Democratic Convention in many years. Even some of his political supporters thought it was an unnecessary and petty thing to do.

You don't measure Mr. Roosevelt's capacity as a political leader by this incident in New York. It would have been appropriate for Roosevelt the Governor. But Roosevelt the President is a man of larger dimensions. His presidential years are sprinkled with incidents of this kind, but they are not the real measure of the man. Years ago I read somewhere, probably in Emerson, that the mark of a great man is not an absence of weaknesses but an abundance of strength. Add up your judgment of what Mr. Roosevelt has done through these chaotic years, check it all into a balance, and you probably will find that although he has done many things of which you disapprove, they still do not deprive him of his stature. The very rage of his most unyielding critics testifies to his strength. They do not waste their rage on weakness but upon strength that they cannot master.

That's about the net of my attempts to pack an estimate of Mr. Roosevelt into a capsule.

He is protected by an unusual ability to relax at moments of hardest strain. Throughout his working day he snatches relaxation by exchanging stories with callers. Having finished talking business,

Mr. Roosevelt is apt to push away the papers on his desk, lean back in his chair, and tell the visitor a story or some bit of gossip that Secretary Marvin McIntyre or Secretary Stephen Early has brought him.

He is always on the lookout for a good story, and everyone around him is quick to carry a new one to him. One afternoon he was riding down in the White House elevator, escorted by Charles Claunch, a White House usher. Claunch told him a story which he liked so well that half an hour later he opened another strategy talk with Mr. Churchill by telling it to him. It was the story about the sailor who walked into an auction shop and began bidding on a parrot. The sailor bid $5, was raised, bid $10, was raised again, and finally got the parrot for $35.

"Thirty-five dollars is a lot to pay for a bird," said the sailor as he emptied his pocket. "Can the bird talk?"

"Can the bird talk!" exclaimed the auctioneer. "Why, that parrot was bidding against you."

Over the years Mr. Roosevelt has become tired at times, somewhat irritable during exceptionally difficult days, but on the whole I don't think anybody around Washington who has known him over these 10 years feels that he has changed to any degree. He is always supremely self-confident, sometimes angry, eager to exchange gossip, quick to make a humorous dig at the expense of some opponent or critic, and especially of a stuffed shirt. He is usually inclined to be casual about the future, disposed to delay a decision. He is never thrown into a black mood by pessimistic advisers who are trying to convince him that the worst is about to happen. He has a duck's back and trouble rolls off it easily.

No matter how badly things are going, and at the height of confusion in Washington, Mr. Roosevelt has the air of a man who is in complete control of the situation. This is a source of protection to him. If he wore his nerves on his sleeve, he would soon be torn to pieces in the intense pulling and hauling which surround a man in his position. Such a man must insulate himself against it. Nature has done that, fortunately, for Mr. Roosevelt.

Yet this sometimes causes him to procrastinate and temporize, as he did in neglecting to reorganize O.P.M. last winter and in delaying to put the Baruch committee to work on the rubber shortage until 8 months after Pearl Harbor. It leads him to be too tolerant of incompetents, misfits, and buck passing among his associates.

Mr. Roosevelt is able to dispose of an enormous volume of business, which is the first requirement of the office routine at the White House. He knows a vast amount about our government because he has a gift of carrying detail in his mind. Yet, for all of his experience, he has shown a good deal of weakness as an administrator. He has always been indifferent to economy of operation, has permitted offices and agencies to continue with fat staffs long after the peak of need had passed. Time and again he has dodged economy demands by asking his critics in Congress to say what agencies should be cut, a gesture intended to throw the onus of firing on Congress—Mr. Roosevelt knowing the chances were good that there would be no cutting down if the job were left to Congress.

He has been slow to delegate authority in clearly defined concentration.

Mr. Roosevelt has always shown what seems to me a sure intuition that approaches genius in the field of democratic leadership, in sensing the needs of the times and leading the country toward them.

His readiness to experiment, to try devices with total disregard of precedent or supposedly immutable rules of classroom economics, broke the rigidity of the national government at a time when it was permitting a national economic breakdown out of a sheer sense of helplessness at Washington. Many mistakes were made, but the important thing was that at last the national government was attempting to deal with the distress of the people. Mr. Roosevelt's bold, unintimidated aggressiveness in that respect was timely and fortunate.

2/9/39

Roosevelt himself isn't going to change. He can't. He's a Roosevelt, isn't he? Roosevelt blood is strong. It requires action. It drives with abounding restless energy. Roosevelt can no more be quiet and study his lesson than can a healthy small boy who must always be wiggling, jumping up and running around, roughing playmates, banging here, banging there, taking a watch apart and putting it together so it will almost run again.

1/18/41

Well, here we are, going into that third term. On this occasion, the first in our history, one is bound to reflect upon the past and to wonder about the future.

A year ago I did not think this day ever would come, and I hoped that it would not. As anyone knows who has read this column over a long period, I have been sympathetic toward most of President Roosevelt's policies. I felt that he had displayed a little too much appetite for power and was too eager to hold on for a third term. Yet it does not seem to me that he has seriously abused the additional power which he has garnered. On the whole he has used it for ends which have seemed to me desirable.

Even so, I felt that, everything considered, a change to Wendell Willkie would have been healthier. His courageous support now of the Administration's position only strengthens that feeling. Before he endorsed the pending war-aid bill, Mr. Willkie was urged by some who had been most influential in his campaign to oppose the measure as an excessive and unjustified grant of power. In rejecting such argument, Mr. Willkie said, I am told, that if he had been elected President he would have been compelled out of his sense of responsibility to ask for the same powers and could not therefore in good conscience oppose giving them to Mr. Roosevelt.

Mr. Hoover sat in the White House, and it is hard to understand how he can think that extraordinary situations do not sometimes require extraordinary powers. But that always was his weakness. His own Federal Reserve Board could not even prod him into action in face of the banking emergency just before he went out of office. He sat like a bump on a log while the Federal Reserve Board begged him in vain to close the banks and stop the panic—the action Mr. Roosevelt took as soon as he became President. In the light of his own experience as President, Mr. Hoover's judgment as to the emergency powers that a President should have does not seem to be the best guide. He couldn't act when the roof was falling in around him, and he waited for Mr. Roosevelt to come to the rescue.

Every believer in democracy naturally must be suspicious of political power, because it is the weapon that tyrants grab and must hold. Democracy's rise is a history of taking power away from somebody, and lodging it in a larger group. The barons took it from King John. The French people took it from the Bourbons. The American colonies took it from the British Parliament. Our Constitutional Convention withheld it from the chief executive in our series of checks and balances—and seriously considered a limit on the number of years he could serve.

But if power is made safer by placing it in the hands of the people, it is also made less wieldy, and must be used at a slow-motion pace. Ordinarily that is no serious handicap. But in emergencies it is.

Democracy has difficulty in finding the means of retaining ultimate power and yet keeping it sufficiently flexible and quickly available. We are having trouble in gearing its speed to the lightning speed of modern events. It is well geared to the speed of the sailing ship but painfully slow in the day of the airplane. We are now trying to find some means of increasing its pace.

If congressmen and senators would speak their pieces quickly and vote quickly, there would be less demand for lodging so much discretionary power in the executive. So long as Congress is prodigal with time, there will be demand to save time by short cuts such as the President's war-aid bill.

It is inevitable that there should be much hesitation about giving President Roosevelt large additional powers. But Mr. Willkie has said that this should not prevent giving him the power needed now. Republicans had their chance to persuade the country to throw Mr. Roosevelt out. The country put him back for a third term. Republicans are trying to fight the election all over again.

I have had my questions about Mr. Roosevelt's love of power. But as between trusting him with the power that seems necessary for quick and flexible action, and trusting those who seem blind to what is going on in the world and who would sit down flat because they don't like Mr. Roosevelt, I'll feel safer riding with him.

3/37

The strong man meets his crisis with the most practical tools at hand. They may not be the best tools but they are available, which is all-important. He would rather use them, such as they are, than do nothing.

Spring, 1942

I have always believed that Mr. Roosevelt, far from plotting his way towards dictatorship, hoped to be known to history as the man who adapted democracy to the new needs of a modern industrial nation. Those who, in the phrase of Romain Rolland, lay huddled in sleep on their moneybags, hated Mr. Roosevelt for disturbing them. He had to fight them or surrender to them. He was thwarted by a reactionary Supreme Court, which as Harlan Stone, now Chief Justice, said in a dissenting opinion, was writing its own economic predilections into its decisions. And more clearly than most of us, Mr. Roosevelt saw the totalitarian nations preparing their pincers movement against the free world. Again those who did not wish to be disturbed in their sleep cried out that he was a warmonger.

Throughout it all, Mr. Roosevelt was trying, with longer vision than most of us, to protect democracy.

The weakest part of Mr. Roosevelt's story, it seems to me, is his defense of his participation in the so-called "senatorial purge" in 1938. He devotes a good deal of space in the introduction to the 1938 volume to his conduct in that campaign. He defends it as an attempt to preserve the liberalism of the Democratic party. Yet he was not content to lay down a yardstick by which voters might judge which of their candidates measured up. He went himself into several states and spoke to the voters against sitting Democratic senators. To the voters, Mr. Roosevelt seemed to be intruding, to be using his enormous power to punish men who had voted against some of his measures. Popular sympathy rose to the support of the senators thus attacked in their home states by the powerful President of the United States.

That episode, more than any other, verges on the dictatorial. Yet I think fundamentally it was an unwise outburst of temper rather than any studied scheme towards dictatorship.

8/25/42

In the meaning of the war, in its danger to us, and in the grand strategy that was called for, the President has taken rank with the most aggressive and imaginative war leaders of our time.

Today, Mr. Roosevelt stands opposite Hitler—the leader of the free world against the leader of the slave world.

1/30/42

The American people have the deepest reason to wish President Roosevelt on his sixtieth birthday continued health and success.

His leadership at this time is most essential to us. We have no other dependable source of leadership except in Roosevelt and some of the men around him. That is a terrible thing to have to say about a democracy but I believe it to be true.

The other sources from which true leadership ought also to come seem almost bankrupt. The Republican Party? What a pitiful thing it is. What has it offered us during the last nine years except stupidity, five-cent criticism, and complete misunderstanding of our main problems, domestic and foreign?

Once, by accident and not because the leaders of the party wished it, a real leader appeared—Wendell Willkie. He was forced on the party. But as soon as the election was over the party leaders tossed him out. The Republican Party was even unable to recognize a real leader when it had the luck to find one on its doorstep.

That is about the story all over the lot. The bankers, the industrialists, the groups that have had the advantages of education and experience in affairs and who are efficient operators in their businesses, are the ones to whom we would naturally turn for guidance through this bewildering and violent revolution. But they have had nothing to offer except nostalgic pleas that we go back to the gay nineties, back to a world that had disappeared without their knowing it.

Roosevelt is not the perfect leader. He, too, has misjudged and made errors. He had no full conception of what was going on. Nobody could have had. Nobody does have. But he was on the right side of events. In both domestic and foreign affairs he knew from which direction the enemy was approaching.

In the prewar years he knew that new mass forces were on the march and that they had to be recognized. He knew that people demanded more security, that the workman was determined to have the right to bargain collectively with the big corporation, that the ranks of hard-working employees would not be content any longer to bet but would insist upon society doing something for them when economic conditions forced the closing down of whole industries. Roosevelt saw that and insisted that Government assume the responsibility before mass indignation forced it by violence, or before some American Hitler used it as a vehicle for a ride into personal tyranny.

Where are the bankers, the industrialists, the professional groups, the people with education, the people who had experience in affairs, the people who had traveled and studied history? Where were they during all of this? They were fighting Roosevelt with every means they knew. They were clinging to the little narrow-minded leaders that the Republicans managed to dig up. They were trying to deal with these irrepressible forces, not by channeling them into social and economic reforms but by ignoring them. They thought if we pretended the problem wasn't there, it would disappear.

In foreign affairs, some of these people have a much better record. Some of them saw the dangers as clearly as Roosevelt. Many of them, long before the war, put aside their bitter prejudices against Roosevelt's domestic policies to support him most earnestly and effectively in his judgment of foreign affairs. That is one shining exception. Unfortunately the Republican Party cannot share in it, for it rode on the isolationist side—in a kind of desperate straddle. Even in foreign affairs the Republicans as a whole, the top insiders in the party organization, couldn't see that anything was happening.

So, as an American citizen who sees many day-to-day things to criticize in Roosevelt, I find myself in the fundamentals looking to him as the public figure who seems more than anyone else to know where the dangers are and to make an effort to grapple with them, whether they be at home or abroad. What worries me is that these dangers won't end with the war. Where can we turn for the understanding leadership in the years to come when democratic order and control must be organized around these violent forces?

10/40

On the other hand I do not think that the Roosevelt Administration, however innocent its intentions may be, has taken care to preserve the confidence that must be preserved if popular government is to remain healthy. This is not to say that it should have refrained from pressing reforms even though some of those affected resisted. That is one thing. It is something entirely different to allow to grow up, in a large and powerful class of our citizens, an almost universal suspicion as to the ulterior purposes of the government.

12/23/42

The state of mind of people toward the Administration which is their Government is not a happy one today. We might as well face it. The relation of the people to the Administration is clouded by so much doubt and suspicion now that unfortunate consequences could result.

It is a terrible thing when a majority of people lose faith in the Administration they have put into power, and such a thing would be especially tragic now.

We saw the tragedy happen to Wilson and Hoover. In each case the country went through a period of violent stress while its faith was finding new foundations. In the case of Wilson the country was shaken from the idea of collective security back into the idea of safety through isolation. In the case of Hoover, the country was shaken from its confidence that business prosperity would keep two chickens in every pot and it turned to the idea that Mr. Roosevelt would have the Government maintain an ever-normal two-chicken pot, for one and all.

This Administration and all of its friends may well take stock now, before it is too late, if indeed it is not too late already. It would be a tragedy if the nation had to finish this war and begin shaping the peace under an Administration in which a majority of the people had already lost confidence as in the case of Wilson.

Some of the criticism of the conduct of the war is overdrawn, a substance of the truth blown up into grotesque proportions. To a considerable extent that will right itself in time. But beyond that people are affected by this war in a strange way. It is an offshore war and so much is secret that its magnitude is difficult to grasp. So it reaches out like an unseen hand to clutch people by the throat, with rationing, with goods disappearing completely, with sons and husbands disappearing into the unknown where they may be either alive or dead. The psychological strains of such a war are heavy and lead to bitterness against those regarded as the authors of these circumstances.

President Roosevelt and his whole Administration need to work on this and work hard. There has been nothing more important in our generation than that America make this victory stick. We can't afford to have the chances wrecked by an internal upheaval that would wash everything down the drain again.

Mr. Roosevelt missed one bet in not making better use of Wendell Willkie. He must, for the sake of ends that are bigger than he or his Administration, leave nothing undone to deserve and hold the confidence of a majority of the country so that the task that destiny has lodged in his care can be carried forward.

2/20/43

Before Mme. Chiang Kai-shek came down here the other day, I looked back over the notes of my visit with her for tea in Chungking last April. I thought perhaps I had been overly impressed. The first few lines in my notebook run as follows:

"Then Holly Tong took me to see Mme. Chiang. She more than

lived up to build-up. Speaks English—no accent—cigarette in long holder—Colonel Chennault was leaving as I arrived and she introduced me—she has everything—looks, wit, vivacity, and intelligence."

She asked about the airplane trip, whether it was hard, the route, how many days, and other traveling details. She said she might go to the United States for treatment soon. She talked about the Indian situation, and at length about abolishing extraterritoriality, and said she was "hitting from the shoulder." I believe that what I wrote about Mme. Chiang at that time laid it on fairly thick. But on the basis of her first few days in Washington, it seems to stand up. She has conquered all here thus far. Even the newspaperwomen have gone all out for her—so she must have something that even Clare Luce hasn't got, because the lovely Clare had to work her way through.

Newspaper correspondents who were at the White House press conference when she appeared with the President participated in a show such as we probably shall never see again.

It was high state drama, played by the real characters. Some day they may put Helen Hayes in the part but she'll never do it any better than Madame acted it in real life. It was the delicate, feminine, shrewd, quick, witty, and powerful first lady of the East against the great master himself. As the press conference began the President asked the reporters not to put any catch questions to Madame. She in turn played to the President as the big strong man who could work miracles.

Mme. Chiang, tiny, with feet dangling from the high-seated Roosevelt chair, was working smoothly, while toying with her compact, to coax a promise out of President Roosevelt for China. Mr. Roosevelt, the master of the press-conference technique, was trying with equal smoothness not to melt too much under Madame's technique.

Imagine the scene. Two hundred reporters in on the show, Mme. Chiang sitting between the President and Mrs. Roosevelt, who laid her hand protectingly on Madame's fragile arm.

Madame makes a lively little greeting, with delicate flowers for everyone. A reporter thrusts a direct question as to whether China's man power is being fully used in the war. Madame holds her poise, but with a touch of feeling replies that China's men are fighting to the extent that munitions are available for them. When more munitions are sent to China more men will fight. With the greatest of ease, she has thrown the ball square into the lap of the President. He explains that we will send munitions as fast as the Lord will let us. Madame, smiling and making it all so polite and sweet, says she hears there is a saying that the Lord helps those who help themselves.

About that time President Roosevelt indicated it had gone on long enough and suggested that if the reporters had any questions for him they'd better be getting on with them.

As we left the President's office, the three were sitting inscrutably in a neat row. Mrs. Roosevelt's hand was no longer laid protectingly on Madame's arm. Madame, not a hair ruffled, had a pleasant impersonal gaze from which no thoughts escaped. The President was busy with parting words to straggling reporters.

Whatever it was that Confucius said, it sure was a mouthful.

5/8/43

War is not only deep personal loss. It is also a mass of trivial irritations. The small irritations of today are the big antiadministration votes of tomorrow. Quick and easy victory in the last war did not save Woodrow Wilson and his administration from quick and overwhelming defeat immediately thereafter.

A President may win the war but may at the same time suffer retribution for the small inconveniences that were inevitable in the process of winning it. People may not turn against a President because he sent their sons to war. They are, however, liable to dislike him because they have had to restrict their automobile driving, fill out complicated forms, submit to food rationing, and undergo other irritating inconveniences. These are the little things that add up to furious popular indignation against an administration.

There is growing recognition of the logic that if Mr. Roosevelt remains in shape physically, he will be the best one to finish the war and initiate the peace.

1/8/42

For two hours the other day I sat with other Washington correspondents in President Roosevelt's office while he explained the war budget. More important to me than anything he said was the fact that he was holding the conference, or seminar, as he calls it.

He had just been engaged for two weeks in the wearing conferences with Churchill and the strain of the loss of Manila. That very morning Mr. Roosevelt had gone to Congress and delivered his message calling for the unprecedented program of war production. He returned to the White House about 1 o'clock. After lunch he undertook to explain the war budget in order to assist the Washington reporters who would be writing their dispatches about this complicated array of figures. For two hours he tried to reduce the matter to simple terms for us. He patiently answered questions, some intelligent, some not, and some only repetitious. Though he must have been unbelievably tired and pressed with critical business, he never showed impatience and he stayed with it until all questions were exhausted.

I left thinking not much about the budget but a lot about whether a man who could go through that performance with such patience and good will had very much of the dictator stuff in him after all. If he were of the dictator stripe, he surely would not have used precious hours just so the public might better understand what the Government was trying to do. Dictators don't explain. They tell you.

I had a feeling, too, that Mr. Roosevelt was coping with astronomical figures with the same sense of being unable to grasp them that we all experience.

Dollars are now only symbols on the books. A budget of 59 billion dollars is not anything you or I or President Roosevelt can comprehend literally. It is hardly more than a way of saying that we must have a whole lot of weapons. It is a way of trying to say that about half of the effort of the American people must be put into the war. You might as well say we are going to use up 59 billion ergs on the war.

10/17/40

There are some people who recognize that, everything considered, it would be better to reelect Roosevelt than to risk a change of crew when time is so important and when wise day-to-day decisions depend so much upon knowledge and experienced judgment. Roosevelt has them in a box. He becomes the lesser of two evils. Some newspaper editorials in his behalf are written in this spirit, with the heart not in them.

Businessmen are no more reconciled to Roosevelt than ever. Now he has lost the inner support of others who will cast their ballots for him with regret that he is running.

A Roosevelt victory this time will not be a mandate, certainly not a thinking mandate. It will be a return to power voted by many with reluctance and with strong inner doubts. His victory, if it comes, will come from those to whom he has been a meal ticket, from those who place party regularity first, and from those who regard the choice as far from ideal but think it better than the alternative.

One does not have to scratch the surface very deep to see these things and to get the feeling that victory this time will have some ashes mingled with the sweet.

New Deal

1/25/34

IN THE rush of the Roosevelt Administration to attack the problem of recovery as fast and from as many directions as possible, problems have had to be met catch-as-catch-can. Professors have dug their lectures out of brief cases and in the twinkling of an eye they have become law. Idea men in the Administration have been grinding out new plans every hour on the hour. There has been no time for coordination. It has been felt that the thing to do was to get action and risk the dangers of mistakes and conflicting policies.

3/34

Popular faith in the sincerity and disinterestedness of Mr. Roosevelt, and of most of the men around him, has obscured one of the most important implications of the New Deal—the fact that the almost incredible power and discretion which have been vested in the executive branch make it absolutely imperative, for future safety, that standards of political conduct and ethics be raised. Some may have doubts about the wisdom of the Roosevelt policies, though nobody doubts the courage, independence, and honesty of men like Ickes, Wallace, and Harry Hopkins. But imagine a type of "statesman" different from Harold Ickes being in command of $3,300,000,000 of Public Works money, to be passed out in accord with his own sweet will.

11/33

President Roosevelt looked around carefully for the man to take this responsibility. He must be in sympathy with the policy and understand that the money must be distributed quickly; he must be deaf to politicians on the scent of pork; he must distinguish between projects of lasting social and economic value and those resulting from local greed.

That political Cinderella, Harold L. Ickes, who had just been lifted from the obscurity of a fighter for defeated causes to be Secretary of the Interior, met the specifications. He was still almost unknown except to those Chicago grafters who had felt his unavailing lash. Overnight, with a flourish of the presidential wand, he became America's biggest spender.

Mr. Ickes went to Washington. Democratic politicians were not particularly enthusiastic over this former Republican. Stocky, square-jawed, with a grim, sardonic humor and a suspicion of politicians generally, Mr. Ickes was not exactly the kind of man they wanted to see in the Interior Department. The new Secretary seemed to have no appreciation of their political problems; he gave them scant attention. But the fact that he was a good "no" man impressed President Roosevelt.

Grim but cheerful, Secretary Ickes is at his office with his coat off working from 8 A.M. until after midnight. This old war horse of reform, reinfused with the spirit of his early days, is converting the Interior Department, one of the dead spots of Washington bureaucracy, into the most active spot of the new Administration.

1/1/34

Under the protection of what amounts to an extension of the political truce of last March, President Roosevelt is moving into his big test year with more freedom to make his leadership effective than is the usual lot of peacetime executives.

All indications are that Mr. Roosevelt, with the breath-taking audacity which nearly a year ago rallied a heartsick, shell-shocked nation, will push even further into uncharted territory. New departures are hatching.

The Tennessee Valley experiment, in which it is sought to build a new modern civilization over a relatively undeveloped area, may be repeated in other sections of the country. The Administration's move to finance small householders in buying electric irons and washing machines is significant of the still unflagging aim to carry into the humblest home the simple tools which a new age has offered to mitigate the daily toil of millions.

Overhanging it all there is growing up a gigantic Federal bureaucracy which is reaching out to control the roadside gas station and the little corner grocery store and so many other small activities that the danger of its collapsing of its own weight is seen by some.

1/3/34

The Administration is about to launch a revolutionary land policy which contemplates purchase of millions of acres of poor farm land to be taken out of active cultivation and returned to forest or other noncrop status.

During the pioneer days every incentive was offered to colonize the vast open spaces of the West. The Government gave land away to anyone who would settle on it. Even after the best land had been taken and the reason for the policy had disappeared, it still persisted and thousands of farmers have been induced to settle on soil from which the most expert agriculturalist could not wrest a living. Millions of Government money were pumped into irrigation and reclamation projects on which the carrying charges sometimes exceeded the total value of the crops produced.

Under the impact of the depression, the economic-planning group began to insist that it would be cheaper to buy much of this land back than to go on indefinitely subsidizing farmers to produce wheat, corn, hogs, and cotton for which there were no customers. As a temporary expedient, the A.A.A. attempted to cut down crops by paying the farmers directly for planting less.

Retired land will be turned into national parks or forests, used for improving the condition of Indians, or blanketed back into the public domain and left to lie until some future day when perhaps the growth of the country or the opening of new world markets will make it worth while to put the plow to it again.

10/34

Red tape is the big threat to the New Deal. Even in sections where businessmen and farmers give the Administration credit for trying to do a constructive job and where there is much sympathy with its aims, there is strong protest against the red tape involved.

A county agent in southern California cites the papers filed by one farmer near San Miguel, California, as an example. He had leased five ranches and had to sign wheat contracts with A.A.A. for each parcel of ground. When his papers were all in order, they bore exactly 411 signatures, including those of the owners, the renter, witnesses, and other persons. Multiply that instance by several million farmers and it is no wonder that A.A.A. was so late in getting out the corn-hog checks.

1/30/34

The Administration, it became apparent yesterday, is preparing to push its program of social reconstruction into new fields.

One field is unemployment insurance. Legislation is being drafted for introduction in Congress, probably late this week, through which Federal tax pressure would be exerted to induce states to set up unemployment-insurance funds.

In addition, the Federal Emergency Relief Administration is planning to move thousands of persons now on relief to other communities where opportunity for work will be greater. For instance, in the coal regions, the Administration believes that no degree of recovery will provide enough jobs to go around, as thousands were idle at the peak of the boom. Surplus men in such regions would be encouraged to let the Government transplant them into more promising sections.

Twenty-five per cent of the farmers have total incomes of less than $500 a year. So that, while T.V.A. officials expect the toes of private enterprise may be stepped on slightly, they hope to find the chief outlet for the valley's Government-sponsored industries in an increased standard of living. In short, they hope to create a new market and supply it on the spot. So far as possible, they will attempt to stimulate small retail businesses by providing expert accounting, merchandising, and management advice. They will sponsor wholesale cooperatives to reduce the cut of the middleman. By such assistance they hope to put the small retailer on a basis of equal competition with the chain store, which supplies such services to its branches.

2/3/34

The green pastures of world trade seem likely to be the next grazing spot in the recovery effort.

Two developments yesterday gave significant evidence of this.

First, it was announced that the Government is setting up an export and import trading bank with R.F.C. funds. Its purpose will be to give financial assistance to American business in buying and selling with Russia primarily and also with Latin America and other parts of the world.

Second, President Roosevelt indicated he expects to send a tariff message to Congress at this session. The purpose of this is to open the way for a greater influx of imports so that foreign countries can in that way pay for the increased purchases it is hoped they will make here. What the President will recommend is not definitely known, but he probably will ask authority to negotiate reciprocal-trade agreements so that imports can be correlated to domestic production more directly than at present.

Last summer's wave of intense nationalism which followed the disillusionment of the London Economic Conference is passing. For a time the Administration seemed to despair of looking abroad for any help in recovery. It turned its effort inward with almost furious intensity, to drive through a program of economic self-containment.

Picturing the United States as working inside a high protective wall, N.R.A. was counted on to force up wages. P.W.A. was expected to stimulate buying power with its $3,300,000,000 kitty. A.A.A. was to hold down farm production to domestic needs and thus boost rural purchasing power.

That was the picture last August. Officials, or many of them, realized that this could not remain the complete picture. Secretary of Agriculture Wallace has gone up and down the country warning that either $1,000,000,000 of foreign goods would have to be admitted every year to finance farm exports or else millions of farms would have to be put into idleness for lack of mouths to be fed. Secretary of State Hull, even in the midst of the wave of nationalism last summer, continued to preach the doctrine that the United States would in the end have to come to reciprocal trade.

Russia, for instance, can sell to the United States manganese, furs, tungsten, platinum, and vodka without treading seriously on the toes of American industry. America can sell all sorts of machinery to Russia.

If the tariff policy works out as contemplated, this process will be refined down to the point where an administration policy board will attempt to determine what American industries legitimately need protection, what ones are sturdy enough to stand on their own feet, and which are so intrinsically anemic that they might as well be left to shift for themselves against an open import door.

2/11/34

President Roosevelt's cancellation of air-mail contracts is viewed by some here as one of several strides yet to come in the direction of taking Government aid away from a favored few and giving it to hitherto unfavored millions.

It is, within the field of Government control, a miniature process of redistributing wealth that is now going on. It is in harmony with the larger purpose of President Roosevelt who began his march to the White House with a promise of help for the forgotten man.

In time, it is widely believed here, promoters of steamship companies who have profited richly from Government subsidies, also will find their access to the Federal treasury restricted. Investigations are going on in Congress now to lay the groundwork for taking the huge profits out of war supplies.

This is an Administration which believes in doing things by the millions, not only in dollars paid out but in the number of beneficiaries.

3/6/34

It was in a colorful setting, in the D.A.R. Constitution Hall, erected by the descendants of America's first revolutionists, and against a background of tapestry pictures of the heroes of the first great American experiment, that President Roosevelt stood yesterday as the champion of another historic adventure.

The hall was packed. New Dealers crowded the platform, with a few Old Dealers, just a few Old Dealers inconspicuously holding down rear chairs.

At 11 A.M. the band sounded the presidential bugle call, flood lights were turned on, and President Roosevelt entered, accompanied by General Johnson. Many of the spectators had ringside seats at the inaugural ceremony a year ago and thoughts inevitably ranged back to the contrast. The President, wearing a double-breasted blue business suit and a soft white collar, seemed a little older, a little more drawn, with the inevitable marks which a year of almost superhuman struggle has chiseled into his face. His voice seemed to some a little more weary, and with not quite the strong, bell-like ring of his inaugural hour.

A year ago the day, like the weather, was bleak and full of dark forebodings. Banks had closed in most of the states. There was fear everywhere and grave doubt as to whether anyone, let alone the untested man who was just taking the presidential oath, could save the nation from utter collapse.

Yesterday, he appeared to report, not victory by many lengths, but progress. As a climax to his report he asserted that the "willingness of all elements to enter into the spirit of the New Deal becomes more and not less evident as it goes on," and read a telegram from the president of the American Bankers Association, Francis M. Low. It said:

"On this, your first anniversary, please allow me, in behalf of the country's banks, to express our full confidence and our sincere desire to cooperate in your courageous efforts to bring about recovery. The banking structure of the country is sound and liquid and banks have improved to the point where it is no longer necessary for banks to be superliquid. There is a definite call now for banks not to extend loose credits or to make improper loans, but for a most sympathetic attitude toward legitimate credit needs and for a recognition of responsibility for their proper and vital part in the program of recovery."

Departing from his prepared text, Mr. Roosevelt added, "If the banks come along, my friends, we'll have three great elements in American life working together—industry, agriculture, and banks, and then we can't be stopped."

3/30/34

The Civilian Conservation Corps, one of the most novel experiments of the Roosevelt Administration, will begin its second year next week by offering about 120,000 men outdoor work with board and keep and $30 a month pay.

These workers have built 17,000 miles of truck trails and 243,000 erosion dams to keep topsoil from washing away into rivers. They have spent 579,000 man-days in fire-fighting.

And it is no laughing matter to report that they have pulled up more than 80,000,000 wild gooseberry and currant bushes. It is in those bushes that the costly little pests known as the white-pine blister-rust spores, or germs, hatch. One of those little fellows can only fly 900 feet but when he and other numerous members of his immediate family land on a white-pine tree, they dig into the bark and that is the end of the pine tree. So by pulling up every gooseberry and currant bush within 900 feet of a pine tree, the C.C.C. workers are doing a wholesale birth-control job on a microscopic tribe that menaces a national stand of white pine valued at $420,000,000.

Each month some 300,000 families are receiving $20 to $25 each sent by sons and relatives out of C.C.C. pay.

6/8/34

These sudden floods, which have swept rivers out of their banks, washed railroad tracks away, flooded whole farms, sent streams of yellow water running down highways, constitute only the latest of a series of visitations which, like the plagues of Biblical Egypt, have pounded despair into the hardy sons of the dauntless pioneers who wrested this rich breadbasket from nature.

It seems as if nature, in a revengeful mood, were swooping down from all directions to claim it back.

Drought, flood, voracious grasshoppers, and hustling little hungry chinch bugs, all have combined to wreak their temporary damage. As if this wasn't enough, the pesky little starlings heard clear back East about this field day of woe and the malicious little creatures are beginning to appear on the scene, destroying large quantities of fruits and vegetables, spreading weed seeds, carrying deadly chicken diseases, and otherwise making noisy nuisances of themselves.

But most dismaying of all, especially in the Dakotas and other states around Iowa, the windstorms, like mighty invisible dredges, are stripping off the crop-growing topsoil and carrying it eastward, leaving once fertile farms standing as barren desert land. Travelers coming in from South Dakota report pathetic scenes of struggling farmers, whose land has been thus stripped, hauling topsoil back in their wagons, laboring over their large farms like a Chevy Chase gardener trying to resurface his lawn. Thousands of these farms have been ruined for all time.

With disaster thus piling up in a greater heap than ever this year, on top of a decade of hard years filled with starvation prices, bank closings, and mortgage foreclosures, and upsetting within a few weeks the man-made calculations of A.A.A. experts at Washington, it is not to be wondered that people, in their despairing helplessness against the forces which defy all human ingenuity, are appealing to Divine aid.

It is easy to be self-confident when you are prosperous, when you have your environment under your thumb; when you can, if you are good enough, get that customer to buy a suit of clothes or persuade him to sign up for that life insurance; or when you can order your stenographer to take a letter; or send out that gang to dig a hole for a new building. Those are the jobs for self-made men.

But when you have been out plowing from dawn to dark, and when you have drilled your seed, and then wake up in the night and hear the howling wind, and go out anxiously at dawn and see your seed hundreds of feet up in the air, blowing away with your very farm and leaving you nothing but the hard, barren understrata, you can't order a gang of farm hands to go out and bring that farm back. You can't do anything but wring your hands and wonder how the kids will eat next winter.

But the story of this epic tragedy is one that statistics cannot reach. It seems unlikely that such a calamity will fail to leave its mark on the minds not only of the adult generation but of the children whose earliest memories will always be of nature that would not give a man a break.

7/13/34

On his way back from Hawaii, President Roosevelt will visit the Bonneville Dam project on the Columbia River, Grand Coulee Dam in Washington, the Fort Peck power project in eastern Montana, and will view the dredging work on the Upper Mississippi, below St. Paul.

This visit will serve to dramatize and publicize the great power projects which are part of the New Deal program and which in years to come may be its chief physical monuments.

8/4/34

This writer has traveled 8,300 miles in the last two months, observing conditions, talking with persons in every line of activity. A 3,000-mile trip in June covered the drought area of the Middle West. The last three weeks have been spent in the Far West with 3,000 miles of flying from Cheyenne to the Pacific Coast and from Los Angeles to Vancouver, B.C.

There can be little doubt but that there is widespread bewilderment and doubt as to the future of the recovery experiments. This has not reached the stage of rebellion against the leader. On the contrary, the people appear still to be clinging to him as their one hope. They still have confidence that he will pull them through.

But they are not as sure as they were a year ago that he has the perfect formula. Instead of implicit confidence in what he is doing, the people now appear to have confidence that he will recognize what they regard as mistakes and correct them. They heap their criticism largely upon the presidential advisers. They feel that in some instances Mr. Roosevelt has accepted bad advice. So they do not blame him. They are able to retain their confidence that he will correct the mistakes of his advisers.

That, insofar as such a complex situation can be reduced to generalization, appears to be the picture in the West. That is why this country west of the Mississippi is for the moment the real battleground of the New Deal. There is irony in the fact that this should be the trouble area. If ever a President has worked for the agricultural West it is President Roosevelt. The West has always held grievances against the "money-changers." Mr. Roosevelt has swung his heaviest clubs against them. He has poured millions into the agricultural-adjustment program, more millions into drought relief, still more into the gigantic power, irrigation, and navigation projects in the West like Bonneville, Grand Coulee, Fork Peck, and the Upper Mississippi.

What is causing the restiveness in the West? Most fundamentally of all it is a feeling that the present policies head toward regimentation and will lead in time to curtailment of individual liberty. New Dealers are inclined to scoff at those who raise this objection. They say that there was regimentation under the old order by powerful private interests, Wall street, the steel kings, Mellon, Insull, that the people were at the mercy of powerful private forces.

1/31/36

Volunteer warriors fear that Roosevelt is making the country communistic.

This worrying would be much more to the point if it were directed at the failure to put the unemployed back to work, and at the dismal prospect that we are in serious danger of having some 10,000,000 unemployed with us indefinitely.

We have just felt the impact of 3,500,000 war veterans demanding their bonus. What is the potential dynamite in 10,000,000 American citizens condemned to permanent idleness?

We have been assuming that recovery would solve the problem. That assumption is crumbling before our eyes. Within and without the Administration grave doubts exist that any probable amount of recovery will put this idle army back into private jobs.

All of the billions thus far spent have done little except to keep the unemployed from starvation. The relief load is as heavy as ever. Some in Congress expect that another $4,000,000,000 will be needed for the coming year.

About half a million additional employables come of working age every year. New jobs opened up by recovery are offset by this yearly crop of new muscle.

Then there is our old friend, technological unemployment. During a private discussion of unemployment here this week, Senator Guffey of Pennsylvania said the steel industry is spending millions of dollars installing laborsaving machinery.

Take the new strip-sheet mills being erected around Pittsburgh. The old-type mill using hand labor needed a force of 375 men working around the clock. They would produce 60,000 tons a year. The new-type mill needs only 126 men—one third as many. It will produce as much in a month as the old-type mill in a year.

10/17/36

Is Roosevelt—as the Republicans now assert in the major charge of their indictment—hell-bent on setting himself up as a dictator to destroy the private capitalist system?

If he had any such purpose, he missed the boat. The time to have accomplished it was in the crisis of 1933, not now in the bloom of recovery when the more rugged individualists are, as Roosevelt said the other night, throwing their crutches at the doctor. In March, 1933, the country was scared. It wanted Roosevelt to save it. Anything he asked was his. Even Landon had just said he would rather have a dictator than paralysis.

Roosevelt is a shrewd politician. If he had nursed secret ambitions to become an American Stalin, he would have struck while the iron was hot.

First of all he would have attended to certain important details.

Under pretext of safeguarding the national welfare he would have done what would be done in wartime. He would have seized the radio and put the press under a curb. To avoid future troubles he would have jammed through a law increasing the size of the Supreme Court or curbing its powers to veto acts of Congress.

Then he probably would have cultivated the Army more assiduously instead of making the Navy his pet. He would have played it up, staged military spectacles. He would have sought to condition it mentally for possible home-service duty and in various ways would have kept it before the public as visual evidence of his might. He probably would have made the Civilian Conservation Corps into a military body of personal storm troopers instead of excluding military features from its routine.

Roosevelt, as a politician, would have recognized that such measures were essential to maintain a dictatorship beyond the brief honeymoon he was then enjoying. He would have attended to those matters while the country was in a mood to let him get away with it. Actually, they are so out of line with Roosevelt that it seems fantastic, almost ludicrous, even to mention them.

Also look at the opportunities he passed by. A Socialist or a Communist would have grabbed the railroads in 1933. Instead, as John T. Flynn points out, Roosevelt lent them millions of dollars to save them from bankruptcy and to ensure private ownership. He would have nationalized the banks instead of setting them up on their own feet again and guaranteeing their deposits.

Still, Roosevelt did obtain vast discretionary powers. But we forget the temper of 1933. Read the newspaper files of the period. Iowa farmers had dragged a judge from the bench, put a rope around his neck, smeared him with grease and stolen his trousers because he refused to promise not to sign any more mortgage-foreclosure papers. The farm-holiday strike was spreading. Everything else had been tried and farm leaders wanted crop control. Roosevelt agreed to try it on a voluntary-contract basis.

Congress was about to pass a mandatory inflation bill requiring the President to issue $3,000,000,000 in greenbacks. Roosevelt persuaded Congress to make that action not mandatory but discretionary. He then put the discretionary power in his pocket and forgot about it. Instead of bringing inflation, he averted greenback inflation being forced on the country by Congress. Read the record.

We have forgotten also how N.R.A. got into the picture. The Black-Connery 30-hour-week bill had passed the Senate and been favorably reported to the House with certainty of passage. It would have thrown all industry into a strait jacket of 6 hours a day, 5 days a week. Industry was alarmed.

But industry also had been clamoring for suspension of the anti-trust laws, so that it might combine against cutthroat competition. The oil industry was clamoring for Federal intervention. Oil-state governors, including Landon, came to Washington pleading for help, saying they were helpless to curb destructive overproduction. Roosevelt rolled all of these problems up into one ball of wax and shoved N.R.A. in as a substitute for the 30-hour-week bill. President Henry I. Harriman of the U.S. Chamber of Commerce pronounced it a Magna Charta of labor and industry. Dr. Tugwell, according to Ernest K. Lindley, was dubious. He thought the bill went too far. But nobody paid any attention to him.

Just to keep everything in perspective, it is well to remember that the income tax was denounced years ago as socialistic.

10/20/36

Governor Landon calls upon the President to say whether he "still intends to make N.R.A. principles live and operate in the American Government by one device or another."

Of course, the intent of this question is to put Roosevelt in a hole. Nevertheless, it deserves an answer.

Principles underlying N.R.A. were:

1. Abolition of child labor.
2. Limitation of hours of work.
3. Minimum wages.
4. Collective bargaining.
5. Cooperation of business to prevent unfair trade practices and cutthroat competition.

The method was to obtain agreements carrying out these principles among competitors in various industries, subject to approval by the Government, which in turn waived the antitrust laws to make such agreements permissible.

The objects were to stimulate reemployment, increase purchasing power, ensure fair treatment to labor, and protect decent businessmen against chiselers who would stop at nothing to undersell a competitor.

N.R.A. was the first experiment of the kind, undertaken hastily in a period of desperate unemployment and business bankruptcy. Many mistakes were made, resulting in the whole experiment getting out of hand and bringing down upon itself vast disapproval and finally the veto of the Supreme Court. It probably was Roosevelt's most unhappy experience. You can hardly blame Landon for taunting his opponent with this ghost of the Blue Eagle and pointing in admiration, as he did at Detroit recently, to Henry Ford, who defied N.R.A. and got away with it.

Still, Roosevelt cannot afford to dodge the painful subject. It would be better to face it now than to duck until after election and then, if he tries to return to the principles of N.R.A., be confronted with another broken-promise charge.

For Roosevelt already has given pretty clear indication that he is not through with trying to do what he tried through N.R.A.

At Detroit, he said, "I do not accept the conclusion of many Republican leaders that major depressions are inevitable in modern life. . . . I believe it is the duty of government to bend every effort to prevent another major catastrophe. . . . There are still a thousand and one things to be done. . . . The automobile industry and every other industry still need great improvement in their relationship to their employees. . . . It is my belief that the manufacturers of automobiles and the manufacturers of many other necessary commodities must, by planning, do far more than they have done to date to increase the yearly earnings of those who work for them.

"Your Administration has that kind of objective in mind. It is my belief that the people of Detroit, like the people of the rest of the country, are going to ask on Nov. 3 that the present type of government continue rather than the type of government which in its heart still believes in the policy of 'laissez faire' and the kind of individualism which up to only three and a half years ago frankly put dollars above human rights. . . . History will record that the outstanding issue of the campaign was this: Shall the social and economic security and betterment of the masses of the American people be maintained or not?"

But Roosevelt should be more specific. The issue isn't whether he is determined to repeat the mistakes of N.R.A. Only a fool would propose to do that. The question is whether the country wants its Federal Government to endeavor again to establish the five principles which N.R.A. sought to serve. Does Roosevelt propose to reestablish them? Does Governor Landon pledge himself that the Federal Government shall wash its hands of those principles?

It would be a healthy thing for both candidates to declare themselves. If democratic government means anything it means putting such fundamental questions as this squarely before the voters.

12/37

Mr. Hopkins is driving on with hopeful enthusiasm, a hard-boiled practical sentimentalist.

By nature he is cocky and tough. He didn't play basketball and run campus politics at Grinnell for nothing. Social workers are supposed to be generally mild, meek, and long-suffering. But the years Mr. Hopkins spent in social work before he became a public-relief administrator only deepened his sympathies without softening his skin. It is obvious, as he sits talking through the curling cigarette smoke, that his vocabulary has survived unexpurgated.

Mr. Hopkins has retained a buoyant lightheartedness which is not unlike that of President Roosevelt's. The two are extremely congenial. The President likes having him around. Their ideas harmonize, and Mr. Hopkins is never gloomy or bowed down with worried alarm over the state of the nation, as are so many of those who see the President.

They first met in 1928 when Mr. Roosevelt was running for governor of New York. Mr. Hopkins was helping in the Smith presidential campaign. Both the President and Mrs. Roosevelt took an immediate fancy to him, and, if he has had any stronger friend during the stormy days of the New Deal than the President, it has been Mrs. Roosevelt. When the depression set in and Governor Roosevelt turned to establish his state relief organization, he asked Mr. Hopkins to take charge. When Mr. Roosevelt moved to Washington, he brought his relief man down with him, at a $3,000 reduction in salary.

President Roosevelt's humanitarian impulses have been strengthened and implemented by Mr. Hopkins. From him the President obtained the idea of dramatizing the one third of our population which he describes as ill-fed, ill-clothed, and ill-housed. His persistent repetition of that theme is a result of the Hopkins influence. It is probable that there is still more to come in the direction of improving the lot of this group. Behind the Great Humanitarian stands Hopkins, the Expert Humanitarian, feeding ideas on what to do.

1/34

He [Hopkins] has hardheadedness with good humor, consumes many cigarettes, and dispenses old-fashioned profanity. His small, dark, brightly shining eyes see through a lot of things. They have a "hells-bells" glint in them that gives a cocky touch to his confident energy. And if anybody needs it, this young Samaritan does.

4/4/42

You have to think of Mrs. Roosevelt as you would about the strong man at the circus. She simply has several times the physical energy of the average person.

I never realized that until long after Mrs. Roosevelt had moved into the White House. It was the time she drafted several of us broken-down, flat-footed newspaper correspondents into one of her Virginia reels.

None of us had done the Virginia reel since we were kids. We all knew it was too late to start in again. But when Mrs. Roosevelt decides it would be nice to do the Virginia reel, you do the Virginia reel. She may be gentle and humble, always eager to understand the other person's problems. But when it comes to dancing, she is a woman of iron will. You dance.

Well, a dozen of us were rounded up at the White House one night to rehearse. Mrs. Roosevelt decided to put us into bright-colored colonial satin breeches, with tail jackets and lace ruffles on the cuffs, so we could do a really old-fashioned Virginia reel, Mount Vernon style, at the White House newspaper party that year.

Rehearsal night found Mrs. Roosevelt all ready to go. She had returned to Washington that morning about 5 A.M. from one of her trips down into a West Virginia coal mine. She had written her column, entertained guests at luncheon, seen half a dozen people by appointment, taken a horseback ride, finished off an early dinner, and when we arrived in the East Room, there she was, waltzing around the empty floor with her brother, the late Hall Roosevelt.

We lined up and for half an hour swung our partners until we were gasping. We couldn't go on any longer, so Mrs. Roosevelt gave us a 10-minute recess. We dropped exhausted to the floor, but Mrs. Roosevelt took her son Elliott around the East Room in a fast waltz while we recovered our breath. Then we went back at the rehearsal for another half hour. As we dragged ourselves out of the East Room that night, Mrs. Roosevelt was still waltzing around the floor, waving good-by to us over the sagging shoulder of brother Hall.

After that I knew it was no use to try to judge Mrs. Roosevelt by what you would expect of an ordinary person.

And on the night of the party, Mrs. Roosevelt swung us around so heartily that several of us were tossed halfway out of our bright satin minstrel jackets, so that we barely escaped disastrous exposure, as it was a hot night and we had stripped down to nothing underneath our satin clothes and lace ruffles.

Mrs. Roosevelt's triumph was complete. She had put a troupe of spavined old fire horses through what no doubt seemed to her the gay and light-footed spirit of the dance. She was sure that it did our souls good, as it had done hers.

Sweet, gentle, and kind—yes. But don't fool yourself. There's a core of iron, too. There wasn't any more chance of our escaping that Virginia reel at the White House than there was of electing Alf Landon President.

Most of Mrs. Roosevelt's troubles flow from a really good heart. She can be perverse and headstrong and she can blunder into unfortunate controversies. Yet, if these incidents are studied from her point of view, it will be seen that usually they are the eggs which, in spite of the mother instinct, hatch out into ugly ducklings instead of into the expected adorable little cotton-ball chicks. These cruel tricks of nature leave Mrs. Roosevelt baffled but unshaken in her maternal loyalty to her brood. She mothers each and every one, for better or for worse.

Mrs. Roosevelt's belief in people and their good intentions often overpowers her judgment. During her years in the White House, Mrs. Roosevelt has been exposed to all of the scheming, selfish, grasping, clawing side of human nature that storms so fiercely around that throne of power. Still, Mrs. Roosevelt sees no evil, hears no evil, thinks no evil. Some call that being plain gullible. But she goes on, looking for sorrow and trouble to heal, telephoning the State Department to ask if they won't please get a visa for some poor victim who wants to get out of Europe, never realizing that she is thereby shoving a favorite case in ahead of hundreds of others, all possibly equally heart-rending. She does not seem to realize—or does she?—that her slightest word, spoken ever so softly to an official appointed by her husband, has the impact on his mind of an executive order.

Once Mrs. Roosevelt was invited to visit a charity institution. She found a delicious hot lunch, with meat balls and everything that those housed in the institution could want. But she was suspicious, and returned a few days later unannounced. That time she found the regular luncheon was weak, watery soup. She was able to thus prod the management of the institution.

As a newspaper columnist Mrs. Roosevelt is able to bring to public attention many conditions which need airing and which can be corrected by simply giving them publicity. True, she has been criticized for writing professionally, and for her hopping about the country, some 40,000 miles a year, often driving her own car, but the criticism never really took hold. After all, she had always led her own life. Although some criticized her, they had to agree in the end that, even though she was the wife of the President, she had a right to conduct her personal affairs as she pleased.

Sometimes Mrs. Roosevelt seems so naïve that you wonder whether it isn't something just a little more subtle. When anyone who has spent a lifetime in politics seems naïve, watch out. It is the most baffling technique in the business, and so completely disarming that I have never understood why the ordinary politician didn't make more use of it, since politicians try every other crafty trick they can think of.

Mrs. Roosevelt may be gullible and naïve, but when she throws her heart into a cause she works at it with persistent skill. She is a most effective and formidable propagandist.

She was one of the first to take an interest in the Okies of California, long before *The Grapes of Wrath* was published. She visited the miserable Okie camps and called the attention of the nation to them.

Mrs. Roosevelt did the same kind of work in behalf of Negro share croppers who were evicted by landlords wishing to avoid sharing A.A.A. benefit payments with them. Out of that experience grew her great interest in Negro problems.

Her mother instinct led her to listen sympathetically to the problems of youth. Mrs. Roosevelt was largely responsible for creating the National Youth Administration. She has had a long series of embarrassing experiences with the American Youth Congress, which has been at times under fire by Congress.

Mrs. Roosevelt has given the shelter of the White House to the leaders of these and other movements. She opened her summer home at Campobello Island for a seminar of youth leaders. She invites them to tea, to discussion dinners, and sometimes to remain as house guests. When they seem to be wandering too far off in their views, Mrs. Roosevelt argues with them. Often they have argued back, as on one night when her son Franklin said they didn't seem to have very good manners. Mrs. Roosevelt excused them by saying they had not had the opportunities he had. Always she remains loyal and tolerant.

5/27/39

It is supposed to be sound economy if a hospital is built privately, but Government waste if it is built publicly. A. A. Berle, Jr., testifying before the O'Mahoney Temporary National Economic Committee, said the Government does create wealth in the form of parks, public buildings, and public hospitals. It is absurd, he said, to say that a public hospital is not "wealth" because it serves the area without charge, and that a private hospital is "wealth" because it charges each patient. What is the difference whether the charge is paid by the patient, or is distributed over the whole community, so far as the useful value of the hospital is concerned?

Mr. Berle used an apt contrast in citing the Brooklyn Bridge and the George Washington Bridge. It is absurd, he said, to consider that the Brooklyn Bridge is not wealth because it is a free bridge and paid for by the whole community, whereas the George Washington Bridge is a toll bridge and is paid for by the units as people pass over it.

Toll roads were once private business institutions. They constituted wealth. Take off the toll and let everyone use the road and charge the whole community for it through taxes. That doesn't change the fact that the road is wealth. You only remove the monopoly character from it, and release the facilities for fuller use.

The vital thing about public spending is to ensure responsible scrutiny of projects. The attack on spending could be constructively directed to that question, not to mention the importance of taxation, which the Administration has neglected and which it is being forced to take up in Congress now. We'll all be talking about taxes next week.

But before leaving the subject of spending, note the distinctions made by Dr. Alvin H. Hansen, Harvard economist, before the Temporary National Economic Committee.

He said the ordinary run of Government expenditures, operating expenses which in modern times must include social-service, relief, and welfare expenses, should be balanced by tax receipts over an entire business cycle. This portion of the budget should be balanced, in other words, not necessarily every year but over a short span of years.

But when public investments are made in long-term durable projects like a bridge, it is sound, Dr. Hansen thinks, to borrow if provision is made for amortization and interest charges within the lifetime of such projects.

"When an individual builds a house," he said, "and borrows the funds to defray part of the cost, his personal budget cannot be said to be out of balance if his income is adequate to cover interest and amortization."

State and local governments always have done this, and the same accounting should be adopted by the Federal Government.

Again I cite those historic attacks on proposals to establish public schools, those editorials in *The Philadelphia National Gazette* in the summer of 1830: "It is an old and sound remark that Government cannot provide for the necessities of the people. . . . Some of the writers about universal public instruction and discipline seem to forget the constitution of modern society, and declaim as if our communities could receive institutions or habits like those of Sparta. The dream embraces great Republican female academies to make Roman matrons. . . . The scheme of universal equal education at the expense of the state would be a compulsory application of the means of the richer for the direct use of the poor classes; and so far an arbitrary division of property among them."

Now there's an issue for those who are alarmed about present tendencies. Go back to fundamentals and get rid of this Government spending for public schools. It is competing with private schools. If public money shouldn't go into hospitals, why should it go into schools?

1/31/40

Maybe the National Youth Administration is one of those extravagant New Deal spending agencies. Possibly it is one of those expenses we could get along without. Even Mr. Roosevelt himself seems tempted to give it the ax.

But I spent a little time on the receiving end of N.Y.A. out here in the great open spaces, and I know there are ambitious young fellows in Texas working out an education in ways that would be impossible without the assistance of N.Y.A. Some of our well-fed, well-heeled economizers in the East, who were fortunate enough to be educated by wealthy parents, no doubt subscribe to the theory that it is only pampering these youths to help finance a college education for them. Let them stay on the farm! Don't arouse ambitions in them that can never be fulfilled.

Well, I discover in going around that some of our leading citizens who are so violently opposed to institutions like the National Youth Administration are not so opposed to subsidizing college students for football teams. In one Middle Western city I happened to be in a business office. My host proudly pointed out a strapping young fellow working in the large office which we were passing through.

"He's a star back on our team," my host said. "They have given him a job here and he is a good worker. This office always provides a job for one man on the team."

At another stop I learned that several boys—six, I think—at the near-by college were carried on the police-department pay roll as undercover men. Some question was raised about using college boys in that way. It developed that it was only a practical way of financing a few students who were needed on the football team. So the city taxpayers willingly accept the expense of that subsidy. The boys help make a good team and the team brings thousands of dollars' worth of business into town during the football season. Those college-boy undercover men are considered a good civic investment.

At Amarillo, Tex., you can drive out a few miles from town to West Texas State Normal College and find something that will restore your confidence in postdepression youth. If anyone in the East thinks that the American spirit is dying out of the younger generation, that it has succumbed to defeatism, let him take a look at any college in the Western country.

At West Texas College, N.Y.A. is helping 100 students, men and women, work their way through school. Part of my income tax, and some of yours, goes toward paying them $15 a month. In exchange the students work 50 hours a month. Some I met were working as library assistants. Others were cataloguing the rich Texas historical material, which is being accumulated here in one of the most remarkable collections of frontier source material to be found anywhere. As they work they are learning. They are doing some of the most useful work at the institution. They are at the same time training themselves to become teachers of the next generation. In my time I have seen a good many billion dollars appropriated in Washington and none of it could go to any more useful or more constructive purpose than this $15 a month that goes out to these young Texas men and women, who come mostly from hard-pressed ranch families.

N.Y.A. also is supporting a large squad of boys who are somewhat below college grade. About seventy of them are here, learning to be carpenters, airplane mechanics, sheet-metal workers, welders, stone and brick masons. They are building school dormitories and school buildings while learning their trades. They receive $30 a month and work 4 hours a day for it.

I visited dormitories where students do their own housework on a cooperative basis. Thus they obtain their college education at a cost of $15 a month. They may bring food from their ranches and sell it to the college commissary at market prices. In one dormitory the girls have managed to cut their expenses to $13 a month. That takes hard work, planning, and sacrifice which the manicured dolls in Eastern girls' schools would consider far beneath them.

Even if N.Y.A. is going to add a few million dollars to the national debt, I as a taxpayer consider it a good investment—insofar as the money goes to these students and not to padded overhead. For here you are giving a chance to the most ambitious young men and women, the ones with real stamina. They are willing to put themselves through work that would be disdained by Eastern college boys who are being educated on dad's checkbook to grow up as smug reactionaries. This country will be better off for these young people who, in two or three years, will be out teaching the next generation.

I could write much more and give you more facts. But it isn't popular copy. Some people might think I was a red—those people who don't know Americanism when they see it.

3/4/38

Five years have seen the New Deal rise to a peak of hopeful enthusiasm and then settle down, where it is now, into a cautious and bewildered middle age. These have been five years of mingled successes and failures, of quick-changing and baffling currents. They have left Roosevelt not sadder but certainly wiser. He knows now there is no slide-rule formula for running a democratic country. If democracy is the easiest form of government to live under, it is the hardest to run.

In 1933 Roosevelt took the stage promising action, "action now." But in 1938 the emphasis is upon no action, reflecting Roosevelt's response to the reversal of opinion.

Once Roosevelt seemed to think that if the right laws could be drawn and passed, our troubles would be cured. It was mainly a job of finding the right laws. Now it is evident that he has less faith in laws alone. He realizes more keenly that under a private capitalist system cooperation cannot be conscripted. So the wages-and-hours bill fades quietly into the background. Only the ghost of N.R.A. is left and the monopoly question, it appears, is to be approached with exceeding caution, and then only after long preliminary investigation. He approaches it as gingerly as Hoover approached prohibition repeal.

Roosevelt is reflecting only the bewilderment and loss of confidence which the whole country is feeling. After a pump-priming expenditure of some $17,000,000,000, the business cycle is down again and there has been a loss of public confidence in spending as a cure. If it is sound in theory, it has not, for one reason or another, worked satisfactorily in practice.

NEW DEAL

Throughout most of his Administration, Roosevelt has been engaged in a kind of bloodless civil war with the business community. Both sides were stubborn and bitter. In a private capitalist system both Government and private business share the real power. Both occupy large areas of control. It does not seem possible to operate such an economy when the two most powerful groups in it are engaged in war with each other. A stalemate has resulted and the whole country is feeling the effects of it.

11/19/39

The days of the New Deal as such appear very likely to be drawing to a close. Roosevelt may drive on for a short time longer but already the page is being turned on him. This most spectacular and significant political adventure seemingly has run its course. As has been the case with other forward movements, the New Deal has led and driven the country into reforms that were long overdue. Now the country appears to be settling down on the new plateau to rest a while.

Certainly that is the mood of the Middle West, the valley of democracy, whence the great political movements of the past have sprung. This is the heart of America, the mother of political change. The Middle West made Bryan, made Theodore Roosevelt and his progressive movement, gave Woodrow Wilson his footing, gave us prohibition, and then permitted prohibition to go. We went into the European war only when the Middle West consented. The Middle West made possible Roosevelt and the New Deal. Where the Middle West goes, America usually follows.

The Middle West found in Roosevelt the answer to its needs. It found in him a man willing and courageous enough to undertake reforms long wanted. But if I have correctly gathered sentiment in a number of key states in this area, the Middle West believes Roosevelt has done the job he was called to do, or as in the case of agriculture has demonstrated that he cannot do it, and people here are ready to let up for a while.

Roosevelt's major reforms—social security, stock-market control and securities regulation, Federal enforcement of collective bargaining, Federal wages-and-hours standards, Federal responsibility for unemployment relief, assistance for soil conservation—all of these are now part of the accepted American way. Roosevelt made them so. Some changes may be made in details but in principle his major work will not be erased.

10/7/43

Politically the war is changing everything. It is changing the New Deal almost beyond recognition. I think the term itself is ceasing to have much significance. We are more and more referring to the Roosevelt Administration rather than to the New Deal.

President Roosevelt seems to many to be moving to the right, to be deserting the New Deal. I would state the situation in different terms.

I have been observing this Administration closely from the time when Franklin Roosevelt was talking about the forgotten man back many months before he was nominated for President in 1932. I never have thought there was anything very revolutionary about Mr. Roosevelt. Representative Dies has been worried about Communists here but they have existed largely in the woodwork and meant nothing much in Washington.

The New Deal to me has always been a mild affair. It has been improvised and usually played by ear. Its original purpose was to break the depression, bring about reemployment, use public works for those who could not find employment in private industry. Relief and reemployment came first.

Then there were several reform measures, such as stock-market regulation, which were not revolutionary but moderate regulation of private enterprise.

A third line of activity was in behalf of organized labor—and there the Roosevelt Administration encouraged unionization and collective bargaining, which are matters that are regarded as radical nowhere in civilized countries—and I might add that in no other country are labor unions afflicted with so much racketeering as here.

That's about all there ever has been to the New Deal.

One of the most realistic descriptions of the New Deal comes from a Canadian, W. D. Herridge, formerly Canadian minister here in Washington.

He says the New Deal was "a generous and progressive thought emotionally developed by amateur economists and cynically exploited by professional politicians."

One economist who has been considered sympathetic to the New Deal is Stuart Chase and he has written recently in the magazine *Common Sense* to the effect that the war has finally accomplished most of what the New Deal set out to do. The war has given every workman a job at high wages, removed him from dependence on charity, and through rationing has leveled off the upper crust until the rich man cannot buy any more of many things than the poor man. The common man, in other words, is getting a better break through the war than the New Deal was able to give him.

The wealthy class is being taxed into moderate circumstances now. What would have once been resisted as an intolerable New Deal social-reform measure is now a matter-of-fact war necessity which is taken for granted.

I never have thought much of the terms left and right as applied to political affairs here in Washington. I grant that sometimes these are convenient labels. But I believe they are grossly overworked. Some try to force men and measures into left or right categories artificially. On the basis of personalities around here and the changes in faces that President Roosevelt has made in the last few months, I could fix you up a good argument to show you that he has gone to the right and also a good one to show you he has gone to the left. Neither one would mean very much.

He is putting some businessmen in high places now—Averell Harriman to Moscow, Stettinius into the State Department, Leo Crowley to direct our foreign economic activities. Harriman is chairman of the Union Pacific Railroad and one of the richest businessmen in America. Stettinius formerly was chairman of the United States Steel Corporation. Both of these men are tame businessmen brought conspicuously into the Administration picture to balance it off. They have more in common with Harry Hopkins than with a bitterly anti-Roosevelt industrialist like Tom Girdler.

During the war Mr. Roosevelt has had more businessmen than New Dealers around him—probably more Republicans than Democrats. The War Production agencies have been rather thoroughly manned in key positions by Republican businessmen and then you have also Secretary Stimson and Secretary Knox, who were anti-New Deal Republicans.

The best case for the rise of conservative influence in Washington is in the high power now of Judge James F. Byrnes, and Judge Carl Vinson, who run the economic front—and the significant thing is that standing around near them, in a close advisory relationship with them, is the shrewd elder statesman, Bernard M. Baruch.

Yet under businessman Crowley, Mr. Roosevelt has placed as executive officer of the Board of Economic Warfare one of the original so-called New Deal economists, Lauchlin Currie. An original brain truster from the 1932 campaign, Judge Rosenman, has just been brought into the official White House staff from the New York State bench. An original New Deal member of the cabinet, Secretary Harold Ickes, is still on the job and has a considerable amount of power, especially as Oil Administrator. And the man who has been at Mr. Roosevelt's side from May, 1933, until this very day is Harry Hopkins. Most people would call him a New Dealer. Yet he is one of the men who is strongest for Secretary of State Cordell Hull. I could go on scrambling these names but it would only add to the confusion. My point is that if you want to have the real picture of Washington, don't be too quick to shove every man and every measure into a neat little pigeonhole marked right or left. It won't add up. You get a much simpler picture of Washington but one that is somewhat misleading.

For instance, although Harry Hopkins once was in charge of work relief and devoted most of his living hours to the problem of reemployment, he probably never gives that sort of thing a thought now. He is engaged entirely on work connected with the war, with munitions assignments, international relations, and all kinds of matters which come to him as the closest adviser to Mr. Roosevelt. In these days he is no more left or right than a soldier is left or right in trying to win a battle. Ideologies are at their lowest ebb in Washington today.

If Mr. Roosevelt is a candidate for President again, I should think he would minimize the ideological cleavages which have centered around the New Deal in his earlier campaigns. Mr. Roosevelt's natural role in the present situation would be to avoid arguing over domestic issues at all and to stand for a vote of confidence on the conduct of the war.

Republicans will try to make the campaign turn on domestic affairs. They believe that the memory of the New Deal is unpopular and that they can capitalize on it.

But it will be largely talk. Whatever party is in power when the war is over will do what the Roosevelt Administration did when it took office in a period of acute unemployment—it will move heaven and earth to find some way of putting men to work, either on private pay rolls or on Government pay rolls.

In that sense Roosevelt is not deserting the New Deal and in that sense Republicans will have to accept a fundamental New Deal policy if they should come into power.

Republican Party

6/11/40

WHAT chance has the Republican Party? Very little, if it is thinking only of winning the election. People have no patience for ordinary politics now. They are not interested.

But if the Republican Party is thinking, as some of its leaders are thinking, of rising to the challenge of this fateful hour, when the clock is telling off perhaps the end of the world that we have known, then the Republican Party has an opportunity the like of which it has never known.

What is the challenge? The challenge is to throw aside all considerations of political expediency. It is to forget the usual prattle of politics. It is to strive only for a sense of responsibility to the needs of the nation.

The challenge is to realize the hard fact that in Europe democracy has failed, failed miserably, shown itself to be incompetent, fumbling, too slow, too ignorant, too paralyzed by its own internal politics, helpless to use science and invention effectively for its own self-preservation—a tragic victim of its own internal weaknesses. In Europe democracy has been tried and found wanting. We may not see it restored there for a long time.

Republicans can nominate somebody who looks good in ephemeral straw votes, or some plodding politician whose profession is running for office. Or they can take a bold and audacious course, look at the job to be done, and select, regardless of tradition, the man best qualified to do it.

12/15/34

For years the Republican Party has existed as an alliance between Eastern financiers and industrialists on the one hand and Western farmers and small businessmen on the other. That was the result of trying to maintain a national party on a geographical basis rather than on community of economic interest. Often these two wings of the party are directly opposed to each other. Eastern creditors line up on one side and Western debtors on the other. Industry wants tariff protection, whereas agriculture wants cheap factory products and dear foodstuffs.

The Western group was powerful in Congress throughout the years of Republican domination at Washington because it was able to form a bipartisan alliance with the Southern agricultural bloc of the Democratic Party. Though powerful in Congress, the Western group never has dominated the national party machinery. By a policy of broad tolerance, the Republican Party allowed its La Follettes and its Norrises to have as much rope as they wanted. But always the party machinery was in the hands of the Eastern industrialists and financiers. At national conventions and at the White House it was Penrose, Hilles, Ogden Mills, and such leaders of the Eastern group that dominated and picked Presidents. Westerners went along under this Eastern domination of the party machinery because they had their outlet in Congress.

5/6/34

In May of 1934 Senator Borah of Idaho, the hair shirt in the Republican Party for a generation, told the press that the party must be reorganized from top to bottom and be divorced from the economic and financial influences which have dominated it in recent years.

He said, "The Republican Party is pretty close to the brink and unless it has an organization free from the influences which brought us to our present plight it will die as the old Whig party died—of sheer political cowardice.

"There is just one hope for the Republican Party instead of a new party and that is the young Republicans all over the country who have a new outlook, new spirit, and cleaner, higher political ideals.

"If they can take charge of the party and divorce it from the economic and financial influences which have dominated it recently then we can have a Republican Party."

He added that "the rank and file of the Republican Party is still loyal and there is a majority of Republicans in this country if given the proper leadership."

7/29/34

You leave the low-roofed Spanish home on top of San Juan Hill just above the red-tiled quadrangle to Stanford University wondering whether Herbert Hoover will return to active politics to seek vindication or whether he will be content to let time render its true verdict.

What thoughts turn over in his restlessly alert mind as Mr. Hoover sits calmly on the unroofed veranda of his quiet retreat and gazes out across the peaceful Santa Clara Valley and reflects, as he surely must sometimes, how the curious fates have played upon his busy life with triumph and disaster both in unparalleled degree?

His story is epic meat of the kind which fed the ancient Greeks and Shakespeare in their great tragedies. There were the youthful struggles and quick success. World fame came at forty when he took over the Belgian relief. Three years later he was wartime autocrat of America's dinner tables. Finally there was his comet-like sweep across the political firmament when he returned after 20 years of exile and ran away with the presidency from a field of lifelong professionals. Even while he was still being cheered as the ideal man, by virtue of his administrative and business experience, to lead the nation through the glorious flowering of the machine age, the ominous thunder of the greatest depression began to crash on his ears and he was turned out of office, carrying only six states.

Mr. Hoover will be sixty years old Aug. 10. For the first time in his life he has nothing to do. For a year and a half he has been among the unemployed. No one thought, after the life he had led, that he could just go out on the porch and sit down and be quiet for 18 months. For 20 years he roamed the world taking on one trouble job after another. He was the hardest worker the White

House ever saw. This is the first time in his life that responsibilities have not been piling down on his shoulders. For the first time there is nothing that he has to do tomorrow.

He likes it, at least for the moment. Or he thinks he does. Yet you wonder. For though he has nothing to do, he is not idle. His mail is heavy. On light days there will be only 200 letters possibly. When some highly controversial issue is up at Washington his mail will react instantly and run up as high as 1,500 letters a day. Two stenographers are kept busy. Mr. Hoover tries to answer every letter. It is a source of private gratification when friends or strangers take the trouble to write him. But every answer costs a 3-cent stamp—widows of former Presidents have the franking privilege, but not former Presidents. Mr. Hoover once estimated to friends that it cost him $700 a month out of his own pocket to answer his mail.

He reads. Last week he was reading James P. Warburg's *The Money Muddle* and wondering how popular this young former Administration adviser might be in Washington now, and how many people in the country had read this devastating analysis of the monetary policy. Mr. Hoover, whose proudest campaign boast in 1932 was that he had kept the country on the gold standard, still has his ideas. You pick up echoes of them from friends. Devaluation of the dollar has struck hard at university endowment funds. As a trustee of Stanford University, Mr. Hoover has come face to face with the problem. There it has meant cutting down departments, slicing off professors, and reducing salaries. Endowments and foundations such as the Rockefeller and Russell Sage Foundations have suffered severely, and Mr. Hoover frequently laments to friends that this is one of the calamities of the attempt to manipulate the currency.

Friends here report that in Mr. Hoover's rambles around Santa Clara Valley he talks with small merchants and businessmen and finds them resentful of N.R.A., with restrictions which have permitted large business to thrive and develop into a guild system more rigid in its control than those of Elizabethan times. These friends gather from Mr. Hoover that he sees a parallel between N.R.A. and prohibition and would not be surprised if the country turns on

N.R.A. and tears it out by the roots, regardless of any meritorious elements it contains, just as they turned on prohibition and wiped it out completely.

When these little groups of friends gather with Mr. Hoover and get to discussing the basic point of attack which is likely to be made against the New Deal, the drift of the conversation almost invariably goes to the Bill of Rights. The belief is expressed that the average man eventually will center on that as the point at issue.

Mr. Hoover has little to say about the show on the Washington stage. Washington is a long way off. The news goes on page 6 and foreign news goes on page 9 and Mr. Hoover looks on as a distant observer.

The outside world thinks of Mr. Hoover as a man brooding in silence. He is silent so far as the outside world is concerned and he has firmly rejected all offers to write or to discuss national affairs. But it is not a brooding silence. Nor the silence of a man who has lost his interest in life. It is the calm self-restraint of a man who is observing and thinking a great deal. It is a relaxed, attentive silence like that of a performer who has had his turn on the stage and is now watching the performance of others.

He watches the act with an experienced professional eye and he is alert to some of the fine shades of the performance which might pass unnoticed by the audience. He probably does not think the performers are doing as thorough a job as he did, but if he does, he does not call out to the audience to say so.

It is some such role as that which Mr. Hoover appears to be playing at the moment. He motors about the state and reexamines with unceasing interest the spots where he worked as a young geologist years ago. Sometimes he will address a group of Boy Scouts. He serves as trustee for a few public institutions. He turned the first spadeful of earth for the gigantic San Francisco-Oakland bridge. He went to San Francisco and walked in the rain in the funeral procession of the late Governor Rolph, though they were never mutual admirers. He is courteous to all visitors, important or obscure. Ruddy color has come back in his face. His hair is whiter and thinner but he looks younger.

He must have been bitter when he first returned to California, the most spectacular casualty of the depression. But if so, it has worn off now. At sixty he looks out on the world and while obviously he does not find it moving to his satisfaction in a great many ways, he seems, so far as the casual visitor can detect, contented, yet interested. He has no plans for more than a month ahead.

11/9/34

Republicans envy the Democrats for having Franklin D. Roosevelt. They think it must be great to have someone's coattails to ride through on. Everybody was invoking Roosevelt's magic name to get elected. Even Merriam, the Republican candidate for governor in California, insisted that a vote for him was a vote for Roosevelt. Having no Roosevelt of their own, Republicans in many instances were reduced to leaning on the Democratic Roosevelt.

The hypnotic effect of that name in American politics is striking. As one who is desperately ill dwells over happy scenes of his childhood, so the Republicans in their bitter hour seek refuge in their memories, and it is their own Roosevelt—Theodore the First—who rides gallantly into their reveries. His name is recalled in public statements by Republicans like Borah who are urging reorganization of the party. They think back upon what a different history the party might have had if it had accepted T.R.

But the party turned down the right-hand path and coasted in glory for a long time. Now it is at the bottom of the hill smashed and bleeding, and it calls for Theodore Roosevelt. It was Theodore Roosevelt who came nearest to dominating the party with the progressive spirit which a large element feels must be recaptured now.

The two fifth cousins, one in the White House, the other whose spirit comes leaping back across a dark chasm, may in a sense be regarded as the two great political forces of the moment.

6/10/35

National victories do not seem to have much to do with the longevity of a political party. Local machines keep it alive. Through most of its existence after the Civil War the Democratic Party consisted, first, of its Southern bloc, which was steadily whittled away until only ten states were left intact and then Hoover crashed in and took away four of these. The second element in the party was the loose federation of city machines in the North—Tammany, the organizations in Boston, Kansas City, Omaha, San Francisco, and other large cities. These city machines were interested primarily in local control. They wanted the patronage and the city contracts. That was more important to them than winning a national election, or often even a state one.

Time after time deals have been made whereby Democrats would trade with Republicans, putting up feeble opposition to the national Republican ticket in return for push-over opposition in mayoralty fights.

Thus the Democrats maintained their party through one national disaster after another. On the morning after every election, the Democratic Party was solemnly pronounced dead. But all that happened was that Democratic leaders went back to distributing city patronage, dealing out city contracts, and winning more city elections.

So, in a sense, it is with the Republican Party now. It has control of many village, city, county, and state governments. As long as it has these it remains alive.

The question before the Republican Party is not whether it can remain alive but rather how it can resume its place as the dominant national party.

That involves something entirely different. Organization is essential but during the present generation, at least, national elections have tended to be won by landslide proportions. The clearest illustration is the violent overturn from Hoover in 1928 to Roosevelt 4 years later. The Republican who broke the solid South turned up 4 years later with only six states. The respective vote of the Republican and Democratic presidential candidates was almost exactly reversed between 1928 and 1932.

The 1912 election, although split three ways, showed a strong surge of progressive sentiment which was divided between Wilson and Theodore Roosevelt. In 1920 the Harding majority was a landslide out of all proportion to any strength of his as a leader. Coolidge's 1924 sweep was a similar tidal wave. National elections have tended to crash overwhelmingly in one direction or the opposite.

This signifies that the real national victories are won by candidates who stir something deep in the average man, who touch a popular note and sweep the country like a popular song hit. That is what a presidential candidate must shoot at and it is the thing his party must build toward in the preparatory stages.

Republicans are now in the preparatory stage for another presidential campaign. This is the time when they must give thought, not only to the matter of local organization, but also to the broad type of national appeal they expect to make.

They must decide to whom they will appeal.

As for the Midwestern Republicans, if the view privately expressed here by the leaders is to be reflected in the creed to be adopted here this week, the appeal will be not to the New Dealers, but to those opposed to the New Deal and everything associated with it. They expect to appeal to the same voters who for so many years before the depression returned the party to national power time after time—these, plus old-line Democrats who may feel that Roosevelt has betrayed the Democratic Party and that he has left no place in it for them. To such conservative Democrats, the Republicans will offer hospice.

It is essentially an appeal of predepression leaders to predepression psychology. Republicans count on a nest egg of 13,500,000 voters—the ones who stood firm for the Republican candidate in the congressional elections last year. That is not enough voters of course. Hoover polled some 15,000,000 votes in 1932 while Roosevelt polled some 22,000,000. They are counting upon a backswing of former Republicans and of some dissatisfied Democrats. How their calculations will come out nobody knows. But there is an important long-range factor involved in this which goes beyond 1936.

Voters die and new voters come in, some million a year. In the long run the party that stays on top nationally is the party that brings in these younger voters.

Oldsters never realize that a new generation is moving in behind them. Men and women will vote in the next election who were born in 1915, after the First World War broke out, after the *Lusitania* was sunk, who can't remember Harding and don't know what "back to normalcy" meant, to whom "Keep Cool with Coolidge" conjures up no recollection. Rather their first sharp recollections about public affairs are more apt to begin about the time the stock market crashed, when they heard around the family dinner table that something pretty terrible had happened to father. These young men and women were just fourteen then, when the world went suddenly askew.

Almost 30,000,000 persons of voting age were born after the turn of the century. The oldest of this group were entering high school when the First World War began. They were marrying and starting homes and families when the depression began. This vast group in the population has, with few exceptions, felt the effects of the depression keenly. Thousands have finished college and found no jobs. Others have lost their jobs. They have had to support relatives.

This is the class to which the political party of the future will have to appeal to win. What this class is thinking is the key to the political outlook. Is it as a group tired of experiments? Does it think Roosevelt is seeking to introduce European forms of government into the United States? Does it think he is crippling individual initiative? Is it fearful of regimentation of the farmers? Does it think professors in government are a vicious influence? Does it believe that if the New Deal were wiped out the country would go back to the prosperity of the twenties?

Politicians who can guess the answers to these questions correctly are the ones who are going to put their feet under the White House table in the future.

6/11/36

The remorse of a guilty conscience undoubtedly had something to do with the fervor with which the Republican convention saluted Herbert Hoover.

You could not mistake the warmth in the demonstration. Newborn affection showed itself in the way the thousands in the convention hall remained standing afterward, calling in vain for Hoover to come back. They wanted him to hear once more the sweet music of earsplitting cheers which had been lavished upon him during the short time he was in the hall.

For three long years, as we say now, or more, Hoover has occupied an unhappy place in the esteem of his fellow Republicans only slightly higher than that in which they hold Roosevelt. For three long years, Republicans have been willing to take anybody but Hoover. He was an unwanted Jonah.

But last night they were in a far different mood. Hoover came before them as a man who had served faithfully, giving the best he had only to meet with ill fortune which they now realized he had borne like a man. If he had any ambition to be President again, they knew he had forsworn it. Yet he did not sulk. He continued to labor for the party. They were touched by the sporting way in which he had carried on. So they sought by applause, which is the only coin with which they could pay, to make reparation.

Perhaps also the sight of Hoover evoked among the Republican delegates fond recollections of better days, when they were deputy marshals, postmasters, collectors of internal revenue, long before the strange tribe of New Deal job holders, A.A.A. agents, N.R.A. compliance officers, P.W.A. eurythmic-dancing directors, appeared like a swarm of 17-year locusts. Those were the good old days. It was pleasant for an hour or so to recall with Hoover their departed glory. There must have been in their applause a touch of belated gratitude for these blessings no longer enjoyed.

This occasion also gave the Republicans release from the drab enervation which has hung heavily over the labored convention proceedings. Hoover not only entertained them with some of his brighter sayings, but he drew a bead on one simple issue which no delegate could be too dumb to understand—the issue of liberty.

With a far more adept hand than he showed in his greater political days, Hoover skillfully touched the issue which in Republican Party history is wrapped in the warmest sentiment.

The party was born in the cause of liberty—abolition of slavery. Hoover stood last night for rebirth of the party in the same cause of liberty—a fight against making the citizen the slave of the state. He fears the New Deal may enslave the citizen as European dictatorships have. He puts the New Deal government in the same class with Simon Legree. The "Battle Hymn of the Republic," the great hymn which inspired the Republicans in the Civil War, is becoming the unconscious theme song of this convention.

But Hoover's conception of liberty is not exactly that of the Middle Western progressives who are, through the Landon movement, setting a new temper for the party. He may be a little out of key with it. Liberty seems to Hoover a totally negative thing. Government seems to be interference with individual liberty—a policeman trying to cramp our style.

Middle Western progressives also believe in individual liberty. It is their strongest inheritance from pioneer days. But the farmer saw prices fluctuate so that he had to pay his Eastern creditor twice as many bushels of wheat as the mortgage called for at the time it was given; therefore he wanted some kind of currency control, or management, which would protect him against these violent fluctuations of the yardstick by which the wheat was measured—the dollar. He also found himself the victim of extortionate freight rates, and monopoly prices, and he wanted the Government to protect him from them.

In short, he came to see that the Government was useful in protecting his individual opportunity. Liberty to him is a process which includes regulation of economic traffic so that he will not be run down as he crosses the street.

It is that kind of liberty which the new leadership in the Republican Party seeks. Hoover's conception is somewhat narrower, unless we misunderstood him.

At any rate the party is turning to the new Middle Western leader. As it does so, it pauses to say to Hoover, hail and farewell.

8/10/37

In its thriving years the Republican Party was a bedlam of internal conflict. Its Penroses and elder La Follettes were at each other's throats. Its Norrises and Smoots were on opposite sides of practically every economic and social question. In Wisconsin the Republican Party was a La Follette party. In Nebraska it was the Norris party. In Pennsylvania it was a Penrose Tory party.

The reactionary leaders in those days were smart. They knew that the way to play the game was to rule with an easy hand. They let the insurgent Republicans talk wild in Congress. But when election day came, the progressive Republicans went along, helped elect Republican Presidents, and helped constitute Republican majorities by which the conservative group retained control of the House and Senate machinery. Insurgent Republicans got practically nowhere in Congress with their programs. So the conservatives paid a small price indeed for their tolerance, which returned such large dividends in national power.

But in the early twenties the Republicans, in their great strength, became arbitrary and highhanded. They expelled a group of Republican insurgents of the Norris-La Follette brand from the Senate Republican caucus because this group bolted Coolidge for the La Follette third-party ticket.

That purge was the work of young, hotheaded Republicans, intent on revenge. They were comparable in temperament to the extreme left-wing New Dealers who are yelling now for a party purge. The old heads didn't care much for it. Old Penrose was gone. He would never have permitted it. He knew that the Republican Party, to remain dominant, must accommodate itself to western progressives. He learned that in 1912. But the young Republicans insisted on their purge and the western progressives swung aboard the first hospitable band wagon that came along, which happened to be Roosevelt in 1932.

National political parties exist not so much because of principles as because they are necessary machinery in getting things done. This country has so many sections with conflicting interests that a national party must be loose enough to accommodate a number of these conflicting groups within itself. They struggle inside the walls for control of the party machinery. But if dissident groups are purged, the party whittles itself down into a weak minority. It attains harmony by throwing out all dissenters. And then it gets thrown out itself.

It would be a calamity for this country to lose its two-party system and have its politics disintegrate into bloc government which would quickly degenerate into paralysis or would put us at the mercy of minority balance-of-power groups blackjacking their way to power.

12/7/37

Any number of Republicans are concerned, as they well should be, about the future of their party. Many of them are offering public prescriptions to cure what ails it. Not many, however, have the courage to say all that needs to be said. They all condemn Roosevelt's management of affairs. That's easy and is to be expected. Having said that, most of them lose their nerve. A few would go on and nudge the party's stuffed shirts out of the front row.

But it remains for Governor George D. Aiken, of faithful Vermont, to blurt out the frank advice which no one in the family has yet had the forthrightness to give. Having fought, bled, and won for the Republican Party in Vermont, Governor Aiken now addresses an open letter to the Republican National Committee. This letter, if any attention is paid to it, would prove a turning point in the party's sad history.

"We have become a party of old men," Governor Aiken says. "Unless we can become also a party of and for young men and young women, the party will die—and the processes of dissolution have already begun."

Registration figures in many localities will support the governor. Most Republican politicians know the reason for this but they are afraid to admit it, because it would make a good deal of what they have been saying appear ridiculous. But Governor Aiken faces the painful task without gagging.

For one thing, he said, it will be necessary to "purge the party organization of its reactionary and unfair elements."

But that will not be enough. The Republicans, the governor says, must also "accept in general the social aims which the opposing party has had the wisdom to adopt, but has lacked the ability to put into efficient operation."

That is exactly the policy which many of Governor Landon's friends urged him to pursue in the 1936 presidential campaign—to attack Roosevelt's methods, not his objectives. Instead the Republicans pictured Roosevelt as a revolutionary who was seeking to undermine the American form of government and of course the American voters gave them the horselaugh.

Governor Aiken urges the Republican Party to reject the policy of enormous expenditures and not to attempt to outbid the Democrats. "We should," he says, "be ashamed to try." A strong party, resisting extravagance, is much needed at this time. He makes an exception concerning agriculture to the extent of proposing means for carrying over bumper crops into lean years and for subsidizing domestic crops, the prices of which are fixed in the world market, but without imposing production control.

Concerning industrial problems, Governor Aiken would have the party use the Government's regulatory power to curb monopoly and to protect small business, but with Government regarding business as the source of production, employment, and consumption and with business, on its side, ready "to meet more than halfway the honest overtures of an honest Government."

He warns against the Federal Government taking on powers too great and too complicated to be successfully used. He would resist blank-check legislation and large grants of discretionary power to the President, but he believes the presidential office and its supporting staff should be strengthened in the gathering of information and in the making of recommendations.

Governor Aiken was trying to suggest a general course rather than draft a detailed program. The important thing in his letter is the approach that he recommends, a recognition that in these times governments have broader duties, and an attempt to rise to those responsibilities in a practical levelheaded way.

It isn't the kind of letter that the Republican National Committee likes to receive and this is apt to be the last that will be heard of it, unless the governor was smart enough to write it on asbestos paper.

12/10/37

Almost every Republican who speaks for publication now says that the party must be progressive. That sounds up and coming and suggests a change of policy toward something more in line with what is expected of government in a modern industrial world. But when you say the party must be progressive you are tossing around another one of those trick words that anyone from Hoover to Stalin can appropriate and make mean anything or nothing. Coolidge used to say the Republican Party ought to be as progressive as science. Then he always added—but as conservative as the multiplication table.

12/24/37

In the matter of developing unified sentiment at this time, the biggest and most pleasant surprise which the White House has had during the Japanese crisis came at 6 P.M. Monday when the telegraph room brought to Secretary Stephen T. Early a day letter from Topeka, Kan. It was signed by Governor Landon and pledged his support to the President while criticizing members of both parties in Congress for agitating a war referendum during such a tense situation.

That is what comes of being a free man in public life. Landon had recently shut the door against any further presidential aspirations. He had no political entanglements to consider. This step meant crossing with his political ally and close friend, Senator Capper, who recently entertained him in Washington. It meant also leaving his Kansas Republican congressmen on this issue. Furthermore, when the White House asked him if his telegram could be published, Landon didn't have to stop and consider whether it would damage his chances of getting the Republican presidential nomination.

In other words, all that Landon has to gain is the satisfaction of having time decide that he acted with good judgment for the national interest. His only risk is to have time decide that he acted unwisely for the national interest. When you have men acting from that interest and no other, then you get the best they have to give. In this world of human frailty that is all anyone can give. If enough people gave just that, it would be sufficient, more than sufficient.

1938

Roots of the party, although sadly undernourished, are still alive and waiting only to be revived. These seem likely to persist for a long time. There is no reason why, as a minority party, the Republicans are not assured of an indefinite existence, unless they should deliberately choose suicide. The Democratic Party subsisted as a minority for years, feeding on Southern states and a few Northern city governments.

But the Republican Party need not be content with this minimum-subsistence level. The political decision in this country still is in the hands of a large balance-of-power group, loosely joined to the Democratic Party at the moment, but traditionally Republican and only driven away from its own party because that party offered it nothing that seemed worth while. These moderates want to see democracy succeed. Republicans proposed nothing except to render government impotent in the face of problems that demanded attention. Roosevelt proposed to deal with these problems. His methods might not meet the approval of the moderates but better Roosevelt's methods than nothing.

You can go through the debates on practically every measure proposed during the Roosevelt Administration and find it attacked as a threat to the American way of life. Social security. Regulation of the stock market. The attempt to use the idle water power of the Tennessee Valley to produce cheap electric power and lift the conditions in a backward part of the country. The minimum-wage-and-hour proposal to require employers to pay their help at least $16 a week, barely enough to enable a human being to keep body and soul together, if that. These and many other proposals were resisted by Republicans as un-American, as threats to democracy, as steps toward dictatorship, as betrayals of the liberties of American citizens.

What has the Republican Party offered in the last few years to inspire among American citizens any confidence that it has anything to contribute toward making democracy work in these times except to sit down with folded hands and let nature take its course? No wonder that the voters have taken advantage of every opportunity to remove Republicans from Washington. To the very end of the last session of Congress, Republicans seemed completely oblivious to the experiences of the last four years. Nowhere have they shown the slightest effort, or have they appeared to sense the need, to adjust our government to the handling of problems which press upon it in a rapidly developing industrial age.

10/13/38

Dewey will make a fight which will be a real contribution to the cause of good government and toward the restoration of an intelligent and constructive opposition party, which even the Democrats must agree is desirable in a democracy.

I have been nosing around here and I think it is a mistake to put Dewey down as merely a boy prosecutor, limited to the role of racket-busting. His horizon is vastly broader than that as will, I think, become evident as his campaign unfolds.

To the contrary, Dewey is an unknown quantity outside of the one role in which he has grown up. In Washington some people think he has no social philosophy. Some think he is a fascist. Others think he is just a plain, second-generation Hoover.

Those guesses seem grotesque in the presence of the facts. Dewey must be classed clearly as in the progressive wing of the Republican Party. I have no doubt on that score now. I am quite certain that he realizes the world has changed, that government has social obligations which it must not dodge.

Dewey will have much to say concerning labor. His fight, in the district attorney's office, to free labor unions from the clutches of racketeers, won him the gratitude of many rank-and-file labor-union members. In one instance, the union membership doubled after the racketeers were removed through Dewey's prosecutions.

Dewey is done with the obsolete slogans which froze the viewpoint of the Republican Party into a groove that was heading toward virtual extinction. It is not impossible that under the more modern and intelligent outlook of Dewey and the group with which he is working, the Republican Party will undergo a reformation such as the British Conservative Party underwent a few years back and which resulted in its complete restoration and eventual return to power.

12/7/39

In his later presidential speeches, no doubt, Mr. Dewey will let us in on some of his thoughts about national questions. Inasmuch as he is preparing a series of addresses, he might better have selected one of his more meaty manuscripts for the campaign kickoff at Minneapolis. The one which he used as an opener contained laudable sentiments, but it could more appropriately have been held for delivery to the Pawling, N.Y., Boy Scouts.

America, Mr. Dewey said, is suffering from defeatism. He picked up a couple of old quotations from the December issue of *The Reader's Digest* to show that pessimism was nothing new in the world and explained that optimism always had prevailed in the end.

"Tonight," Mr. Dewey said, "I propose that we Americans, of whatever party, make up our minds that we do believe in the continued growth of this country. . . . The one thing that I want to do in whatever way I can is to help make the courage of eternal youth run once more in the veins of my party and of my country."

The late Arthur Brisbane said it better, "Don't sell America short."

This was the typical speech of a cautious candidate, putting himself squarely on record against sin. If Mr. Dewey has anything to offer this country as a presidential figure, it is youthful drive, a clearheaded, courageous attack on very real difficulties. By his record as prosecutor in New York, we look to him to break away from the clichés of the shopworn politician and strike out with the driving realistic methods which have brought such salutary results in cleaning up New York rackets. If Mr. Dewey has anything to offer, it is his demonstrated ability to tackle sacred rackets. National politics is as ripe for the man who can do this as was New York City when he moved in.

We already have been given the Coué treatment by Mr. Hoover and Mr. Roosevelt. We have been dosed with confidence for years. We had eight years of a businessman's paradise with Harding and Coolidge in the White House, and then came Mr. Hoover, who not only had all of their sympathy with private enterprise, but knew a good deal more about it. We heard him in 1928 tell us that we were within sight of the day when poverty would be abolished. Campaign advertisements told us that this was the land with a chicken in every pot and two cars in every garage. Even the elevator boys had confidence. They were playing the stock market long. In 1929 nobody was selling America short and confidence was unbounded.

Americans have plenty of courage and plenty of confidence in the possibilities of this country. If you want to see courage look at the dust-bowl farmers fighting through year after year. But confidence alone doesn't solve the problem of these farmers, of the share croppers, of the self-reliant families turned into the wandering tramps of *The Grapes of Wrath.* Confidence isn't enough to solve the problem of those in Cleveland who can't get work though the town is throbbing with industrial activity.

We want to hear Mr. Dewey get down to cases. The American people know that this is a land of almost infinite possibilities. They are conscious of its great natural wealth. What they want is somebody who can show how this wealth may be used to make life reasonably comfortable for the whole population.

The people have plenty of confidence. The place where confidence and courage are needed is in our political leaders.

3/28/40

In his St. Louis speech, Thomas E. Dewey makes the gravest charge that has been laid at the door of the Roosevelt Administration.

"Underlying all its policies," said Mr. Dewey, "there has been a fundamental lack of integrity—a cynical disregard of the principles of common honesty."

Who are some of these policy-making people in this Administration who so glaringly lack integrity and common honesty? Cordell Hull? Henry Morgenthau? Harry Woodring? Robert Jackson? James A. Farley? Charles Edison? Harold Ickes? Henry A. Wallace? Harry Hopkins? Frances Perkins?

Are they the ones Mr. Dewey says are lacking in integrity and common honesty? Evidently he has had no contact with any of them. They can be criticized for many errors of judgment but not for lack of integrity. In some 20 years here I have seen several batches of Cabinet officers, going back to Harding's time. For integrity and honesty of purpose I'll put this Cabinet against any that has been in Washington since the war. It is the one thing that does truly distinguish this group. There is not a shady one in the lot. Some of them may be too idealistic. Some of them may be impractical. Some of them may be too stubborn. But that these Cabinet members are lacking in moral fiber, in "fundamental integrity," or in "common honesty" is something that not even a district attorney can demonstrate.

Go down the line to some of the lower ranking policy-making officials. Who are the ones there lacking in integrity and common honesty? Aubrey Williams of N.Y.A.? Thurman Arnold? Jerome Frank and Leon Henderson of S.E.C.? Sumner Welles and Adolf Berle? Eccles? Henry Grady? Steve Early?

Average up the Roosevelt crew and the one thing that does mark it is the exceptional devotion to the general ideals of the New Deal, and the incorruptibility of the group as a whole. Judge these men by political standards and that is the one thing that stands out in their favor. If any of them are ever caught handling little black bags, I'll be amazed. Republicans ought to be cautious about bringing up a subject that recalls so much history.

Mr. Dewey attempts to peg his case on such circumstances as Mr. Roosevelt's failure to carry out his 1932 economy pledge and his abandonment of the gold standard.

In his first presidential campaign Mr. Roosevelt definitely promised a 25 per cent cut in Government expenses. It was a foolish campaign pledge because it was an impossible promise. Whether Mr. Roosevelt knew it at the time, I don't know, and I doubt if Mr. Dewey does.

At any rate, after he went into office Mr. Roosevelt began slashing expenses. He cut veterans' allowances. But there were millions out of work and something had to be done. The Federal Government started spending money. With that the pressure in Congress to restore the veterans' cuts became irresistible. In the summer of 1932, many thought that the worst of the depression was over.

But you remember February and March of 1933. Conditions were infinitely worse. If the Republicans had been in office, they would, I hope, have done about what the Roosevelt Administration did. They would have faced the situation and done the necessary thing. I hope Mr. Dewey doesn't mean that in view of his pledges of economy he would refuse to approve more expenditures if he should enter the White House and find that business had collapsed, as it did under Mr. Hoover.

Mr. Dewey is talking with his tongue in his cheek. If he became President he would try to meet the problems that faced him and he wouldn't be stopping to thumb back over his campaign speeches, I hope. He would, I believe, be statesman enough to brush aside the past and wade into the job with whatever was required. Every man of affairs, who has been responsible for the success of large enterprises, knows what I am talking about and so does Mr. Dewey.

Integrity in public life means the higher integrity of fidelity to the best interests of the country. If that requires a public official to forget something he said when he didn't know any better, he had better forget it and the quicker the better. You can't walk backwards, reading old campaign speeches, and be a good President.

6/27/40

Did you ever see a dream walking? Well, I did. It's the Republican National Convention. Some morning the Republicans will wake up and read the newspapers. Let us hope that it will not be too late. For the moment they prefer to live in a dreamworld. They mumble a platform which has less relation to the reality around us than *Grimm's Fairy Tales.*

Reading the Republican platform you would never suspect that at this very moment some of the most decisive events in all history are heaving up over the horizon. They are destined, as surely as I am writing these lines, to cause the most profound changes to us. I don't want to seem frantic about this. But the appalling blandness of this convention, its apparent ignorance of what is about to happen, give one a sinking feeling. Is this great political party competent to face the drastic world changes that are now coming out of the womb?

Do you realize what is about to happen? Read your newspapers.

Did you read that statement by Senator Key Pittman, chairman of the Senate Foreign Relations Committee? He said it is no secret that Great Britain is totally unprepared for defense against the German attack that is about to come. He said nothing the United States has to give could do more than delay the result—he means delay the inevitable defeat. He urged the British to transfer their navy to Canada immediately, implying that this was the only way to save it from falling into Hitler's hands. Senator Pittman made the statement in a purely personal capacity. I am reliably informed that his judgment of the situation is shared in high official quarters at Washington. Think of it! The defeat of England is considered inevitable and the chairman of the Senate Foreign Relations Committee extends the British an urgent invitation to send their fleet to the Western Hemisphere so that at least this portion of the world can be made safe for survival of what is left of the British Empire.

What Senator Pittman doesn't say but what he has in mind is that if the British fleet falls into German hands as the French fleet has, the United States will thereupon become an inferior naval power. Remember that in the Atlantic we have no Hawaii standing as an outpost. We have no outer line of defense. Our outer line of defense has been the British navy dominant in the eastern Atlantic. That guard is about to be lost.

Read your newspapers. Did you read the dispatches from Japan? The Japanese Minister of War addressed his entire war-office staff and told them that Japan's hour had come. Japan, he said, must not miss this rare opportunity. Japan, he said, must act drastically against the powers who obstruct her policy.

The controlled Japanese press explained that Japan was preparing to issue a new declaration of policy proclaiming the autonomy of East Asia. Under this new policy "Japan will not allow any foreign power to interfere in East Asia, including French Indo-China and The Netherlands Indies." This means Japan is about to throw her clutches around one of our important sources of rubber and tin. It means the white man is to be driven out of the Far East.

Read your newspapers. Did you see the dispatch from Buenos Aires that Germany already has offered to purchase immense quantities of foodstuffs from Argentina, and proposes to pay for them by electrifying the Argentinian state railways and by building hydroelectric plants? But I see by the Republican platform that America must keep Argentinian products out of the United States. The Republicans didn't mention Argentina; they did it by declaring for an "effective quarantine" against imported agricultural products. That's the old question that has so embittered Argentina.

Read your newspapers. Read them and weep. They will tell you in what kind of world we are caught. The Republicans won't tell you. They haven't read their newspapers yet. Their platform goes on fighting the last World War, telling us how much it cost in life and treasure. They don't tell us what this world revolution is going to cost us. Herbert Hoover knows. He is talking about some kind of Western Hemisphere tariff wall, a hemisphere trade cartel, some such thing as the Roosevelt Administration is trying to work out.

But the Republican platform knows no evil, sees no evil, hears no evil. It comes out strong for equal rights for women, Negroes, Indians, and Hawaii.

God save America. The Republican Party will never save it on this platform.

6/28/40

The people have saved the Republican politicians from themselves and have forced them to nominate Wendell Willkie. That's all there is to it, just a determination on the part of a large section of the American people, regardless of economic status, that American politicians should not repeat the fumbling performance of the Chamberlains and the Daladiers. That's what nominated Mr. Willkie—a determination among the people that democracy here should not fall victim to the creeping paralysis that has laid it low abroad.

I can show you letters and telegrams from humble persons and they have said it better than I can say it.

The Republican politicians didn't want Mr. Willkie. Hoover was against him. Landon was against him until the nomination was in sight. Pew of Pennsylvania held out until after Mr. Willkie's nomination had been assured. Those few who did see something in Mr. Willkie—Governor Stassen of Minnesota, Representative Bruce Barton of New York, young Representative Charles Halleck of Indiana, and several others—were looked upon contemptuously as Boy Scouts by the more seasoned politicians who were too slow to catch the meaning of the Willkie boom.

The professional politicians said the Republicans should never take a man who had been a Democrat until recently, who had not worked his way up through the errand-boy apprenticeship of politics. They said the Republicans should not take a man who had supported the Hull reciprocal-trade program. And, to cover up, some of the reactionaries who have been doing political errands for public utilities for years, lifted their hands in pretended horror at the thought of nominating a utility executive.

The plain fact is that the people don't care a damn whether Mr. Willkie used to be a Democrat, whether he is a utility man, whether he lacks experience as a ward politician. What the people want now by every sign on the landscape is a man who has intelligence, energy, and courage. They want a man who has some idea of what it is all about. They want a man big enough at least to realize that we have the toughest problems ahead of us that we ever have had.

The politicians who opposed Mr. Willkie figured the country wanted a change from Roosevelt. Perhaps it does. I don't know. But if it wants a change I am certain it doesn't want to change to some fumbling, dozing fellow who thinks that the job of a President is to go to sleep and let things run themselves. The country may be tired of glamour—and I'm not sure of that either. But it is hungry for efficient action and it wants a big man. A really big man.

That's why this convention was deluged with demands to nominate Mr. Willkie. Sure the utility people were pumping in telegrams. And so were thousands of ordinary citizens with no interest except in seeing the Republicans put up a good man. The convention delegates resented it. Forty-eight hours ago I think they were determined to freeze Mr. Willkie out. Again the delegates heard from the country. The Republicans had been looking for years for a candidate who could stand up against Mr. Roosevelt. But when that man appeared the politicians had to be clubbed into taking him. Well, the people have saved the Republican politicians from themselves.

All that the Republicans start this campaign with is Mr. Willkie. They fumbled the platform completely. By a lucky break, they at least have a strong candidate—a strong candidate and a weak platform. Mr. Willkie will have to write his own platform. Fortunately he is not under much obligation to the politicians, and if they are smart they will lean heavily on him and let him carry the ball.

Mr. Willkie's nomination is a triumph for public opinion. Public opinion has this time been ahead of the politicians. It has been more intelligent than the politicians. For that we can be thankful, because this is the most difficult period that our generation has ever faced. The Republicans have chosen the best man available.

9/20/40

By two tests, the Willkie campaign up to now falls so far short that grave doubts are raised, at least with me, about the kind of job he would do as President.

One test is Willkie's success as an organizer. The other test is to be found in the policies upon which he offers himself for the job. By neither test does Willkie seem to live up to earlier expectations of at least this one of his friends.

At the time he was nominated, Willkie was a highly successful lawyer and business executive. His published utterances, such as those in *Fortune Magazine,* gave evidence of an understanding grasp of national problems. He was equally impressive in private conversations. In all, he seemed, as did Herbert Hoover in 1932, exceptionally well qualified to be President.

Public life is different from private life and Willkie is entitled to have time in which to hit his stride. But that time must be about up.

The Willkie campaign has been notorious for disorganization. Seldom has there been more chaos in a presidential campaign. Congressional cloakrooms echo with stories of confusion, hurt feelings, unanswered telegrams and letters, crossed wires, and general demoralization. Willkie is carrying his campaign in his hat. This condition is well known and is a subject of incessant discussion among politicians here and among newspaper correspondents on the Willkie train, which seems to operate with all the confusion of an amateur road show.

There are always some confusion and friction in a presidential campaign. But this one is so loose-jointed that it indicates poor direction at the top. If the Willkie Administration in the White House functioned with no more unity, coordination, and effectiveness than the Willkie Administration in the campaign, then the Government would be almost paralyzed.

The presidency is more than a business office. It is a political office also, and I don't mean in a tricky sense. The art of herding an army of politicians and public officials and second-string prima donnas into effective handling of the enormously complicated public business centered at Washington requires more than Willkie has shown in the management of his campaign.

By the test of his policies, Willkie is falling short of the standard which he set for himself earlier.

His start was a brave one in which he disregarded expediency and stood for essentials in foreign policy, which encouraged his friends. But he has dropped his standard and has now reached the point of making narrow-minded appeals to sectional interests. He is using the Argentine as a whipping post at a time when we are striving to keep that country from falling completely into the totalitarian orbit. His thrust at the Argentine sanitary convention was unnecessary, and if he carried his attitude into the White House our situation in Latin America would be done serious harm.

Willkie also said, out in the cattle country, that one way to rehabilitate our domestic economy would be "to have the American Navy eat American beef instead of Argentine beef." That was an attempt to reawaken the storm of indignation in the cattle country over the Navy's purchase of about $7,500 worth of tinned Argentine beef a year or so ago. It was fishing for votes at the expense of our interest in Latin America, and it was needless; Willkie evidently didn't know that Congress later passed a law forbidding the Navy to buy foreign beef. If that is the way to rehabilitate our domestic economy, as Willkie suggests, then it has already been done long ago.

The irresponsibility of some of Willkie's other recent talks already has been revealed by his own corrections. He seems to be suffering from a combination of misinformation and bad judgment. If that, coupled with the confusion which he seems unable to eliminate from his campaign organization, gives a fair sample of what Willkie would be as President, then it leaves much to be desired.

10/14/40

The sharp difference between Mr. Willkie and the New Deal centers on the place of capitalism in our national life. Roughly Mr. Willkie believes private capitalism can carry the ball alone. New Dealers believe private capitalism alone is inadequate and that public spending must supplement it. The more extreme New Dealers go even further and question whether private capitalism is not a waning influence destined, not to disappear, perhaps, but to play a far less controlling part in our national life.

These underlying philosophies sound like abstractions. But it must be remembered they give the impulse and direction to a man's specific policies and actions. The real things we see done stem from those viewpoints. So if they sound abstract, they nevertheless are the real springs of action, out of which come things like T.V.A. and Mr. Willkie's long fight against it.

Lately Mr. Willkie has been trying to spell out this issue. He had been promising that industry, if given its head, could give jobs to all. The New Deal has challenged that. At Providence Mr. Willkie said he was happy to take his stand on that issue.

He has a deep, unshakable conviction about it, obviously. That undoubtedly accounts for the extraordinary vitality which stirs him to fight doggedly against great odds. He said he was engaged in a crusade and he is making it such, going into the highways and byways, pleading against stony faces and against boos, tomatoes, and eggs, with the undaunted fervor of an evangelist. In spite of the rough edges which he shows as a campaigner, in spite of the fact that he campaigns with the advantages against him, there comes through an impression of rugged conviction that one does not give unless dead earnestness lies behind the words. In short, Mr. Willkie thinks he has something and he is going to make the nation listen or bust a larynx in the attempt.

To understand why Mr. Willkie believes so passionately that capitalism is adequate to do the job itself, it helps to know he has drawn inspiration from a kind of bible which he has adopted, *Capitalism the Creator,* by Carl Snyder, a close personal friend and sometime economist for the New York Federal Reserve Bank.

To direct public attention to this book, Mr. Willkie made a ceremonial purchase of it at a book store in Washington immediately after his nomination. It spells out what he means when he says that the cure for our troubles is to let private capital go ahead and create jobs.

Mr. Willkie makes some reservations to the thesis, particularly as regards labor and Government regulation, but as it has clarified and strengthened his own direction of thought, no one can be fully informed as to what Mr. Willkie is driving at without familiarizing himself with this source book. Its thesis is that inventors plus capital savings alone have created our modern world and that solely by these two elements can the United States progress.

10/15/40

Although the book, *Capitalism the Creator,* has had strong influence on Willkie in this campaign, it is not fair to attribute to him all the ideas contained therein, since the candidate is speaking much more sympathetically of labor legislation than the author, Carl Snyder, does.

Snyder has combed history, past and present, to assemble evidence supporting his thesis that inventors plus capital savings have created our modern civilization and that they must be given full head to continue it. Labor, Snyder holds, has had little part in the process and none in the creative phase of it.

Throughout history, peoples have risen from barbarism and poverty only by that concentrated and highly organized system of production and exchange that we call capitalism, says the author of *Capitalism the Creator*. Solely by accumulation and concentration of capital, and directly proportional to the amount of that accumulation, have modern industrial nations risen. It has been true throughout history. No agricultural or pastoral nation has grown rich or powerful. Where the will to live, to gain, to discover, and to conquer has waned and a nation is given over to visionaries, doctrinaires, and novices in social experimentation, decadence has begun.

We accept, says Snyder, the idea of exceptionally endowed poets, musicians, and painters. But the idea that the accumulation of great wealth belongs in much the same category, and is of vastly more value to society, seems to incite profound incredulity.

The big powers are the machine powers. This wealth is not the product of "labor." Nine tenths of it is the product of machines. They are the product of brains and exceptional ability, literally the creation of geniuses—inventors, discoverers, enterprises, and accumulators.

The method, says Snyder, is essentially that of placing surplus capital accumulation largely in the hands of a relatively few individuals who have the rare gift for the management and utilization of this surplus—all for the general good. In a single generation this method has provided two thirds of our people with 25,000,000 automobiles.

The price of this system? It is to reward the rich and the exceptionally capable—a bagatelle. Besides, most of the reward is plowed back into industry. The rewards are so slight as to be of no practical importance, whereas the loss to the country of this talent would be indescribable.

The achievements of civilization are not the achievements of the whole human race, Snyder says, but always of a very few nations, and of a few people among those—of 1 per cent or less of the whole population. The genius population does it. To them, Snyder believes, we owe all. Without them and their creativeness, energy, and organizing power our modern world would simply never have been. Ten or a dozen industries produce one third to one half of our total industrial output—all creations of our own day, in electric power, automobiles, chemicals, rubber, rayon, aviation, radio, and the like. The machine is the liberator. It has abolished slavery. Yet a part of the workers, who have contributed so little, would now claim the whole.

Just one concession would Snyder make. He would have Government control of the volume of credit, to prevent booms and depressions. Otherwise give capitalism full right of way. Regulation of any kind is bad, even of railroads and utilities. The economics of capitalism provides its own automatic regulation.

That, in brief, is the Snyder thesis as I read it. His book is long and carefully documented so that it stands as the classic case for modern capitalism. I have tried to give a fair factual summary of it because it goes to the core of the difference between Willkie and the New Deal.

10/16/40

The New Deal point of view is that private industry cannot do the job alone. Such popular interpreters of the New Deal as Stuart

Chase and David Cushman Coyle express the belief that public spending is here to stay, that the stagnation of the thirties revealed the inadequacy of private capitalism to maintain the necessary volume of production and consuming power.

Throughout that period private industry was assisted by public spending. Now we are coming into a gigantic production period stimulated by the defense program—the biggest peacetime spending program on record. As that will continue for some time, there will be no opportunity, even if Willkie should be elected, to test his contention that private industry could carry the whole load on its own.

New Dealers argue that there are many enterprises which private capitalism can't undertake. T.V.A. is cited as one. Before the T.N.E.C. a number of pro-New Deal economists argued that there was not enough industry to utilize the surplus capital—and that this capital was piling up and had to be circulated through governmental nonprofit projects to avoid stagnation. Stuart Chase, one of the consultants in that inquiry, thinks that a two-cylinder pump is needed permanently, one cylinder for private investment and one for public investment.

Henry Wallace, vice-presidential candidate, in a book just published by the Home Library Foundation, entitled *The Price of Freedom,* says that if private capital cannot do all of the job of making it possible for the people of the United States to utilize their resources, then Government capital must do the necessary work. He says it cannot be otherwise in a capitalistic system that fails to provide work for millions of people.

The New Dealers also challenge the contention that private capitalism working automatically without Government interference will operate satisfactorily.

Thurman Arnold, Assistant Attorney General in charge of antitrust prosecutions, has voluminous evidence that private enterprise does not function freely and automatically but that if left alone it sets up its own restrictions—what Arnold calls its own private tollgates. He means monopolistic restrictions, price agreements, allocation of territory, indirect use of patents to restrict production and competition, and similar clogging of free competitive enterprise.

S.E.C. came into being because, among other things, financial managers of industry were promoting enterprises from the point of view of making quick winnings rather than from a production point of view. Holding-company legislation was enacted because financial manipulators were milking operating companies.

Collective-bargaining legislation and wage-hour legislation were enacted essentially because the rigors of private management, in some instances, were bearing down unduly upon employees and it was thought that the general welfare required protection for them.

As New Dealers see it, the vision of private enterprise functioning automatically for the general welfare is not always borne out in reality. There are times, they think, when the profit motive, instead of working directly for the general good, works against it. When such effects are too severe, they believe the Government should cushion them.

Finally, in the immediate picture, they see the defense program making heavy demands on production facilities, creating bottlenecks, requiring special financing because of the uncertain future of such enterprises, and in other ways interfering abnormally with the normal industrial processes so as to require, at various times, governmental traffic control. They see the possible necessity of measures to prevent extreme price changes growing out of abnormal demands.

In brief, they don't see a chance of going into industrial laissez faire. They don't think Willkie could, either, if he should become President, no matter how deeply he believes in the ability of private enterprise to carry the ball alone.

2/12/41

This man, Wendell Willkie, is the hated target of most of the influential politicians in the Republican Party today. They are conspiring to get rid of him. They hate him more than they hate Mr. Roosevelt.

It is just like the Republican Party. After these lean years it stumbles accidentally upon a man with real political sex appeal and promptly proceeds to toss him down the chute.

When one sees how seldom it is that a man appears with natural gifts that give him popular leadership, when one realizes how essential to democracy this gift is, when one thinks ahead and wonders where to turn for the leadership that will follow Mr. Roosevelt, it seems a crime, a tragic waste of priceless talent, for a great political party to set out deliberately to plow under a fellow like this Willkie. It certainly is a good way to make this country dependent upon one man indefinitely—to mow down anybody who might compete with the one and only Roosevelt. But I suppose one should not expect more of the kind of leaders who have run the Republican Party in recent years.

2/13/41

Clare Boothe Luce, at the Republican Club dinner in New York, made probably the frankest and most brutal speech that ever shook a Republican Party occasion. Not being a candidate for office, she could say the things that needed saying.

She said the party must face the fact that, as presently constituted, the Republican Party may never again elect another President.

"Historically," Mrs. Luce continued, "ours has always been an active and dynamic two-party system, and the inescapable logic of the situation is, that if the Republican Party can never again elect another President, the chances are, sooner or later, there will be no more Presidents elected in America."

She said the Republican Party could continue for a long time in its present condition, as a sort of chronic vermiform appendix in the body politic, but that if the totalitarian fever which has swept out democratic institutions in many other countries continued, the Republican appendix would be removed in time.

2/15/41

Not in a long time has there been so much commotion inside the Republican Party as has been stirred by the position taken by Wendell Willkie in regard to the world situation.

Coupled with the inside debate over Mr. Willkie is the secondary excitement over the shift of Thomas E. Dewey toward the Willkie position. Many politicians, knowing Mr. Dewey's finger-touch steering facilities, are taking his sudden change of direction as an indication he has decided traffic is moving in Mr. Willkie's direction and has hastened to fall in. He is thinking also, no doubt, of sentiment in New York State, where he expects to run for governor next year.

A month ago, 24 hours after the lend-lease bill was introduced in Congress, Mr. Dewey issued a statement denouncing it as "an attempt to abolish free government in the United States."

But speaking here on Lincoln's birthday, Mr. Dewey startled Republican opponents of the bill by saying, "The majority has accepted important amendments which have removed many of the original dangers while in no way weakening full aid to Britain. . . . With some necessary further reservations of power to the people through the Congress, I am satisfied the House bill will be adopted (by the Senate). Speaking for myself alone, I hope it will be."

Actually the bill hasn't been amended at all in any fundamental. If it was a dictator bill to abolish free government when Mr. Dewey first so described it, the bill still is that except it gives Mr. Roosevelt only 2 years in which to abolish free government.

Everybody around here simply puts it down that Mr. Dewey changed his position on second thought, and decided discretion was the better part of valor. In other words, Mr. Dewey is fast on his feet and was not going to be caught out on a limb with Mr. Hoover and the other irreconcilables.

Mr. Dewey's speech caused more inside commotion than Mr. Willkie's stand. Everyone was prepared for the latter's bolt. Mr. Willkie is considered a maverick anyway, and Republican congressmen and senators are accustomed to having him jump the fence on them. But Mr. Dewey's leap hurt. He's more regular, and he has a following around the country—or a sufficient one in some sections to cause members to fear the effect on their constituents.

5/8/43

Governor Harold E. Stassen of Minnesota is a young and rapidly rising figure who has demonstrated the same courage and foresight regarding foreign policy that Mr. Willkie has shown. He is one of the most aggressive of the leaders who urge that the United Nations be transformed into a strong world organization after the war.

The length of the war may have some bearing on his future plans. His youth gives him time.

6/3/42

There's a big-framed, thirty-five-year-old governor in Minnesota. He's a Republican, now running for a third term.

When I was president of the Gridiron Club in 1939, Governor Stassen made the Republican speech at one of our dinners. It was one of the best we ever heard. Its wit and wisdom made it a sensation at the time and caused the Republicans to make him their keynoter at the 1940 Republican National Convention which, in spite of itself, was forced to nominate Wendell Willkie for President.

Governor Stassen has a reserve commission in the Navy and will go into active service as soon as the next session of the Minnesota legislature is over.

I mention those facts to show that Governor Stassen is no hothouse intellectual but an experienced, practical, grass-roots politician, one of the relatively few Republicans who has been smart enough to make a success at the business during the last few years.

Governor Stassen made a Memorial Day address to a Baptist convention at Cleveland which is important, it seems to me, not only because of its content, but because it was made by a successful Republican governor from the Middle West. This is something up from the heart of the country. For that reason it seems far more significant to me than what Eastern thinkers might have to offer.

Threading his observations on Lincoln's Gettysburg Address, Governor Stassen asked what the objectives of this nation must be if those who die in this war are not to die in vain.

He said we must have twin objectives. First, win the war. Second, establish a peace "that will be a people's peace"—a peace that will have a chance to endure. He observed that little question was raised about the first objective—victory.

But he noted that, when the second objective of an enduring peace is raised, some say that must wait until the war is over. Governor Stassen asks if we can safely wait.

"If our peace is to be just," he said, "would talking through to it obstruct the best of our war efforts? Surely not. Rather, if the pattern of our peace will be just, will knowledge of it not cause a greater contribution to the war effort, from South America and India and Burma and other lands?"

If there are differences among the United Nations, that is all the more reason to Governor Stassen why we should understand the program upon which this nation is giving its resources—"that we understand the basis on which millions of young men of America are going forth to war, many never to return."

He says this, "Heroic men can die upon the battlefield in vain, because of what occurs after a war, as well as because of what happens during a war."

Governor Stassen said, "I hope that one or two or three or four years hence, when Hitler and Tojo and Mussolini run up the white flag of surrender, there will have developed a plan of action in peace—understood and supported by the overwhelming majority of the people of this country, and understood and accepted by the people of the nations of our Allies."

First of all, Governor Stassen does not think this country is fighting a war just to reestablish the status quo of the prewar period. To do that would simply sow the seeds of another war. He says the walls of American isolation are down and in their place we must build bridges of understanding and constructive influence.

You say the governor is talking beautiful generalities? Yes. But he's been thinking and he has some specific suggestions that sound like good, practical guideposts.

10/17/42

We are about to see an interesting experiment in public leadership in the activities of Wendell Willkie. If it succeeds it will bring something very much needed back into American political life.

Willkie is spending a few days at Rushville, Ind. He has indicated that as soon as he gets his breath he will begin speaking and writing on subjects connected with the war and what is to follow.

Already there is enormous interest in what he will have to say. Many people are prepared undoubtedly to be influenced by what he says, for they are confused by much that they have heard from Washington and would welcome an effective discussion by such a man as Willkie. He has the opportunity to exert large influence on American thinking at this point, and perhaps to do much to shape the public attitude on postwar policy.

The reason I hope he will be successful is a simple one. Willkie is a man without any public office, without any lobby behind him, yes, and without any political party behind him, because a lot of Republican organization regulars hate him, because he was too far ahead of the party. He probably has as many friends in the Democratic Party as in the Republican Party now. In other words, Willkie has nothing but himself, the force of his personality, his character, his courage, and a whole lot more insight into what is going on in this world than many people used to give him credit for having. He has no platform but his own soapbox. He owns no newspaper, no radio, no means of communication except a good-sized mouth with some brains to tell it what to say. He has to work entirely with his bare hands—or bare tongue.

If a man can get anywhere on that basis as a force in American public affairs, then it brings back something that we have lost in America. People say you have to get high public office to be a force, or you have to be head of some big lobby, or own newspapers or radio stations. They think you must have a lot of tools to work with to influence American public opinion, some kind of sounding board, some kind of organization that will do the sewer work for you.

I hope Willkie is able to demonstrate that this is all bunk. I hope he is able to demonstrate that a man who has the vigor and brains and understanding needs nothing more in the United States to be an influential leader in democracy.

We have been drifting into dead waters in this country.

Except for Roosevelt, we have had little leadership of national stature. We have had some synthetic personalities, some who tried to get there by hiring press agents. But mostly it has been second-string stuff.

Perhaps the real talent has been stunted. Men who might have grown, as Willkie has grown, may have become discouraged and given up when they actually had the possibilities of full growth had they felt the struggle worth going through. Nobody can know.

But we do know that at times in our history considerable numbers of big men have appeared, as if perhaps they stimulated each other, in the way a literary group or a group of scientists will develop under the stimulation of each other.

If we ever needed not one big man but many big men in America it is now. We are moving into a new world. It will be vastly different. We can't know what it will be like. All we know is that we will have to deal with problems such as have never before existed for us. Intelligence, understanding, and above all the courage of great convictions will be needed.

It can't be a one-man job. It will require not a big leader but big leaders, and behind them a people that responds to them.

If Willkie can step up now into this vacuum, and start the yeast working, it will be something very good for the country. I have a hunch he maybe can do it. At least I don't discount the man who could step up and give that Russian ballerina a smack that was heard around the world.

11/4/42

The election of Thomas E. Dewey as governor of New York will start a wave of talk for him as the Republican presidential candidate in 1944. Indeed, there has been considerable talk already.

When he accepted the Republican nomination for governor at Syracuse on Aug. 24, Dewey had something to say about his future.

"For my part," he said, "let me say right now that I shall devote the next four years exclusively to the service of the people of New York State."

Thus Dewey himself has given us the basis of judging his good faith. The Syracuse pledge reads like an airtight promise to stick to the job as governor for the next four years. Dewey says he will devote the next four years "exclusively to the service of the people of New York State."

He says "exclusively." He could hardly devote himself for four years exclusively to the service of the people of New York and still run for President year after next. If he became President, of course he would have to devote himself to serving not only the people of New York State but the people of all other states, whose interests might not always be those of the people of New York State. He could not exclusively serve his own state while serving as President of all states.

There are three little words—"for my part"—that Dewey might interpret as giving him an out if the Republican Party nominated him without any effort on his part. But if in his own mind he was pledging himself without mental reservation, as they say, to serve his own state exclusively for the next four years, he would not permit his friends to do the kind of work on his behalf that is always necessary to nominate a presidential candidate. He would not cooperate in the way that is always necessary, no matter how a candidate appears not to be running for the job. He would not allow large sums of money to be raised to finance a preconvention campaign.

The statement either means what it seems to mean, or it is a piece of tricky double talk.

Double talk usually bounces back with quarrelsome echoes.

If there is a hole in Dewey's language through which he could slip out and run for President in 1944, then he is too slippery with words to inspire any confidence in the oversigned.

Time and Dewey's own actions will tell how genuine Dewey's words were. The prevalent belief among politicians and political writers is that Dewey will find some way to get around his words and grab the presidential nomination if he can get it. That is how cynical people in the political world are about it.

All of that may be unfair to Dewey. If it is, he doubtless will find a way to make it clear that he is to be taken at his word and that his statement which seemed to renounce his chances at the presidency next time meant what it seemed to mean.

Public men often have indulged in tricky words. In fact when a fellow who wants to be President has no originality he begins his fight for the nomination by saying he is not a candidate. That means his hat is in the ring.

It is going to be interesting to see what Dewey does about his Syracuse pledge when the campaign to nominate Dewey for President begins to roll.

9/7/43

Something is happening in American thinking when a Republican politician with the sensitive antenna of Governor Dewey says we should have a permanent military alliance with Great Britain.

He accepts, in his talks at the Mackinac Island Republican conference, the necessity of joining with other nations to use force to subdue future aggressors.

Governor Dewey recognizes, as a great many people are coming to recognize, that our attempt to keep our own freedom of action has been a failure. We have refused to make alliances. We have refused to commit ourselves to any future course of action.

But that has not given us freedom of action. Instead, twice in the lifetime of this generation, the United States has been forced for self-protection to go into world wars which it did not start.

Our very inaction, our very attempt to preserve our isolation, has perhaps encouraged the starting of those wars which we found it impossible to escape.

One well-known American citizen talked with Nazi Foreign Minister Ribbentrop shortly before the present war began. He told Ribbentrop that if Great Britain were threatened, the United States would intervene in the war as she had done before. Ribbentrop laughed at the idea. He said America would never go to war a second time. He cited the isolationist sentiment in America as proof that Germany did not need to fear American intervention.

Would Hitler have dared to plunge into war if he had been certain that the whole weight of the United States would be thrown against him?

If the principal industrial nations now join together, and make it clear that they will crack down with force whenever any nation threatens the peace, the chances are that nobody will dare invite certain disaster by starting trouble—and certainly not after an example has been made of the first offender.

This is all very bitter swallowing for men like Senators Taft and Vandenberg, who prefer the plush horses of the gay nineties. They will try to distract attention from the realities and play with wordy generalizations about sovereignty.

10/16/43

The core of Wendell Willkie's thinking today is just the same as it was long before he was nominated for President in 1940 and as it was throughout that campaign: America must have productivity big enough, expanding fast enough, to absorb the unleashed energies and aspirations of all our people. And such productivity can come into being only if America joins with other nations to establish a world at peace in which trade can flourish.

That all seems so self-evident that it is hard to understand how there can be the violent argument about it. I suppose the explanation is that prejudices, incomplete knowledge, and natural fears and timidities about the future combine to prevent people sometimes from thinking clearly or from recognizing the obvious. Certainly Willkie has stated the obvious but his words will be chewed over as if he had daringly voiced some new and surprising thesis.

Evidently what the Republican Party needs is someone who has the courage to say these obvious things, say them simply, and with the warmth and force that have made Willkie a large political figure in a forest of stunted timber. This tendency of Willkie's has made him the only one of the Republican leaders who has, over any considerable period, shown an understanding of his times. He was talking this way in the summer of 1940 when Taft, Dewey, Landon, and the others were still ghost walking in a world that had gone to smash in the fall of France.

It will be a question whether the country will care to change presidents while the war continues. There are reasons which appeal strongly against a change, in spite of the truth of what Willkie says about administrations that stay in power too long and become remote from the people.

But if the country does change, it is not likely to change to nonentity, or to a man of negative inclinations who is able only to complain and criticize and obstruct, and who shows no sign of aggressiveness or interest in leading the country forward. It does not seem probable that people will be looking for one who is merely a competent bookkeeper. Not when the complaint you hear about Roosevelt is that he does not stand up to Churchill and Stalin and fight for American interests as they fight for their respective interests.

That is a tip-off that people in this day want a President of dimensions comparable with Churchill and Stalin. This is no time for Hardings, however honest and conscientious.

So it strikes one as sound warning when Willkie tells the Republicans that the party cannot win if it merely attempts to coalesce under its banners the various negative groups within the country.

5/8/43

Governor John W. Bricker of Ohio is a conservative who takes no stand on anything.

Governor Bricker is the current darling of the regular conservative party leaders who think that it will be politics as usual next year, with the same kind of setup that the Republicans had when they shoved Harding into the sure-thing nomination of 1920. At that time the Republicans knew they would win, and the party insiders who knew what they wanted picked a nationally obscure and colorless candidate. If history is going to repeat, then it's Bricker by big odds.

11/12/43

Here in the political capital of the country, the announcement that Governor Bricker of Ohio would be a candidate for the Republican presidential nomination was an incidental inside story in three of the four Washington newspapers.

But Washington's lack of interest in the Bricker candidacy may not be a reliable index of the governor's chances. In 1920 Harding's early candidacy was widely ignored while all attention was directed to the big figures of the day, Lowden of Illinois, General Leonard Wood, and Senator Hiram Johnson.

He is a popular governor of Ohio, and evidently a competent one, an uninspired man but a tidy public official, with that average air of mediocrity around him that is so popular in American politics.

All of this suggests the country has come to recognize that being President of the biggest industrial nation in the world is a big job, needing the most capable men obtainable. No party figurehead will do.

You can't run U.S. Steel, or Pan American Airways, with a mediocre man. Why think that just because a man is an average decent citizen or even a governor of a good-sized state, he should be qualified to step into the complicated job of steering the strongest power in the world through the tangled period of finishing the war and readjusting to a new kind of peace?

Possibly Governor Bricker has large capacity that has not yet been drawn upon. Roosevelt was never considered a public giant as governor of New York. He gained his stature after becoming President.

All one can say is that thus far Governor Bricker has said nothing to indicate unusual capacity and understanding of what the presidency will require in the coming period. That seemed to be the judgment of many who sized him up during the American Newspaper Publishers Association convention in New York last spring.

A man can grow and he can learn. Governor Bricker has some months yet in which to do that. But on the basis of what has been indicated up to now, he will have to do a good deal of homework.

I don't believe it can be done by moneybags in the old-fashioned way. Some big money has been friendly to Bricker. That will get delegates but it won't put him in the White House. He'll have to make that run with his own muscle.

1/11/44

In politics any man who is widely mentioned as a possible presidential candidate is considered to be receptive to the nomination unless he removes himself categorically from consideration. In that sense, General Douglas MacArthur must be considered "available."

General MacArthur is a natural subject for glamourizing, and he has suffered from that. In conversation he gives a far stronger impression of sincerity, deep conviction, wide intelligence, and of course complete courage.

It is unusual for this kind of copy to come from a military area—a piece like this about the commanding general of that area—but I am assuming as I write this that General MacArthur recognizes there must in a democracy be free discussion of political matters, and that he will interpose no censorship, since nothing herein relates to considerations of security. General MacArthur has been a subject of political discussion for months, and therefore I feel that it is within the bounds of propriety to write here as I would write after a visit to any other prominent political figure who is being considered for a presidential nomination.

One of the questions about MacArthur answers itself instantly when you see him. He will be sixty-four this month but gives the impression of being in his early fifties. He is vigorous, there are almost no lines of age on his face, only a few flecks of gray. On the physical side he seems thoroughly adequate, even though we seldom elected to the presidency a man beyond his fifties.

One serious handicap for General MacArthur, although perhaps not as serious as I had previously felt, is his long absence from the states. Inevitably there are many gaps in his knowledge of domestic events and problems of the last few years and likewise of what has been done in high diplomacy among the Allies.

Furthermore, the election of General MacArthur to the presidency might easily mean considerable changes in the conduct of the war—perhaps new directions in foreign relations. There is no way of knowing at this time. Also, there would be some practical difficulties in the way of leaving his command to return home to participate in the campaign. And it would be necessary for him to state his position on a number of questions which he would hardly discuss while in an active military command. So the more one thinks the matter through the more are the difficulties that suggest themselves.

Yet MacArthur would be a formidable candidate if he overcame those difficulties. There is enormous power in the man. He seems like a caged or wounded lion, suffering deeply. In many ways he seems a deeply tragic figure. His capacity, his stature, his military ability, his power as a leader, seem of large dimensions, yet he has been relegated to a minor part in the war and put on starvation rations. MacArthur unquestionably feels deeply on this, as his occasional statements indicate. Those statements are explained here as not being connected with presidential politics but as designed to answer what are considered here to be unfair or inaccurate statements regarding what has been done for the Southwest Pacific.

For instance, some of the general's friends say that if he had been sent planes in the quantity he is now beginning to get he would have been able months ago to advance his campaign as he is now beginning to do.

Most of the story from MacArthur's point of view cannot be told until the end of the war, but it is highly probable that when the time comes and that secrecy is removed there will be a historic controversy over MacArthur.

1/12/44

The key fact in all this is that MacArthur has not only waged a campaign against the Japs but has felt it necessary to plead a case for the Southwest Pacific, because of the well-known fact that the attention of higher powers is directed chiefly at Europe.

MacArthur is first of all a soldier. When he was ordered out of the Philippines he evidently thought, as indicated by his statement at the time, that he was to be given forces to lead the campaign for recovery of the Philippines. As it turned out, his area had to wait. There has been a period of nearly 2 years of this hope deferred which "maketh the heart sick."

Perhaps every war produces its MacArthur, that is, a strong figure who is forced by circumstances into a position of standing for a cause which has a strong appeal but which apparently conflicts with controlling decisions in the conduct of the war.

11/4/43

Election returns this week indicate the Republican current has such strength as to challenge the ability of the Administration to hold either house of Congress next year.

Republicans are almost certain to take the House of Representatives. Already they are within fourteen seats of the Democrats.

Hitherto the Senate has been considered beyond reach of the Republicans. Seats of twenty-one Democrats must be filled next year. Judging by the way the Republican tide is running now, a dozen of those seats are in debatable states. A change of ten seats would give the Republicans control. It could happen.

The Democratic Administration is living now on borrowed time.

American political control has moved in cycles, each lasting through several elections. One slow swing of the long pendulum began in 1928 when Herbert Hoover was elected. The Republicans had thirty governors then. By 1934 they had lost all except eight of them. Today they are back up to twenty-four, and one more has just been elected in New Jersey, giving the Republicans a majority of the state governments in the country.

The Republicans now have control in every populous state outside of the South, except Indiana. Harrison Spangler, chairman of the Republican National Committee, points out that in the thirty-eight states outside of the South, Republicans control twenty-seven state legislatures, and the Democrats only nine, with control divided in the remaining two.

Thus the Republicans have recovered grass-roots control of the country, except in the South which is a special political realm. They control states which represent, including newly won New Jersey, 328 electoral votes out of 531, a 60 per cent balance.

Most political writers, and most politicians speaking off the record, would agree that Roosevelt is the only Democrat who would have a chance next year. He might be placed above the political battle because of his personal war prestige, the value of his intimate knowledge of the war and its usefulness in future negotiations, and the forceful argument against changing commanders during the war. No other Democrat would have that protection and would be exposed to the full sweep of the Republican wave.

I question whether this is, for the time being, what it started out to be—a revolt against Roosevelt. It is a revolt against domestic policies of the New Deal, accelerated by the natural movement of Republicans back into their normal territory. Reforms produce many irritations, and countless toes are stepped on. There are maladjustments. Times are better. Labor is bitter over wage repression. Taxes are high. Reforms go in waves. Then people become tired. Nostalgia is part of it and we're all dreaming of a white Christmas. People want a change, back to something that they won't get. They won't get it because the clock does not turn back.

Republicans will not abolish social security, or collective bargaining, or the practice of finding work for the unemployed. Willkie and Dewey are promising that. The usual history will be repeated again. The reformers will be kicked out and the reforms will stay.

12/9/43

Republicans who have little or no sympathy with much of the Administration foreign policy are getting on top of the heap in the party now.

Former Governor Landon of Kansas has gone among Republicans in the East talking up criticism of the Moscow conference and emphasizing distrust of the Soviet government. We know nothing of what really happened and that provides a perfect breeding ground in which Landon and others can plant seeds of suspicion and disunity.

Numbers of Republicans have supported most of the foreign-policy moves of the Roosevelt Administration. Some of the strongest support in Congress on matters connected with the war has come from Republicans like Austin of Vermont, Wadsworth of New York, and Eaton of New Jersey. Outside of Congress, Wendell Willkie and many large Republican newspapers have ignored partisan politics to endorse international policies and give them the national backing necessary to make them effective.

All of that has given the impression that the Republican Party is cooperating to provide unity on the large policies connected with the war. But Republicans who feel that way about it had better watch out. The Republican Party is being taken away from them. They are rapidly becoming a rump crowd with no influence in their own party. Willkie, who has symbolized Republican Party support of collaboration with other nations, is becoming a party outcast. Landon, and others, are traveling around the country talking mistrust of the Administration foreign moves as a political issue.

The Republican politicos think they have pretty well ditched Willkie. Landon is talking Dewey on the first or second ballot. Incidentally, Dewey is no longer talking as he once did about serving out his four years as governor of New York and he is being coyly silent over the sure-fire nomination predicted by Landon after talking with him.

Considering that the Republicans are almost certain to take over Congress after the next election, it is significant that the House Republicans have chosen Representative Charles Halleck of Indiana as their chairman of the National Congressional Campaign Committee.

Charley Halleck is a likable young congressman who has plenty of courage, as he showed when he stood up against the Townsend movement crackpots who had intimidated most Indiana politicians. Charley Halleck is several cuts above the run of mine, being exceptionally alert, and one of the most popular men personally in Congress.

Although Halleck made the 1940 nominating speech for Willkie, they don't think alike. Halleck voted against lend-lease, voted against selective service, voted against an authorization for an advanced fleet base at Guam. In fact he voted against practically all of the measures designed to strengthen the Allied side in the desperate days when the Nazis were close to winning the war. The Republican leader of the House, Representative Martin of Massachusetts, voted against most of those measures also, although not against selective service. He is likely to be Speaker a year from January. Halleck may become majority leader of the House.

Those are signs that indicate the wind drift. Republicans who believe that the Administration has on the whole been wise in its foreign moves are likely to find their party back in the hands of those who hate Willkie, who hate the British, who hate the Russians, who think, as Landon still does, that lend-lease made it inevitable that we should get into the war.

International collaboration such as is being carried on now would be impossible with such men in control of this Government. It is a situation that should cause the deepest concern among Republicans who believe that our peace and security depend on working with other peace-loving nations, and not returning to the period of anarchy and mutual ill will that preceded the last two wars.

12/13/43

It is almost a certainty that the Republican presidential candidate will be either Dewey or Willkie.

For more than a year those two men have been far ahead of all others in polls, such as Gallup's, and in the amount of news and radio attention they have commanded, as well as in the way they dominate the discussions, public and private, of politicians. Most political reporters talk chiefly about those two in their speculations.

As the nominating convention is little more than 6 months away, it seems hardly likely that the leading position which those two have had for so long will be materially affected in the relatively short time left. Likewise others who have been talked about for so long, such as General MacArthur and Governor Bricker, and former Governor Stassen, are not likely to advance very far out of the low brackets where they have remained during the many months of build-up effort by their friends.

Former Governor Landon reported on his recent trip here that there were more pictures of General MacArthur in Kansas homes than he had seen of anybody else since the day of old Dr. "Goat-Gland" Brinkley, who won enormous popularity for reasons far removed from politics. The difficulty of conducting a campaign with General MacArthur as the candidate causes doubts among many politicians as to the practicability of nominating him.

It is possible that Governor Bricker will strike fire and come rapidly to the front, although in a year of effort he has made little if any headway. Some prominent Republicans were saying a few days ago that his last chance would be to ring the bell in his Pennsylvania Society speech at New York last Saturday night. From the accounts published the next morning, it did not appear that he said anything sensational or that he shed any new light as a leader on the nation's political and international problems.

Former Governor Stassen of Minnesota, as a lieutenant commander on Admiral Halsey's staff in the South Pacific, is not in a position to campaign, or even to reply to attacks. His friends are, however, insisting on entering him in primaries where the chief effect will be to take votes away from Willkie. Commander Stassen may come home on leave in a few weeks, and if he does he may be persuaded not to allow his name to be used to split Willkie's vote.

Willkie's chief chance now is to demonstrate strength. It will be done not alone through speeches, but by going into primaries, especially the Wisconsin primary in April, where he must make an outstanding showing. Organization politicians, if they are free to make the decision, will nominate Dewey. Only a commanding demonstration of popularity by Willkie can prevent it, it seems to me.

But perhaps events will play a part more decisive than any of the circumstances I have mentioned. By early next summer we may have suffered the most severe casualties and no one can say what effect that will have on the public mind. No one can know what stage the war will be in, nor what the psychological changes in the country will be.

Some anti-Roosevelt Democrats say the President will not run, but will put up General Marshall. But if, as is more likely, Roosevelt runs for a fourth term, and particularly if he picks up as a running mate a more conservative Democrat, such as Justice James F. Byrnes, to continue as a kind of home-front director, the Republicans may not be safe in counting the election in the bag—far from it. Republican prospects in the Northern states, and for taking control of Congress, look better every day. If Republicans want to win the presidency as well, they need to consider which candidate will make the best appearance against Roosevelt.

8/5/42

The principle of democracy would gain new vindication if it were possible for us to go through a nationwide campaign maintaining unity on the deep questions and at the same time free debate and choice regarding the men we wish to trust with responsibility.

12/9/42

It may be difficult to know just what the Republican Party would do with its power if it won the 1944 election. In 1920 the party was divided. Candidate Harding rambled all over the issue, or as we used to say when we were covering his campaign, he was for and against the League. Many leading figures of the Republican Party were strong champions of the League of Nations. Just before the election they issued a public appeal saying the surest way to go into a league was to elect Harding. That appeal was signed by such figures as William Howard Taft, Elihu Root, Charles Evans Hughes, Herbert Hoover, Nicholas Murray Butler, and others whose names also carried a great weight with the public. As soon as the election returns were in, Harding announced that the League was dead, and it was—and all other forms of cooperation with other nations.

Not Taft, not Hughes, not Hoover, not any of the pro-League figures in the party, but a group of insiders who controlled Harding, planned that the Senate's rejection of the League should stand, although they kept their hole card down until after election.

That was a standard political maneuver. It happens often in politics, on issues both big and little, and is practiced in both parties. The important thing is to know that the game is often played that way, and to be on watch for the appearance of the old familiar trick.

Perhaps public opinion will be determined against going back into the kind of war-breeding international anarchy that we have had. Perhaps the Republican Party will be driven by public opinion to take the position Willkie has insisted upon. But judging by performance thus far there is a strong desire among many of the Republican leaders to give Willkie a big kick in the pants and go the other way. That's about all I can make out of it up to now.

Congress

9/18/39

THE responsibility of Congress is great but simple—to discuss with intelligence and understanding the questions which arise and to decide them with a conscience single to the best interests of the United States. There can be no other standard. Adhering to it, we may safely let the chips fall where they may.

2/34

Public debate in a democracy is something more than mere talk. It is a vital part in the process of government. Congress is frequently contrasted with the executive. It talks while the White House acts. This is not entirely fair. There is legitimate complaint against the quality of the talk in Congress. Senators and congressmen waste hours uttering meaningless drool for home consumption. But serious discussion, pointed toward the heart of pending problems, is a good deal more useful in the long run than the antics of some hard-boiled executive who is running about in circles uttering war whoops as he cracks every head in sight.

Dictatorship is the fate which comes to a people too lazy, too indifferent, or too helpless to run its own government. The judgment of a whole Congress, battered out of the cross fire of running debate, is apt to be more sound than the conclusions of the wisest man who may sit in splendid isolation in the oval room at the White House.

9/22/41

There is the great democratic dilemma of local versus national interest. Shall a senator or a representative vote solely with regard to the immediate local interest of his area, or shall he consider what is to the interest of the nation as a whole? Because he comes from a cattle state, shall he fight through hell and high water against a single pound of Argentine beef coming into the United States? Or shall he consider the whole question of trade relations between these two countries and the importance of developing closer ties between them in such a time as this?

If he is going to be hounded by his constituents on every single vote, a senator or congressman must choose between using his best judgment or facing political suicide. Few commit suicide knowingly. When a state or a district expects its member to be strictly a local messenger boy and insists that he fight for it regardless of what might be to the national interest, then it robs the country of the independent judgment of its representatives at Washington.

You do not obtain sound legislation simply by adding up a series of local pressures. More often you get the reverse, because members under heavy fire at home trade with each other and logroll through their respective propositions, thus making the final result only worse. That is why tariff bills have been such patchworks that we have finally had to get away from the logrolling method and delegate more power to the executive branch, which is less subject to the special single-area pressures.

In these times particularly we cannot get the best out of our senators and representatives if we insist that they be merely passive reflectors of their own constituencies, because so many of the decisions they must make are vital to the whole nation. There is an obligation on public servants to try to convince their constituents of what the national interest requires. The process of representative government should be two-way traffic, not simply a one-way traffic of orders from back home. That public opinion is sound in its long-range judgment on broad questions does not mean that it is instantly sound on every immediate question that comes up.

In this period it would help us toward better legislation if senators and representatives were not considered to be messenger boys, obliged to carry out orders literally, and were considered rather as hired specialists, delegated to come to Washington and use their best judgment and best information in deciding what ought to be done.

Nothing like that is going to happen, but there isn't any law against wishing that it could happen.

9/13/40

We hear much now about what democracy is and what it should be, but the spirit of it rarely has been illustrated better than in the attitude of Senator Henry Fountain Ashurst of Arizona, speaking in the Senate on the day after he was defeated for reelection.

He had served as senator ever since Arizona became a state. After 28 years in office a man might well come to think himself indispensable. Some reach that state of mind in much less time.

Instead of resenting the decision of his state to dispense with him, Senator Ashurst thanked his people for having allowed him to serve so long. If we are to remain a free people, Senator Ashurst told the Senate, it is the duty of public servants to accept defeat cheerfully, which he proceeded to do in one of the most remarkable speeches heard in a long time.

Ability to change our officials, and prompt acceptance of change, with a willingness on all sides to make the best of the new situation, are necessary to effective democracy. Had the verdicts of the country in 1932 and 1936 been received with more of that spirit among powerful figures in our business life and among the Republican opposition, much of our trouble would have been avoided. It was the continuing resistance to those verdicts that sometimes drove the Administration to opposite extremes and kept us a nation deeply divided within itself.

Senator Ashurst also paid his people a high compliment when he said that during his entire service they had allowed him to do as he pleased and to say what he pleased. In that he was paying himself an unconscious compliment, because the privilege of political independence is a rare one, bestowed only upon those who show the capacity to deserve it. Lesser men must toe the line, and that is not always good for either the constituents, the public official, or the country.

In a time of such confusion as this, when the difficulty of understanding today is exceeded only by that of seeing into tomorrow, public officials must be allowed much latitude by the country. It is not so much a question of which has the better judgment, the official or the public, as it is one of which has the better information. That was possibly the advantage that President Roosevelt had over those senators who in the summer last year ridiculed his idea that there might be a war in Europe.

In a third respect, too, Senator Ashurst tells us something about what democracy should be. He does not say it in so many words, but it is implicit in the whole tenor of his half-humorous, mildly self-deprecatory remarks, in his philosophical acceptance of the shift from important office to private life. Senator Ashurst bears gracefully the ordeal of having his power shucked off. For most public men that is an excruciating operation, accompanied by loud cries of pain and by scars that leave them forever unhappy, damaged souls.

Unwillingness to surrender power is a curse of civilization, the root of ages of trouble. Some men find the appetite irresistible. They will sacrifice everything else to hold their power. This is seen in its rawest form in dictatorships, and in more subtle form in democracy. Wars have been precipitated, crises manufactured, enemies murdered, and countries have been sacrificed by men desperate to hold their power. Senator Ashurst seems able to take it or leave it with equal grace.

He said, "When my present colleagues here are worrying about patronage, worrying about committee assignments, and about the scorching demands of constituents, I shall possibly be enjoying the ecstasy of the stillness of an Arizona desert night, or viewing the scarlet glory of her blossoming cactus, and possibly I may be wandering through the Petrified Forest, a forest which put on immortality 7,000,000 years ago. Enjoyment and ecstasy arise in human life from the contemplation and appreciation of such things."

But this noble example will be wasted on a world now cursed with the evil and brutal fruits of power-crazed leaders. Senator Ashurst would be the last to write himself down as a great and eventful statesman, yet within the range of his capacity he breathes, as the foregoing points suggest, the spirit of ideal democracy, which if it were more common now would make this world more tolerable. But that is only a daydream of what might have been.

12/22/38

Recent world changes have thrust so many considerations into the problem of national defense that Congress would be justified in resorting to special procedure. The most practical method would be to set up a joint House and Senate committee on national defense.

This would be a special, temporary committee. It would be obligated to survey the whole field. It would ascertain what we proposed to defend. First of all, it would define the problem. Are we going to protect merely the shores of the United States, or the hemisphere? Then it would prepare a rounded program to support the policy, covering Army, Navy, aircraft, industrial preparedness, and the methods of financing. It all goes together.

In this situation, it would be criminal to deal with the problem of national defense in the old piecemeal way. Can we do the job properly by working through some ten House and Senate committees, each jealously going its own way and the others be damned?

Under standard procedure you have the House Military Affairs Committee holding hearings, running its own show. The House Naval Affairs Committee runs its own show. Neither knows nor cares what the other is doing. How can you relate air strength and the Navy, or Army coast defense and the Navy, without considering them together and in relation to each other? How can you decide how many Army airplanes are needed until you know what the Navy is going to consist of? These matters are all tied together and they should be considered together.

You can't have properly balanced national defense when you cut the job up into small pieces and distribute it among some ten different committees each working independently. The working out of the defense program would be scattered piecemeal among the standing House committees on Military Affairs, Naval Affairs, Appropriations, and Ways and Means, and among the Senate committees on Appropriations, Foreign Relations, Military Affairs, Naval Affairs, and Finance. Duplicate hearings would be held, and there would result a long time-consuming scramble in which Army, Navy, and aviation each would grab as much as possible. A joint committee would know where the emphasis was to be put, whether on the Army, aircraft, or Navy, and in what proportions.

The joint House and Senate committee should contain representation from all of these committees just named, plus perhaps that of the House Foreign Affairs Committee, which, while of little consequence ordinarily, does have jurisdiction over neutrality legislation, which must be considered in connection with the whole national-defense problem.

Take two members from each of these standing committees, the chairman and the top Republican, and make up a special temporary joint committee of perhaps twenty members. That would be a smaller committee than most of the regular major House and Senate committees, and therefore not unwieldy. It would represent both houses, both parties, and every standing committee concerned in the problem. By taking the top members, you assemble the most experienced House and Senate members, each well informed in his particular field.

Put such a committee to work, first on a carefully organized program of hearings to gather expert testimony and second on the drafting of a balanced, unified program. Then Congress will know what it is doing. Bring such a program before the full membership of the House and the Senate, under the auspices of such a special joint committee, and it would be entitled to respect. Because of the men on it, such a committee would be powerful enough to protect the program from raiding on the floor.

Such a special joint committee as is here suggested ought to produce the best program that is possible under our system—one that provides enough but not too much, balanced and proportioned adequately to the needs of America at this hour.

12/30/38

It looks as if we couldn't have that joint House and Senate Committee on national defense to make a study of the whole problem. It would be too much trouble.

The idea appears sound to a good many people, to some of the most experienced members of the House and Senate, and to some of the higher officials concerned with national defense.

But as one of the House leaders explained, chairmen of the regular committees in the House are extremely jealous of their prerogatives. That is to say a chairman of the naval or military affairs committee, for instance, would object to coming down from his throne and sitting with a joint committee of some twenty members of the House and Senate to canvass the whole subject of national defense. So long as the chairman stays inside his own committee, he is the head man. He isn't anxious to share his power or to pool it. One chairman said, when objecting to formation of a joint committee, "Someone would dominate it."

Another of the administration leaders pointed out a defect in the idea of a joint committee. It would mean, he explained, that the House members would have to walk over to the Senate side of the Capitol for the committee meetings, or else the senators would have to walk over to the House side. That is a distance of about two blocks. Members don't like to go so far to attend a committee meeting and this particular leader was certain that the attendance would be very poor.

Furthermore, House members object to going over to the Senate for anything, except of course to become senators, while senators feel that it is beneath their dignity to go over to the House side to work—practically slumming, the senators mean.

And anyway some of these chairmen don't see any need of considering defense as a whole problem in which Army, Navy, and air strength are related. As to the larger question of what we are going to defend, what the objectives of our policy are to be—well, that is just something to talk about and is outside the field of Army and Navy appropriations.

Senator Bennett Clark of Missouri says, "The whole question of national defense should be considered calmly in the light of a determination of the national and international policies to be pursued and the means necessary—and only those necessary—to implement those policies."

Senator David Walsh, chairman of the Senate Naval Affairs Committee, urges a "well-devised, carefully planned, practically coordinated program that will be adequate to protect us from invasion."

But when you come down to details, some War Department officials are suggesting 10,000 more planes while others in the Army say that very little, if any, increase is needed. Can the Navy alone give adequate protection against air attack from the sea or must it have the help of the Army air force?

Common sense says Army, Navy, and air strength are all related in defense plans. The Scripps-Howard newspapers advocate that these questions be considered as a whole through a joint committee. *The Washington Star,* referring to the conflict among the experts, says the defense question should be studied as a whole through a joint committee, "not by independent congressional committees pulling at cross purposes."

Yet Chairman Carl Vinson, of the House Naval Affairs Committee, says there is no relation between the Army and Navy, and that each committee should go about its own business.

"The Army's job," he says, "is to protect the land and the Navy's job is to protect the sea. Each has its own job. The Navy has its air force and the Army has its air force. Our committee gives the Navy whatever airplanes it thinks are needed and the Military Affairs Committee does the same for the Army. It is better for each committee to work out its own program."

So those authorities must be wrong who tell us that the mission of the Army is to backstop the Navy, to protect outlying possessions, to defend the home bases of the Navy, and to defend the mainland from attack by land, air, or sea—a job that dovetails with the Navy's assignment. That's one of the questions on which it was hoped a joint committee might straighten us out.

12/12/41

When Congress was put to the test this week, it came through. Congress has been calm and efficient. It has been businesslike and has not wasted time in idle words. To everyone it was obvious what had to be done, and it was done in the simplest, quickest way.

During this week, at least, we have shown that democratic government can meet an emergency without lost motion and without grandstanding. It has been a most heartening experience and it will do much to revive public confidence in the legislative branch.

The war resolutions against Germany and Italy were put through without debate. In the Senate not a single word, aside from the routine mechanical formalities, was uttered. The whole business was finished in less than half an hour. The House was equally prompt. Without anything more than a clarifying question, the Senate voted unanimously to permit the President to send American troops of any kind anywhere.

The fact that there was no debate only gave more force to the action. For it was the silent action of free men. No one was shut off from debate. Senators could have talked by the hour. But they knew that words were unnecessary and out of place in the presence of such compelling events. Both houses have set a high example. They won't be able to live up to it, and in time will fall back into floundering, wandering, irrelevant talk. But by acting without needless words now, Congress will be in better standing when the time comes, as it surely will, that calls for frank and hard-hitting criticism.

Somewhat lost in the rush of bigger actions was the unprecedented political truce, declared just before we declared war on Germany and Italy. This truce was declared in an exchange of telegrams between Chairman Flynn of the Democratic National Committee and Chairman Martin of the Republican National Committee. The truce also was registered in the resolution unanimously adopted at a conference of Senate Republicans. They pledged their full support to the prosecution of the war. The resolution was offered by Senator Lodge of Massachusetts.

This means, it is hoped, an end of the bickering which has hampered the Administration during the last two years in dealing with the dangers created by the war. It will not end criticism and should not. But hereafter criticism will presumably be devoted to making more effective the adopted policy of the Government, whereas before much of the criticism was intended to obstruct and reverse the Government's policy.

The only unfortunate incident that has occurred since Japan's attack is Senator Tobey's attempt to force disclosure of military secrets about the damage at Pearl Harbor. Around Congress they know Tobey. He is cantankerous but is not taken seriously. He embarrasses his own fellow Republicans more than he does the Administration.

Eventually details of Pearl Harbor will be exposed and the blame fixed. Congress is determined to do that. But the responsible Republicans know there is risk of giving information to Japan by going into this now. They are ready to wait until the affair can be hauled out into the open and discussed freely.

In these times there is little for Congress to do but to vote appropriations and scrutinize the conduct of the war. Commons does a good job of it in England. On one occasion Churchill spent a whole evening with an American official being coached to meet questions expected in Commons the next day about the lease of bases to the United States. I found in England that after two years of war there was still free criticism of the government. It was regarded as healthy and stimulating and one of the prerogatives of a free country.

American solidarity behind the war does not mean blind, unquestioning resignation to everything that is done. Our unanimity means that we are all participating in the effort. We are sharing the decision, not merely accepting it. We have a right to know what happens and to pass judgment on it. But we must use better judgment in timing than Senator Tobey is showing. Fortunately most members in both houses of Congress, by waiting until a safe time before demanding military information, are showing a patriotic sense of timing.

3/6/42

We have to change our way of looking at taxes during the war. A lot of people want to help the Government win the war. They need look no further. If no other opportunities are open, they can at least pay taxes.

More than that, they can give their support to every proposal to increase taxes. They can help club down special-interest groups that will try to chisel away the heavy taxes just proposed by Secretary Morgenthau.

Every one of us in civilian life might as well take the attitude now that we must work one or two or three days a week for the Government—or maybe five days a week. Instead of going on the Government pay roll, we stay in private life and contribute the earnings of one or more days a week toward winning the war.

Never has the payment of taxes been such a real privilege as now. People who complain now about their taxes are far more contemptible than the soldier who complains of hard duty. He has some reason for complaint. But the last guy I will be able to shed tears for is the one who crawls in between warm blankets in his bed at home weeping about the taxes he has to pay.

Of course, these taxes will be hard to pay. Of course, somebody isn't going to have a winter in Florida, because he has to use the money for his taxes. As Secretary Morgenthau says, the impact of the new war taxes will be felt in every American home. They will be severe. But, as he said, it is a million times cheaper to win a war than to lose it.

Sure, everybody will agree with those generalities. But a lot of people will be running around Congress trying to persuade congressmen that the taxes hit them unfairly, and harder than they hit somebody else. When anyone turns up with that argument and says he is being discriminated against—then by all means that should be corrected. The way to correct it is to hit the other fellow harder. If revisions have to be made to achieve equality of sacrifice, let the revision be upward to increase the burden, and not downward.

Every dollar taken out in taxes now decreases the future load on the Government. Every dollar taken out now decreases the spending money of the American public and to that extent cuts down the demand for civilian goods which gets in the way of war production. Every dollar taken out in taxes now eases the pressure toward inflation, which is the heaviest and most unjust tax of all.

A lot of high-priced lawyers have been hired to come to Washington and ease down the taxes for somebody. The best way to deal with all such arguments will be to say no without even listening. We will hear about the widows and orphans. But it isn't the widows and orphans who hire expensive lawyers to come to Washington to talk Congress out of imposing taxes. Corporations and rich people are the ones who do that. If somebody is going to have to give up some servants and an extra golf-club membership, that would be too bad. But war is hell. Even General MacArthur has a hard time of it.

Gradually we are learning that we can help with the war even without getting a commission in the Army or Navy. Donald Nelson in his radio talk explained how every production worker is a soldier in this war. Secretary Morgenthau explains how even those who are not in war production can be soldiers in this war.

Yes, even the heavy stockholders can help. They can help more than they realize. Because most of the chiseling on tax bills comes through corporation executives who say they have to look out for their stockholders. Well, this is one time the stockholders can take a cut. Let them call off their lawyers down here and take their rap just as those who work for a living are taking their rap, if you can consider war taxes as a rap rather than an opportunity to help.

Before this war is over there will be work for everybody. So people who have been living off of their stocks won't starve. Mighty few people have starved under this Administration.

5/15/42

A Government official says the Army is switching from rubber to steel treads on tanks. That means a loss of 10 per cent in speed. But the rubber shortage makes it necessary thus to slow down the speed of our tanks.

.rising at eight o'clock every morning, Raymond Clapper exercised in the
'oodpile daily.

Raymond Clapper leaves home for office, kidded by Mrs. Clapper abou
wrinkles in his coat.

Photo by Harris &
Reproduced by special permission of The Saturday Evenir
copyright 1944 by The Curtis Publishing Company.

Courtesy White Owl Cigars

Raymond Clapper goes first to Senate Office Building.

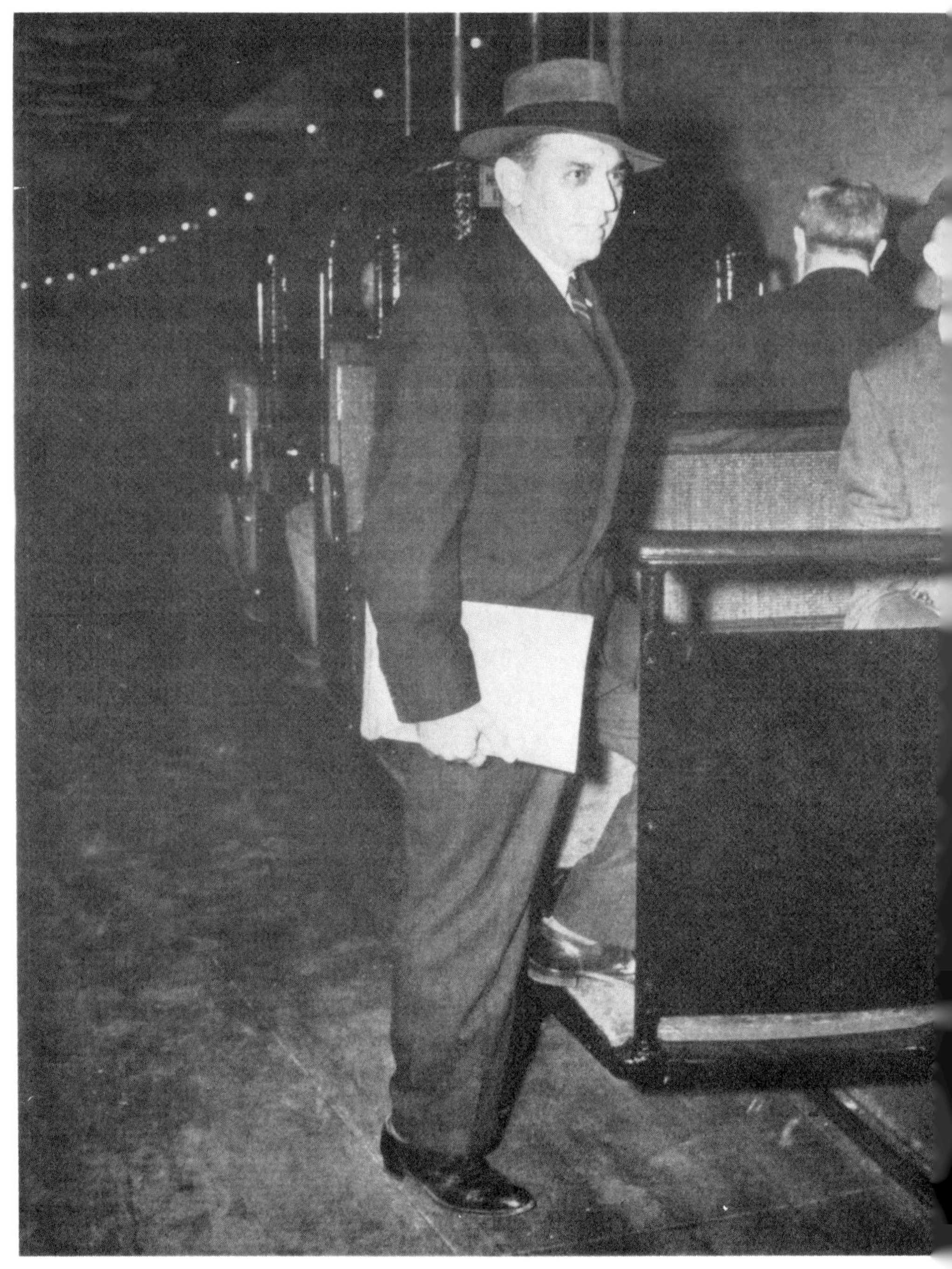

Clapper uses monorail trolley to go from Senate Office Building to the Capitol

Raymond Clapper talks with Vice-President Wallace in latter's office in Capitol.

Raymond Clapper leaves U. S. Capitol after listening to Senate debate.

Clapper checks in at U. S. Supreme Court.

Photograph courtesy J. Walter Thomps

Raymond Clapper entering Polish Embassy to lunch with the Ambassador.

ıring copy for daily
ın.

Photo by Harris & Ewing
ced by special permission of
urday Evening Post: copy-
44 by The Curtis Publish-
pany.

ing statements.

Raymond Clapper en route to White House press conference meets Rober
Sherwood, playwright and presidential adviser.

Leaving the White House press conference. He looks none too pleased.

Photo by Harris & Ewing

At 10 P.M. White Owl announcer says, "And now, Raymond Clapper from Washington."

Checking script of broadcast with latest news coming in on news ticker before going on the air.

You would think that senators and representatives, knowing what a desperate effort must be made to save rubber and gasoline, and to release tankers for carrying fuel to the armed forces, would be the first to cooperate.

Yet on the same day that this disclosure was made about taking rubber treads off of tanks, senators and representatives were staging an obscene spectacle in demanding the right to unlimited use of their automobiles.

I have a lot of sympathy with the need of senators and representatives to get around, and am far less inclined to question the mileage they pile up than I am the spirit—the selfish, obstructive spirit—they display in claiming unlimited privileges. Fortunately they are being so stupid in this that a number of them are apt to pay for it dearly at the hands of indignant voters. We'll find out that some of them are not essential gasoline users after all.

The very men to whom the whole country looks to set an example and to encourage the public to accept the personal inconveniences needed to help win the war are doing exactly the reverse. Instead of trying to cooperate they are cackling like wet hens to hold their special privilege.

They are handing out personal abuse to rationing officials and are denouncing the press for reporting the fact that they are chiseling unlimited gasoline cards. They are claiming that the press and the officials are trying to destroy Congress.

The Senate majority leader, Barkley, instead of appealing to his colleagues to help save gasoline, flies into a rage when Senator Downey of California asks the senators to waive their rights and pledge themselves to restrict their use of gasoline. Barkley says some newspapers are trying to undermine faith in Congress and adds defiantly, "I am going to take whatever I am entitled to without apology."

Representative Faddis of Pennsylvania holds out for his right to unlimited use of gasoline to campaign back home despite "any nitwitted bureaucratic clerk to the contrary."

He and the whole horde of them are indulging in an orgy of morale-destroying chatter. Representative Leland Ford of California says in the House that it is time Congress showed they "were not going to take orders from the bureaucrats downtown." That's outspoken defiance of Government authority.

Representative Wilson of Indiana, evidently nauseated by this line of talk, challenged the need of unlimited cards for congressmen. He was saying that it was hardly a credit to men in their positions when Representative Hoffman of Michigan jumped up and, by declaring the remarks improper, cut Wilson off from further discussion.

The number of unlimited cards being issued is so unexpectedly large that the allowance on all other cards may have to be cut so there will be enough fuel for the unlimited cards.

The attitude of these senators and representatives makes one's blood boil. But more than that, it makes you solemnly wonder for the future of Congress.

5/16/42

Senator Barkley can call this indignation over unlimited gasoline cards for congressmen a tempest in a teapot if he wants to.

But he is the majority leader of the Senate, and as he wants to preserve Congress as a force in our public affairs, he might do well to let down his blood pressure and think it over.

Whether 200 congressmen and a flock of their secretaries get unlimited gasoline cards is a small thing in the relative amount of gasoline involved. If the Senator sees no more in the matter than that, then he is asleep.

As a force in our Government Congress is sliding downhill. It is endangered not by the press nor by the executive branch, but by its own shallow incompetency. It fails to exert the real leadership that the nation must have in modern times.

Congress has remained a collection of 2-cent politicians who could serve well enough in simpler days. But the ignorance and provincialism of Congress render it incapable of meeting the needs of modern government. Consequently the center of gravity has shifted toward the executive branch.

No matter how capable Congress might be, many of its functions would have to be delegated to administrative officers. Regulatory bodies have had to be set up. The power over tariffs, one of the most important held in the past by Congress, has had to be delegated to the executive branch because no large legislative body can handle the delicate and complicated adjustments necessary under modern world economic conditions. Those delegations of power, while removing a good deal of responsibility from Congress, need not mean the decline of Congress.

On the contrary, by getting rid of the details of tariff making and other housekeeping routine, Congress releases itself from a burden of petty chores. It becomes free to fulfill a more fundamental function.

Never was there such need for intelligent and informed debate on public affairs. People are looking to editorials, radio commentators, and newspaper columnists for the discussion of public affairs that they ought to get from Congress. Not the newspaper columnists but senators and representatives should be developing and leading the thinking of the country at this time. Since we have no Webster-Hayne debates, people want to know what Dorothy Thompson and Walter Lippmann think.

Our problems were never so worthy of earnest thought and discussion. The people are hungry for it—so hungry that they sit up nights at the radio and pore over their newspapers eager to soak up what they can from those speakers and writers in whom they have confidence.

Never has Congress had such a chance to make itself a great national forum of discussion. Our supreme debating forum should be Congress—not Town Hall of the Air. The people elect Congress and surely they would rather hear from it. In this democratic struggle they would like Congress to be the great tribunal of the people.

The only reason Congress is not just that is that people don't give a damn what the average senator or congressman says. The reason they don't care is that they know what you hear in Congress is 99 per cent tripe, ignorance, and demagoguery and not to be relied on.

At the Harvard Tercentenary a few years ago I heard Dr. A.

Lawrence Lowell say that great institutions were not killed but committed suicide, and then somebody came along and buried them.

Nobody is going to destroy Congress. It is doing that job itself at the very moment when it is most needed. Members are so busy sneaking through retirement pensions, grabbing unlimited gasoline rationing, hiding wives, children, nephews, and in-laws on the pay roll that they are missing the boat.

And then they say the newspapers are out to destroy Congress. Think it over again, Senator Barkley, please.

6/6/42

Some of my friends in Congress have felt hurt or indignant because of something I wrote a couple of weeks ago.

I was a little heated up at the time by the scramble over X cards and particularly by the cry in Congress that the press, in criticizing the X-card scandal, was trying to destroy Congress. The piece went on to say that nobody was going to destroy Congress; that Congress was doing that job itself with its demagoguery, and so on.

When I read the piece over some days later, after it had cooled off, it seemed a little rougher, perhaps, than I had realized and I thought possibly I had been unfair. You can't long have a sound democracy without a strong, intelligent, conscientious Congress.

Now I read the United Press report about the meeting of an "angry" bipartisan group of 100 House members which unanimously adopted a resolution opposing nationwide gasoline rationing unless a report is filed showing it to be necessary.

The United Press says the meeting rang with denunciations of Price Administrator Henderson, who was described as a "dictator" and a "smart aleck." One congressman said, "We have got to take away some of the power of this bureaucratic monster." There was some confusion when Representative Hope of Kansas, a Republican, pointed out that the rationing decision lay not with Henderson but with Donald Nelson, chairman of W.P.B. But the congressmen went on pummeling the executive officials who are charged with the responsibility of trying to do the things necessary to win the war—one of them being to conserve rubber now that Japan has cut off our source of supply and left us in an extremely serious predicament. One congressman said, "I'm fed up on this bird Henderson," and so on.

When I said the other day that what you hear in Congress is 99 per cent tripe, ignorance, and demagoguery, possibly I was unfair. But if this kind of stuff that I have just been quoting out of the antirationing meeting isn't just that, then you name it.

Senators and congressmen believe it is popular with their constituents to scream against gasoline rationing. None of us likes rationing. We all want to drive our cars. Senators and congressmen, who know they are in bad with the public, are now taking the cheap way out to curry favor. They are in effect—although putting in the weasel words to protect themselves—telling the public that this is all the bunk about rationing, pay no attention to what the Government says, go on and race your car around all you want to, use up that gasoline, and to hell with this bird Henderson or Nelson or whoever it is that is trying to keep you from joy riding in your car.

That's the gist of what they are saying. The object of it is to incite public resistance to whatever rationing plan the Government decides is necessary. It's pretty cheap stuff and just the kind of thing that makes people disgusted and makes them lose respect for Congress. Many members of Congress are out now to grease the public at the expense of the war effort. They are trying to get reelected this way, and in the process they are undermining the strength of Congress at the mainspring of democracy.

The Truman Committee of the Senate spent months investigating the rubber situation. There was a lot that it could not find out. But it found this out and reported it—this conscientious, hardworking committee of the United States Senate, "Driving must be curtailed on the basis of the present rubber outlook. Therefore, national gasoline rationing on a sensible basis must be given serious consideration."

That's not a bureaucrat speaking. It is a committee of the Senate speaking, a committee which is not playing politics and trying to grease the voters, but is soberly considering what is needed to win the war. Executive officials who are dealing with the rubber problem all agree that conservation of rubber is urgent, and nobody has suggested an alternate to gasoline rationing as a way to do it.

Maybe I was wrong. Maybe what you hear in Congress isn't 99 per cent tripe, ignorance, and demagoguery. Maybe it's not more than 95 per cent.

9/25/42

This is something I never expected to write.

For the first time since I have been reporting in Washington, I believe we are in danger of going over to dictatorship.

I don't mean the temporary, quasi dictatorship that war always brings to a brief life. I mean dictatorship, period.

There can be no immediate return to normal when the fighting stops. If Congress cannot recover its sense of responsibility and its independence from pressure groups like the ravenous farm lobby, it will be no more capable of dealing with reconstruction than it is capable of dealing with war problems.

We are seeing before our eyes this week the breakdown of legislative government. Congress is not legislating, it is carrying out the orders of a handful of farm lobbyists who hover around the halls at the Capitol and give their orders. They are the Congress—people you never elected and whose names you probably don't even know. It has been going on a long time. Now it has reached defiance of an urgent need to hold the economy of the country in balance. To see this thing happening at a critical time like this is an appalling event which sends a shudder through your frame if you want to keep this a democracy.

Time and again I have said that dictatorships rise up out of the decayed ruins of parliamentary government. Time and again I have said that those who accused President Roosevelt of trying to become a dictator were silly. They were silly so long as we had a strong, healthy Congress which did not have to eat out of the hand of one lobby.

I have never seen any danger in delegating power so long as the agency delegating it is in good health. Modern government requires quick decisions and flexibility not easily provided by the legislative process. But strong executive power must be kept in a framework of policy set by the legislative branch. Congress is daring President Roosevelt to put his war powers to the test in a way that will mean White House defiance of Congress on a question in which the public interest is so overwhelmingly on the President's side that he is the likely winner—and democratic machinery the likely loser. Congress is risking destruction of its prestige and influence to a fatal degree.

Weeks ago when I wrote rather bitterly about Congress and its demagoguery, some of my friends in Congress went into pouts. I understand some of the congressional ladies took out their hatchets also. Well, maybe I was a little rough, and I piped down, because coming from Baptist parents I always figure that a fellow ought to have a chance to repent. But do we have to wait forever?

I doubt if the country will wait forever. No other country has been able to wait forever. One fine morning after parliamentary government has failed, some loud-mouthed fellow in a uniform gets up and announces he is boss and that you can call him Il Duce or Der Fuehrer and like it, by God.

The odd thing which every one of us ought to keep in mind is that the people like it—at first, certainly. These Germans and Russians fighting at Stalingrad believe in Hitler and in Uncle Joe. They believe the strong man knows how to lead them to victory. They are glad that unbelievers were jailed or shot. When government breaks down, people turn to the man they think is strong enough to put them right side up again.

You know how this country turned to Mr. Roosevelt that morning in March, 1933. He looked like the man who could save the country from chaos. He's still around. Some things have occurred recently that suggest he is getting into the mood. Congress, you had better watch this. The people won't save you. They'll let you go down the drain if that's where you insist on going, and they'll tie to Mr. Roosevelt as they did in 1933.

Congress, you are asking for it, and it will be a sorry day for the United States of America if you get it.

9/30/42

Uncle George Norris is going to run for the Senate in Nebraska again—at the age of eighty-one and after 39 years in the House and Senate.

Throughout the generation he has been a pillar in democratic government. Perhaps I haven't made myself very clear in some of the things I have written about Congress. What I have been trying to say is that it would be a great thing for our country if both the legislative and executive branches could always be moved by the kind of spirit that I think has possessed Uncle George Norris during his long public life.

This is not a reelection blurb and it is not intended at all as comment on his present candidacy, but relates to one of the problems of democracy—that of having men in public life who have sufficient judgment and force to make a representative self-government effective.

It is not a question of whether you agree with every position that Senator Norris has taken. Neither has the senator been any amateur in the business of practical politics. He has as good a bag of tricks as any of them. But the point is that he has had something more than that.

Possibly the real value of a man like Senator Norris has been largely in his independence and imagination, and his capacity to follow through. His work in establishing the unicameral legislature in Nebraska was a useful experiment in the mechanics of democratic government. It was an attempt to improve our old model T. We need more experiments in improved machinery of government.

The senator's amendment to abolish the lame-duck sessions of Congress is another instance of his passion to make democratic government more effective.

But his real monument may prove to be the Tennessee Valley Authority. It is a large venture in practical democracy. Through imagination and persistence, Senator Norris used the power of the

Federal Government to bring to life the natural resources of the whole Tennessee valley in a way that no private enterprise could have done—at least it was not being done and was not being contemplated.

That undertaking gave new life to the economy and social environment of an area previously neglected. The inspiration of T.V.A. led to development of the great water-power projects of the West. All of them are now proving invaluable to war production.

What do we have a right to expect of our leaders in Washington, whether in the executive or legislative branch?

I read in the *New York Times Magazine* something that General Hershey, director of selective service, said in another connection. He said, "The really great man is endowed with a higher degree of sensitiveness, so that seeing a little sooner and farther than his fellows the coming situations, he can size them up in advance."

Senator Norris has had that quality.

When you call in a plumber you want him to know more about fixing the plumbing than you do. When I am building a house I want that builder to know more about it than I know.

So when a man is paid to come to Washington and work for the people, do we as taxpayers expect him just to keep his seat warm? Or do we expect him to know more about national problems than we know and to be seeing ahead? From which are we going to get our money's worth?

1/43

You who are the new Congress—you have an opportunity. Your opportunity is second only to that which was given to the forefathers.

You have an opportunity to make Congress a living force in our democracy again.

You can rescue Congress from fear-ridden submission to pressure groups—labor groups, farm groups, dry groups, business groups, and all of those special self-seeking lobbying groups that are trying to use the war for their own special advantage.

Those are the groups that swung their clubs over the old Congress now going out. They were beaten only when the President and the general public, and the press and radio sent up a cry that churned up enough strength. The farm bloc was beaten only when public clamor forced it. Nationwide gasoline rationing was finally ordered when public pressure overrode the protests of senators and representatives from oil states. The drys, trying to force soldier prohibition in on the back of the eighteen-year-old draft, were beaten in the first test only by the strongest pressure from the Army and Navy and the public mediums of expression.

Congress has in the last two years sunk to a new low. Only by one vote did the House authorize an extension of the draft in the summer of 1941. Congress slyly voted itself a retirement-benefit plan and then had to repeal it under public pressure. When gasoline rationing was first applied in the Eastern states, the number of senators and representatives who obtained unlimited X cards shocked a good many people.

All of this has produced an impression upon many people that Congress has been inadequate to the needs of these times, that Congress could not be counted upon to do the work that had to be done, that the legislative arm was withering, and that we had to depend on the White House.

This disintegration of Congress is dangerous to our democracy. It can lead to only one thing—dictatorship. That has been the outcome of parliamentary decay in other countries. It would be the outcome here. The outcry against Congress is not a cry to get rid of Congress. It is a cry of dismay. The American people, I believe, want to save representative government. They want Congress to be a strong, effective agent of the nation.

Democracy in America cries out now for the very best that is in you. It needs and wants you to give all of your intelligence and conviction and courage to help. It wants you to help first in those things that must be done to win the victory. It wants you also to help in those things that must be done to rebuild an order for freedom at home and security abroad. We recognize, I think, the need of strong executive leadership. But we do not want it to become a monopoly in Washington. We want a strong executive seasoned with the cooperation of a strong legislative branch.

This is not a small thing to ask of you who are the new Congress.

You may be crucified. Your only reward may be such as you can derive from your own conscience. That's the risk you take. It may not be that bad. But there is no use trying to deny that you might offend powerful minorities who could bring about your defeat.

But if you of the new Congress would take those risks, what might not be accomplished?

You might be the Congress to show the world that parliamentary government still is the way for a free and efficient people.

You of the new Congress can show that when there are men adequate for the responsibility, legislative government can serve effectively in modern government. Your Congress can check the drift toward executive control which has become dictatorship in other countries and pseudo dictatorship here.

You of the new Congress have this rare opportunity. You will pass it by at your peril.

The task of restoring the country back to a peacetime basis, of reconverting our whole national activity from war back to civilian pursuits, will be attended by many dislocations. There will be shortages, inflationary dangers followed perhaps by deflationary dangers, problems of the return of millions of soldiers, the return of huge war factories to civilian life. Will the people trust Congress to fix policies on these matters? Or will they insist, as they have recently, that the Congress step aside and leave it to the President? Won't the answer to that depend on how much confidence your new Congress inspires in the people during the months to come?

You of the new Congress are going to serve during a two-year period which is likely to bring vast changes in the world, and in our place in the world. At the end of the war we will be the strong, productive nation. Much will be expected of us. We shall have to do much if there is to be any kind of orderly restoration and a system of security created.

In the beginning we shall have to do policing, restocking, feeding famine populations, rebuilding of devastated war zones, and assist in supplying raw materials. We shall have to open markets so that the economies of the various war-torn countries can begin to function and work their way back to a self-supporting condition. It will be either that or chaos, civil war, anarchy, and constant threat of new trouble.

If we are going to try to do anything to help put the world back together, and to reduce the chances of another such devastating war, we shall have to make some economic sacrifices. But better economic sacrifices for a while after the war than to face the prospect of making more human sacrifice such as this war is imposing on us.

To play its part, Congress will have to legislate for the nation. Members will have to consider the best interests of the nation, not only the interests of their own localities without regard to the needs of the nation as a whole.

Congress has been a collection of people legislating for their respective states and localities instead of for the nation as a whole. That, I believe, has had much to do with the growing tendency of the country to look to the President as its chief policy maker. In view of the part which the United States undoubtedly will play in world affairs from now on, the challenge to Congress to think in national and in world terms, as contrasted with local interests, will become more insistent.

In this dangerous period, when representative government has collapsed almost everywhere else, isn't it worth risking your reelection chances to do your part in bringing health and vigor, intelligence, and informed, free judgment to the legislative arm of the Government?

1/19/43

Out of all the complaint over time-wasting committee methods in Congress only one small change has been accepted by the Democratic leadership.

That small concession to total war was made grudgingly in deference to the rise of air warfare, news of which finally appears to have made its impression. Speaker Rayburn is wedded to the House rituals and to committee privileges as if they were some religious sanctity, instead of being merely tools to work with. He has, however, finally given his reluctant blessing to permitting an exchange of top members between the House Naval and Military Affairs Committees.

That was proposed by Chairman Vinson of the House Naval Affairs Committee. The chairman of the two committees and the top Republican member of each will have membership and voting rights in both committees. Representative Vinson feels that the need of a unified air program makes this slight amount of overlapping between the Military and Naval Committees advisable. Chairman May of the House Military Affairs Committee would go further. He would adopt a similar arrangement between these two committees and the two subcommittees that handle military and naval appropriations, so that all four committees would interlock. But that is practically heresy.

Except for the little Vinson change, the machinery of Congress must creak along as it did in the happy days of Rutherford B. Hayes. Hundred-billion-dollar budgets must adapt themselves to moss-covered traditions. Old-timers who run the House—and it is about as bad in the Senate—are as sentimental over their old rules as ivy-league alumni over their college traditions. It matters little that General Marshall and Admiral King must commute to Congress and repeat testimony among four different committees every time they want money. One day not long ago General Marshall spent the morning before a Senate committee and then repeated his story to a House committee in the afternoon—all because the senators and representatives are too jealous of their prerogatives to sit in a joint meeting and save half of the time they take from the men who run the war.

12/11/43

Only on rare occasions does the Speaker of the House leave his chair and speak from the floor as one of the elected members. When Speaker Rayburn did so the other day, he obviously was moved to say something very close to his heart.

What was the heart of the message that the Speaker was so

moved to deliver? It was that representatives elevate themselves to be leaders and not merely followers. The Speaker suggested that when congressmen return home over the holidays, they try to stamp out among the people some of the dangerous trends that now threaten our unity and the progress of the war.

This is an attempt to restore members of the legislature to the more responsible role for which they were intended under the principle of representative government.

As the art of mass pressure has developed, representatives have become less and less independent. They have not been delegates chosen to exercise their judgment and understanding, but rather rubber stamps to vote as organized minorities direct. Only five out of ninety-six senators stood against the railroad labor organizations the other day in the vote to direct a larger wage increase than the executive branch approved.

In other days a senator or representative was chosen as a man of consequence in his community, and in whom his neighbors had confidence. One of the best examples was Senator Borah. His constituents were proud to sponsor him so that to a large degree he exercised his judgment as to what seemed best for the country. At the other extreme is the Indiana congressman who a few years ago voted for the Townsend old-age-pension plan, although at the same time he told his banker he was against it and regarded it as unsound.

To hit somewhere between those two extremes is about as much as we can hope for. Senators and representatives will never, and should never, be divorced from the interests of their people. Yet their opportunities for learning more about the interests of the country as a whole, their opportunities in mingling with members from other sections to develop a broader and more balanced viewpoint, should have a chance to be felt.

Why should a man chosen by a state or a district of several hundred thousand people, shrivel at Washington to the role of a terrorized messenger boy for a pressure minority?

Under British parliamentary practice, a member, if out of step with majority sentiment of his constituency, can shift to another constituency in which his viewpoint will be more agreeable. That system is far from perfect and encourages the virtual purchase of seats through large contributions to the party by wealthy men ambitious to be in Parliament. Yet it does give protection to the serious public servant. He knows that defeat in his district is not fatal. He can find some other constituency.

But in the United States, a representative, defeated in his own district, is virtually banished from public life. He can become a lame duck at Washington if his own party is in power, but he has little opportunity to continue on his own feet in a legislative career.

So he has everything in one basket. His whole political future is at the hands of any organized group in his district powerful enough to cut his throat. He must yield to such groups or risk his whole public career. That places too great a strain on human nature. Men do not ordinarily go into public life for the purpose of committing political suicide.

Some halfway meeting, between legislators who will lead as well as follow, and voters who welcome intelligent leadership rather than servile errand boys, is sorely needed.

Labor

9/5/38

YOU don't have to look very hard to find black spots on the labor map. Many years will pass before they are rubbed out, if ever, because there are certain catchall basins where the dregs settle, where the least intelligent and most helpless people sink, victims not only of hard conditions but also of their own incapacity. Share croppers, fruit pickers, cannery workers, and others drifting about in seasonal unskilled occupations, will never live the life of Riley. As the French say, stones are hard everywhere. The best that can be hoped for is that these handicapped persons will be protected from too-cruel exploitation.

Your more intelligent workman, the man who is able to look out for himself, is pretty well over the hump in his rise from industrial serfdom. He is now in a position to obtain decent hours and a fair wage. He suffers chiefly from the poor functioning of our system, from the layoffs, the shutdowns, the technological changes. In this he is a joint victim with investors and management. He is in a position to do very well if the employer can keep the business going. They have a joint stake in making our industrial wheels turn at a more even pace.

Labor's role as a helpless industrial serf is about over. Even in the last year labor's emergence has been further accelerated and protected. The Wagner Act, whatever modifications may be made, has been vindicated by the courts and is here to stay in its essential, which is Federal protection of the right to organize. Wages-and-hours legislation throws the protection of the Federal Government around the unorganized employee.

The Harlan County, Ky., mine-union agreement is not only a real advance for labor in a hitherto blood-soaked sector, but it is symbolic of the surrender of the last outposts of union haters. Few employers now doubt the inevitability of union organization. Some are still fighting it, but they know it is a losing battle. They are moved more by pride and stubbornness than by any rational expectation that they can win in the long run. Most employers have become reconciled to collective bargaining as inevitable and are merely trying to make the best possible terms.

To appreciate how far we have come, you have only to thumb back a few pages in history. Less than a hundred years ago children in English mines and factories worked from 5 A.M. to 8 P.M. Older children worked from 3 A.M. to 8 P.M. In the mines, women crawled on all fours hauling tubs of coal. In 1842 an English royal commission reported that in the mines "girls and women worked like boys and men; they were less than half clothed, and worked alongside men who were stark naked." These were the days when the advocates of laissez faire denounced as enemies of the country anyone who wanted to change such conditions. Agitation for a 10-hour law was bitterly resisted and it was asserted that the one thing necessary to economic salvation was to give capital as free a hand as possible.

In America we followed the same pattern, with a little less cruelty, or perhaps a different kind of cruelty. We never worked women and children as brutally as the English in mines and factories. But men who tried to organize unions and to improve their conditions of work were treated without mercy. Strikers were shot down in countless localities during the seventies and eighties. Recent tactics exposed by the La Follette Civil Liberties Committee were nothing to the savagery with which employers sent their hired gunmen against strikers a half century ago. The workmen had no rights except those the employer deigned to grant, and even those were revocable at will. If you don't believe we have advanced, read the history of labor warfare back in Cleveland's time, as told in Harry Barnard's recent life of John Peter Altgeld. It almost makes Tom Girdler look like a sissy.

No, labor's fight from here out will be less to control employers than to control itself, to make itself responsible, and above all for labor leaders to keep their heads, to check their personal vendettas which are damaging not only the public interest but labor itself.

5/27/38

William Green, president of the American Federation of Labor, has lost his United Mine Workers union card, but in his case this is not the tragedy it would be to some less prominent coal miner, because Green had never intended, anyway, to go back to swinging a pick. Union officials never go back to the mines.

No branch of politics carries with it as much social security as labor-union politics. Once a union man peels off his overalls and puts on a white collar, he never takes it off again except to send it to the laundry. When the calluses leave his hands, they go forever.

In regular politics you are the people's choice one year and next year you are in the ash can. Law offices the country over are cluttered up with former political job holders who have had to go back to work.

But your labor-union official has the system. There is no third-term prejudice. Once elected president of a labor union, you have practically a life franchise. Reelection is a mere formality, often accompanied by the gift of a gold watch or a new automobile or, for the more personally vain, a diamond ring. It is one of the sensations of the labor world that Charles P. Howard, for years president of the International Typographical Union, is threatened with defeat in his reelection fight. He would have been in no trouble at all if he had not become involved in the C.I.O.

Many of our national labor leaders, particularly in the A. F. of L., haven't worked at hard labor in 30 years. They all hold on, and there is no room at the top for an ambitious young fellow.

Green hasn't carried a dinner pail for 40 years. He already was a subdistrict president of the United Mine Workers in 1900, before McKinley was shot and before many of you were born. John Lewis took off his overalls and became a labor-union lobbyist 30 years ago. John P. Frey, one of the inside old guard of the A. F. of L. and a leader of the bitter-end faction against Lewis and the C.I.O., is supposed to be a molder, but 35 years ago he had deserted the choking pits to handle a pencil as editor of *The Molders Journal.* Matthew Woll, the fair-haired boy of the late Sam Gompers, rose to be vice-president of the A. F. of L. but is now retired. He was president of the Photo Engravers Union for 25 years.

And our old friend George Berry. He is a United States senator now, a businessman, a banker, a millionaire despite the fact that his $5,000,000 claim against T.V.A. was found worthless, and still he is president of the Printing Pressmen's Union. Thirty years ago, when I was a printer's devil earning a journeyman's card in old Local No. 60 of the International Typographical Union, George Berry already had graduated from the ranks of toil. He was president of the Pressmen's Union and he hasn't fed a press since. Year after year he has been reelected. His seat in the Senate would be safer if he could handle the voters of Tennessee as easily as he does the members of his union.

But who can blame them? Anybody would rather be a big shot in Washington, and have his picture taken on the White House steps, than work for union wages. It's nice work if you can get it. The handsome new offices of John Lewis are finer than President Roosevelt's. He has an automobile that sizes up with the limousines of the Cabinet members.

These labor-union officials have to fight, and their enemies are rich and strong. All that union members ask is that their leaders get results. If they don't get results, they still have their union machines to save them, anyway.

Which is a better arrangement than most regular politicians have. All that the political officeholder can do is to relax and enjoy it while it lasts. He knows that the free haircuts, the official automobiles, the White House invitations, and the soft jobs for his in-laws and children are in constant jeopardy. But the labor-union officeholder is practically indestructible.

3/18/41

Until recently we heard businessmen screaming bitterly about New Deal measures. They were leading to regimentation or communism or something. But today one reads in the annual report of Alfred P. Sloan, Jr., chairman of General Motors and an undying foe of the New Deal, that the Government must do some things. He would have shuddered to think of them a year or two ago.

Businessmen are accepting the intervention of the Government on a scale that a year ago would have been regarded as intolerable. That is what the necessity of this war situation is bringing about.

Sacrifices of privileges also are being asked of labor, but whenever that is suggested, labor puts up a terrific cry that its rights are being infringed.

Labor now is acting much as the economic royalists acted during the previous Roosevelt years. Labor is insisting upon its right to tie up vital defense work by silly jurisdictional strikes like the one at Wright Field. Thurman Arnold, Assistant Attorney General, has some appalling evidence of how extortionate labor-union fees have restricted union memberships so that Army construction work is heavily embarrassed. Labor, which has enjoyed such real progress at the hands of this Administration, now repays that help by threatening defense production at a number of points and by threatening the twin coal and steel strikes that would tie up the two basic industries of the country on Apr. 1.

It took the economic royalists eight years to learn their lesson. One would think that labor leaders, at this late date, would not try the dubious experiment of imitating that unfortunate example.

3/20/41

Some friends of labor in the Administration are very deeply troubled. They are troubled, and I think with good reason indeed, over the fact that labor is working itself into a role of irresponsible obstruction to war production.

Friends of labor within the Administration fear that if labor persists in some of its present attitudes and practices, it will bring down upon its head public condemnation so severe that the real interests of labor will be set back for years.

The foregoing is directed to labor leaders rather than to the rank and file. Administration officials do not regard workmen, individually, as any different from the remainder of the population, nor any less patriotic. They do see that labor leaders, in some instances, bent upon playing union politics, bent upon gaining power, are using this situation in irresponsible ways that ignore the urgent needs of the nation.

The Roosevelt Administration has fought hard, and risked public disapproval, to win gains for labor. More than any other administration in history, it has rescued labor from economic slavery and the dictatorship of management, given labor material rewards and a self-respecting place in the scheme of things. Now, when the Administration is midstream in a tough crossing, labor leaders forget all that and set their time bombs.

This is a sure way to invite fascism. Don't think that thousands of families, into whose homes conscription has reached, will not support the Roosevelt Administration if it is driven to take the hard-boiled way. Mr. Roosevelt will have public sentiment fully behind him. Labor will be isolated, branded, and ruined for years. Those are some of the things being turned over in the minds of some officials here today.

3/28/41

Where is the big, strong Government that is supposed to assert the national will and make it effective above the selfish interests of management and labor groups alike?

So far as I can see, the Government is lying down on the job. It is being defied and ignored with impunity by both sides. The Government is going through some fainthearted motions. But its spirit is plainly so timid and halfhearted that neither management nor labor is taking the Government seriously in these labor disputes. They are brushing it aside as a meddlesome interloper. The call to keep defense production going without interruption is just so many words.

When the showdown came here on the Allis-Chalmers strike, which for more than two months has tied up production essential to powder plants and Navy destroyers, where was Sidney Hillman, the C.I.O. official and cochief with William S. Knudsen? He had slipped out. Secretary Knox and Mr. Knudsen issued a joint statement calling upon both parties in the Allis-Chalmers strike to resume work. But Mr. Hillman did not join in that appeal. It was given out that he was on his way to Florida for a vacation. There are still telegraph wires and long-distance telephones. Why didn't he throw in his word as the labor spokesman on O.P.M.? Mr. Hillman is serving two masters, and that is the trouble with the Administration.

Where is the new Defense Mediation Board? It is hiding under the table. It was created at a moment when serious tie-ups had already thrown defense production for a severe loss. It was confronted with the Bethlehem tie-up, involving a row between C.I.O. and a company union which is wet-nursed by the Bethlehem management. Also, there was the Allis-Chalmers strike, which was driving the Army and Navy to distraction. And around the corner is the March 31 deadline in the coal and steel industries, which are under threat of strike.

Yet the Defense Mediation Board holds one short session, most of which is devoted to having its picture taken. It haggles over whether to move in on these situations or to lie low and wait for a fair wind. It finally decides to lie low, and adjourns to meet in a week or two. Neither the chairman nor the vice-chairman is in town. Philip Murray, a labor member, resumed his role of C.I.O. head and began blasting at William S. Knudsen and Secretary Knox, demanding to know by what right they demanded an end to the Allis-Chalmers tie-up. That does not show much desire to resume work first and adjust differences later.

The Mediation Board appears to have been diluted down into a part-time commuting affair, with some members utilizing the remaining time in adding fuel to labor troubles. This project seems to have been affected by the spirit of weakness and timidity that permeates the whole atmosphere here.

The Government's prestige and moral power are at stake. In Chicago the International Harvester management rejects a union proposal that the dispute be referred to the Mediation Board at Washington. In Milwaukee the appeal of Secretary Knox and Mr.

Knudsen for an end to the strike brings the defiant word from the union spokesman that the strike will go on until the union votes otherwise. The Government is ignored.

Yet the Government dictates what the machine-tool industry shall do, what shipowners shall do with their ships, and it rations aluminum.

In these fields there is no timid and helpless bowing to private rights. Private rights just have to get out of the way of Government needs, and if there isn't a law handy, other ways are found to turn on the heat.

Congress and public opinion have supported the Government in thus overriding private interests. Congress and public opinion are ready to support the Government in overriding private interests in labor disputes. If the Government cannot assert itself in these situations, if the national need cannot prevail over local quarrels between labor and management, then we have a Government without real authority.

12/1/41

If men and women who belong to unions are going to become a special group indifferent to an emergency, determined to strike and slug under any circumstances, then you have a large part of the citizenship refusing to discharge the first obligations of citizenship, and your democracy is folding up to make way for the strong man. We have to assume that the bulk of the citizens who belong to labor unions are like all other Americans and will respond in the same way when not misled by union officials. If we can't assume that, then our form of free government is going to change.

4/3/41

Of course labor alone is not responsible for all of the strike trouble which the country is suffering now. In some of these situations the responsibility lies at the door of management as well.

The Ford strike is the outgrowth of an antiunion policy which has persisted down to this moment. The Bethlehem Steel strikes have been provoked by a similar antiunion policy. The Allis-

Chalmers strike has been prolonged and embittered because the management refused some weeks ago to accept a settlement plan.

Several years ago we wrote into Federal law the policy of collective bargaining. Public opinion has accepted the right of employees to organize and bargain through agents of their own choosing. Most employers have accepted that policy, some willingly, some reluctantly. Although abuses of union organization are many, and although collective bargaining is far from the perfect mechanism that it ought to be, most employers are trying to make the best of it. Hundreds of industries are moving along smoothly with peaceful labor relations. They recognize that the time has gone by when the principle of collective bargaining can be rooted out of a democratic system. It is here, deeply embedded in our system as it is in every other democratic country, and the only practical course is to try to make it work.

But we still have some die-hards who are trying to turn back the clock. They have fought with every weapon, and sometimes with very ugly weapons, as the records of the La Follette Civil Liberties Committee show. They made fester spots.

Bethlehem Steel is still fighting in the courts. The National Labor Relations Board outlawed its company unions and ordered them dissolved. The case has dragged in the courts and still is not decided, although it was more than a year ago that the Labor Board ordered the company unions dissolved. Yet recently the company insisted upon going through with elections of company-union officials, on company property, although it knew that this would provoke a strike—which it did, not only once but in each plant successively when the election was held. No doubt the company had aggravating conditions to contend with, but its insistence upon carrying out the elections showed little disposition to sacrifice a point and to cooperate for defense.

The Ford strike now bursts open in violent form. And so far as I can see the Ford company has asked for it by four years of high-handed refusal to have anything to do with unions. The Associated Press just now quotes Harry Bennett, Ford personnel director, as having said 3 weeks ago that if the C.I.O. did win an election, "we'll bargain till hell freezes over, but bargaining doesn't mean you have to say yes."

A month ago the union filed notice with the Michigan state labor board of its intention to strike. Still the Ford company refused to negotiate with it, or to recognize its existence.

Back of this attitude is the bitterness of Henry Ford himself toward unions. Recently he was quoted as saying that unions are losing ground and haven't a leg to stand on. The Ford management, it seems to me, has long invited trouble. Now the trouble has come and there is interruption of production, violence, and an ugly mess that comforts no one except Hitler.

Ford people complain that Communists are mixed up in the strike. It would be surprising if the Communists were not in it. Ford has given them just the kind of situation on which they thrive. He has been one of their best assets in stirring up discontent among American workers. His stubborn refusal to try, as other automobile companies have done, to work out some method of getting along, has fed labor agitation until now the situation has broken out of hand and is a public menace.

It is getting pretty late for that kind of industrialism.

4/9/37

A vast business, to which are contributed the efforts of many, is no more to be considered the exclusive possession of one man than politically people are to be considered the slaves of an autocratic ruler.

1/13/42

It likewise follows that a monopolistic labor union—which has millions of dollars in operating funds collected for it by employers through the checkoff, which can practically deny a man opportunity to work at his craft, by refusing him union membership or by expelling him, and which has the power by ordering a strike to tie up an entire industry—such a union is as much a legitimate object of public regulation as is a bank or a building-and-loan association.

If an institution holding power over individual savings is a legitimate subject of public regulation, how much more so should be an organization holding power over the means of livelihood of hundreds of thousands of men.

Corporations are compelled to follow certain procedures as to the handling of funds, the voting of stockholders, the rendering of accounts. And they are forbidden to make campaign contributions. It is difficult to see why labor unions should be exempt from similar regulations.

Democratic government cannot tolerate an uncontrolled force stronger than it—whether the rival force be an industry or a labor union.

11/23/43

Maybe labor knows what it is doing, but some of the things that happen don't make sense from anybody's viewpoint, so far as I can see.

For instance, what I saw at Pittsburgh the other day wasn't anything criminally vicious like some of the affairs that Pegler exposes. What I saw was just dumb. You would think American workmen would be smarter.

It was in the Mesta Machine Works at Pittsburgh. They make big guns for the Army and Navy, and drive shafts for cruisers and destroyers, and other heavy work that few other plants can do. I went up there with some Navy officers to inspect the Mesta works where a new unit built for the Navy was to be opened.

Whether the workmen knew the Navy officers were coming through that morning and wanted to put their worst foot forward, or whether it was coincidence, I don't know. But you should have seen the faces of the Navy officers when they went into the foundry and found nothing going on.

It was like going into a giant's tomb. There was no noise. Workmen were loafing around. Several workmen were pitching horseshoes. The clink against the pin was the only sound in that vast, murky shed. The naval officers stood there aghast. But it didn't interfere with the horseshoe game nor with the interest of the workmen in watching it.

Those workmen were involuntarily idle. They couldn't work because during the night the crane operators went on strike. Heavy material could not be moved.

The strike came in a trivial dispute over Sunday work. About seventy-five crane operators went out and tied up most of the rest of the plant employing 4,500 men. The midnight gang started the walkout. At 2 A.M. they telephoned Lorenz Iversen, president of Mesta. He got dressed and went to the plant. He waited until nearly 5 A.M., but the C.I.O. spokesmen still had not arrived and the men wouldn't talk, so Iversen went back home. That the dispute was trivial was indicated when the men went back to work 24 hours later, after Government conciliators said there would be no negotiations until the men returned to work.

Recently, A. F. of L. electricians walked out on the new Mesta Navy plant because power lines were brought into the plant by the power-company electricians, who have their own union. It was a penalty strike, just to register a protest.

That kind of protest strike has occurred before on Navy work in the Pittsburgh area and Navy officers have become bitter about it. No wages are involved—only jurisdictional privileges. There is more work than all can do. Time is essential and every hour counts. Doesn't it seem stupid for a handful of workmen in a plant to walk out on the Navy or the Army just as a petty penalty? The theory is that labor gets even with the company by delaying war orders a day or two.

I don't see how this kind of thing makes sense from anybody's point of view, except perhaps Hitler's. And I don't believe at all that those men are interested in helping Hitler. As I walked through the rest of the plant, where most of the workmen were standing idle by their machines, I saw several huge steel columns, material for giant steel presses to be shipped to Russia. On one of the columns was chalked a patriotic pun as follows:

"You can't spell victory with an absentee."

These men want to keep their freedom. They don't want Hitler to win. Yet Navy officers go up from Washington to show their interest and appreciation, and see idle machinery and workmen pitching horseshoes in the plant.

These labor boys may be clever, but I don't think so. They are just dumb. They are making themselves easy meat for the big anti-labor swing that is on the way in this country.

12/28/43

After a visit among the men at the front, General Eisenhower expressed amazement at the way American and British soldiers had adapted themselves to the miserable fighting conditions in Italy.

The soldiers are up to their knees in mud.

They can't demand a raise. They can't pull a strike.

They just have to take it. Why? As a punishment for some crime? No. Those American boys are over there taking it in the mud so that the United States will be safe from outside attack.

How are we here at home adapting ourselves to the war in order to help those men get it over with as quickly as possible?

Do you read the strike news with those questions in your mind? When you read of a hundred thousand steel workers walking out, you are reading about a hundred thousand men who give a damn for nothing except to get that raise of 17 cents an hour.

For 17 cents an hour they are willing to tie up one of the most necessary of all war industries. For fewer cents than that, thousands of railroad workers have been threatening to tie up the railroads.

How is it that men can become so avaricious, so greedy for a handful of coins that they—many of them with sons of their own fighting at the front—can lie down on the Army and the Navy? How can a few cents a day induce men to go to such lengths as to paralyze the war?

That is what it is. These men are saying, "Give us those extra pennies or we will stop your God-damned war. You pay us or you'll see how far you can go with this war."

That is what the strikers and those who threaten to strike are saying. They are not saying it in words. They are saying it in something far more effective than words—they are saying it with actions.

I don't believe they have thought it through. They listen to labor politicians. They look back to the old days when labor had to fight to get justice. They are still under the spell of habits and methods adopted when the only way a highhanded employer could be brought to time was to shut up his shop.

But these are not really strikes against employers. In fact the railroads are ready to grant the wage increases asked. These are strikes against the Government. These are strikes by people against themselves. These are strikes against the Little Steel Formula of the War Labor Board. These are strikes against the effort of the Government to prevent runaway wages and runaway prices, those twin evils which always race toward inflation hand in hand.

These are strikes against the best friend labor ever had in the White House—against the man who has been damned for a decade in every country club in America, damned because he was a friend of labor, damned because he was trying to bring about a fair deal for labor, and because he curbed the avarice of the rich.

Now when the interests of the nation require that he curb the avarice of labor, the answer of labor is to strike at the two most vital war industries. Labor's friend in the White House asks that they keep war industries going, and stay at work, and he promises fair adjustment of their demands.

The plea is ignored. Thousands walk out. In some localities the steel strikers carry placards saying, "No contract, no work."

What joy this must bring to Berlin! You know the Nazi propaganda line being put out through Turkey. It is that if the German army will hold out until after the American election, the people in America will get rid of Roosevelt and quit the war. Strikes against war industries help the Nazis keep the war going.

It is enough to make President Roosevelt wish he was Westbrook Pegler.

Wartime Stresses on Democracy —Inflation and Taxation

11/29/43

THE old-timer in Congress will tell the freshman that the way to stay in office is to vote in favor of all appropriation bills and against all tax bills. That is sound advice for one whose object is to be reelected.

But shouldn't some chances be taken, considering it is wartime?

If you swallow what some are saying around Washington you become convinced that the country can't stand another penny of taxes.

Although the Administration asks for 10½ billion more in taxes, Republicans and Democrats alike cry that this will break the country.

Republican members of the House Ways and Means Committee join in solemnly reporting that they would be false to their trust were they to "saddle this heavy additional burden on the backs of taxpayers already heavily burdened." Democrats sided with the Republicans and they appeared in a love feast recommending 2½ billions instead of 10½. Senate Republicans and Senate Democrats indicate they will take the same position. The Administration won't stand for a sales tax. That would be unpopular in the lower brackets.

So there you are.

They do put up two excuses. One excuse is that Government war expenses won't be as heavy as had been estimated some months ago. True. We will spend 92 billion instead of 100 billion. By June the national debt will be 194 billions instead of 8 or 10 billions more.

The second excuse is that the country can't afford more taxes. You can get hard-luck stories from every group in the country.

And by the time the testimony is assembled it appears that there is not a single cent left that Internal Revenue could take.

Taxes are high and we could well believe that they could not go any higher, and that, as the House Ways and Means Republicans say, it takes only one straw to break the camel's back, and that if we put on more taxes now people will slow down in war production and their morale will break. Maybe so.

But it is interesting to look in the back of the newspaper, at the financial-page news. I got so depressed over this crybaby tax stuff that I turned to *The New York Times'* financial section to brace up my morale.

There I found department-store sales, as reported by the Federal Reserve Board, running 20 per cent more than a year ago, and in some cases 40 or 50 per cent higher.

Some allowance must be made for higher prices this year. Even so, there must be a terrific amount of money to spend when department-store sales are up over a year ago by such percentages as these: Akron, 26; Atlanta, 37; Birmingham, 29; Boston, 20; Buffalo, 22; Chicago, 17; Cincinnati, 23; Columbus, 40; Dallas, 61; Ft. Worth, 47; Houston, 51; Indianapolis, 42; Louisville, 31; Oklahoma City, 54; San Antonio, 30; Tulsa, 42.

Further in *The New York Times'* financial section I see the S.E.C. report on salaries, headlined: "Salary Increases Heavy in Two Years." "Many Increases of 100 Per Cent." These are reports of 121 corporations, mostly doing war work. Probably the men are worth what they are paid. As a hired hand I always favor high salaries.

But the figures don't indicate any condition of poverty either on the part of the companies or of the executives. Eugene Grace of Bethlehem Steel remained the individual leader, his salary going from $478,000 in 1940 to $537,000 in 1942. Second place went to Roland Chilton, of Wright Aeronautical, who jumped from $168,000 in 1941 to $372,000 last year. Some jumps appear to cover increased taxes.

People who make good money should be the last to complain of high taxes. If a man is earning enough to pay the Government money that will keep the war going 30 seconds, or a full minute, or that will pay for a hospital where the casualties of those bloody hours at Tarawa can be restored, he ought to be glad to serve as a tax collector for Uncle Sam. Big taxpayers always have enough left to live on.

10/21/43

At best, taxes are not raised easily in a democracy. Candidates who promise lower taxes are likely to be more popular with the voters. Those responsible for higher taxes become easy targets for the political hokum of unscrupulous and irresponsible opponents.

Republicans don't intend to be caught asleep on this. A political campaign is coming next year and the Republicans are behaving so that nobody can accuse them of having anything to do with high taxes.

Republican members of the House Ways and Means Committee banded together in a statement opposing additional taxes. They are against the sales tax as well as increased income taxes. Democrats on the committee say that it will be almost impossible for any tax increase to go through in face of this solid Republican opposition.

The Republicans made it a matter of party policy through the endorsement of the Republican House leader, Representative Martin, who called for further economies before higher taxes are demanded.

With the Republican demand for economy, for curbing wastefulness in the Government, there can be only the strongest support from anybody who sees his money being thrown around like water in some places in Washington. Everybody seems to be on the Federal pay roll. Some of the agencies are cluttered with people who are hard put to think up work for themselves. The arsenal of bureaucracy still is intact. One of the most useful functions of an opposition is to prevent Government waste.

The Republican demand for reduction of waste would carry more force if it were not so crudely used as an alibi for ducking the unpleasant duty of voting higher taxes.

Republicans miss the real point—either deliberately or through ignorance. Even if Representative Taber's optimistic estimate of $4,000,000,000 in economies proved out, that would not remove the need for higher tax revenue and particularly for a sales tax.

This business has two aspects. One is the necessity of holding down the public debt, which is 168 billion dollars and threatens to go to 300 by the end of the war. Every possible economy is desirable. Also the maximum Federal revenue is desirable.

Equally important—perhaps even more so in the long run—is the danger of uncontrollable inflation. That requires ruthless taxation to hold down individual spending. The Republican economy program does not meet that need. We need not only Government economy, we need individual private economy that will take surplus family money out of circulation and stop the scramble of the householder for the scarce goods.

Even though middle-bracket income taxes seem high, reaching 25 per cent at $10,000, retail stores show there is enormous spending money in the country. Sales taxes are needed. As Representative Monroney of Oklahoma tells the House Ways and Means Committee, it is possible to provide sales-tax exemptions for the very lowest income groups. Taxes are severe. But severe measures are needed to prevent inflation.

In that struggle the Republicans are giving the country no help. They are sitting down. They intend to leave it to the Administration. If the Republican refusal to cooperate prevents any tax increase, as is probably to be the case, then the country is left to face the dangers of inflation.

You can't hold the Republicans alone to blame. They are following the lead of the National Association of Manufacturers, which this week registered opposition to any tax increase. They are likewise afraid of the sales tax, following the lead of Philip Murray of the C.I.O., who threatened the House committee with a general wage-increase demand from all labor if a sales tax is voted.

Pressure groups, the reluctance of the Administration to go for a sales tax, political fears, the determination of politicians to play it safe for election regardless of what the situation requires, are all combining to paralyze us on the fiscal side at a time of crisis in our struggle against inflation.

That is a painless invitation to trouble.

11/8/43

A few days ago Henry Morgenthau, Secretary of the Treasury, came back from a visit to the front in Italy. He said our soldiers were worried that back home we would not pay enough of the war costs as we went along. The soldiers felt they would have to fight the war and then come home and help pay for it.

The Roosevelt Administration is trying to put the war as much as possible on a pay-as-you-go basis. The Government is meeting a little more than one third of its war expenditures from taxes. The Administration has hoped for a half-and-half plan and still urges that we pay for about half the cost of the war by taxes and half by borrowing.

Britain and Canada are going about half-and-half, although the British taxpayers do not have our high state taxes.

In the last war, Secretary of Treasury McAdoo at first set a half-and-half goal. Later he scaled it down to one third from taxes and two thirds from loans. If we count in the unpaid foreign war loans, we raised only about one quarter by taxes.

But it was different then. When we went into the First World War, the public debt was about 1 billion dollars. When Pearl Harbor hit us, we had a debt of about 55 billions. A nation with a small debt can wisely borrow more than one which already has a large debt from past borrowing. But interest rates are lower now so that the carrying charge is far less. We can carry 10 billion now for what it cost to carry 5 billion in the other war.

You hear people ask, "How high can the debt go without becoming dangerous?" It is a trick question. The debt can go as high as is necessary to finance the war. There literally is no limit except the resources of the country, the raw materials, the plants, the labor that can be commandeered for the war and the confidence of the people. Before the last war, some economists said there never would be another great war because the cost would bankrupt the nations.

Economists said Hitler would go bankrupt. He continued to build airplanes and tanks.

Once here in the earlier New Deal days some of our economists said public credit would totter if our debt went above 50 billion. But it is now 175 billion and the Government borrows at no increase in interest rates—and you don't know of any safer investment than a Government bond.

A nation's debt must be considered in proportion to its income. If we finished the war with a 300-billion-dollar debt and had an annual national income as a people of 150 billion, which is possible—then our debt would be only twice our annual income as a people. For a corporation, a debt twice the income would be considered safe.

After our previous wars—except the last one—we paid off the entire debt as time went on. At the close of the last war our debt was about 26½ billion. We were paying it off gradually and only owed 16 billion by 1930 when the depression hit us.

But why try to pay it off? Many corporations simply redeem their bonds as they fall due by refinancing with new borrowing.

The conservative British haven't tried to reduce their last war debt.

I was at a White House press conference several years ago when President Roosevelt was talking to us about the size of the public debt. It worried the Republicans. And Mr. Roosevelt was saying that after all, government debt was somewhat different from an individual citizen's debt. The government debt we owed to ourselves. That statement was greeted with howls of derision as loose New Deal thinking. Yet not long ago I heard a very wealthy Republican say substantially the same thing. It means that the people of the United States, represented by their Government, owe the debt to themselves as individuals. You and I have lent the Government money. So has your insurance company, your bank, your college endowment fund.

Practically all of us are paying income taxes. Part of our income tax goes to pay interest on the public debt—interest on war bonds. At the same time practically all of us own some war bonds on which we receive interest, either directly or in the form of redemption values above the cost. We pay income tax to the Government so the Government can pay us interest on our bonds. As Stuart Chase says, the American people are on both sides of the balance sheet.

If the public debt were to be repudiated, most of us would suffer a loss in our capital. But at the same time most of us would gain by paying less income tax to pay interest charges on the debt. Of course, many poor persons would lose more than they would gain, and many rich persons would gain more than they would lose. So repudiation would be grossly unfair, and there is absolutely no possibility of it.

What we are really wondering about is whether the debt will be reduced in effect by inflation—that is, by reducing the value of money or by prices going sky high—and wages too.

A large public debt is safe as long as the national income of the people remains high. If the income falls, then the situation might become dangerous. That is why we must have high economic activity, good employment, good business, after the war.

Deflation would be dangerous because with people out of work, with earnings severely cut, government revenue would fall. It would be more difficult to meet carrying charges, and in fact we should probably be compelled to borrow more money because when conditions are bad, the Government must spend more than when business is good. When times are hard, the Government must finance public works, and relief, and put up money to help banks and corporations over tight spots. It must increase its pay roll to handle these additional services. So hard times and deflation would leave us in a position where we might have to borrow money to pay the interest on the debt, which would be a most unsound position.

On the other hand, inflation would be equally bad. That means our money will buy less. Government bonds would be worth that much less so you would get back from the Government only part of what you paid—in terms of what the money would buy. Inflation is our chief danger. Inflation is one of those things that is feared and denounced in the abstract but in the concrete is embraced without our recognizing it.

Inflation is here now—we are in the foothills of inflation, as Randolph Paul, Treasury tax advisor, said today. There are more customers than there are silk stockings, or fine furs. Storekeepers can get any price they demand on furs. You have price inflation when the volume of goods is less than the demand and when the price is not controlled. Retailers like inflation—at first. They move their goods fast at larger margins of profit. That's in the early days before it is openly recognized or called inflation. It is called prosperity, or good brisk business then. But soon prices rise so fast the merchant, after selling his goods, has to pay much more for his new stock, and he may have to wait to get it. Meantime his money continues to shrink in value.

I saw wild inflation in China a year and a half ago. Merchants literally tried not to sell their goods—they were better off holding the goods than having the Chinese paper money which was being flown into China by airplane loads and which was growing more worthless every day.

The best way to hold back inflation is to levy high taxes. Take the money out of our pockets so we can't throw it away in a wild orgy of spending such as is going on in many places now—take the money to help pay for the war, and to hold down the debt. Leave less for the American soldiers to pay when they come back.

11/9/43

All over Washington the pressure groups are out in hobnailed shoes trying to break through the controls and get foot-loose for an inflation orgy. Sound-money Republicans, so-called, do not lift a voice in protest. The town is full of high-pressure experts.

Everybody is represented in the big push except the little fellow in the middle, the white-collar salaried worker, his salary frozen. He is unorganized. He has no lobbyist or labor leader here to put the squeeze on for him.

Oh, yes. There's somebody else not represented. That's the American soldier who someday will come back. It is a fine kettle of fish we are cooking up for him.

11/17/43

Apparently we are set to be taken for a cynical profiteer's ride into uncontrolled price inflation.

Everything around here points to that.

Unorganized consumers and workers, salaried men and women, millions of them, are for all practical purposes unrepresented at Washington right now. They are about to be handed the big gyp.

Congress is surrounded by lobbyists who know what they want. They want the lid taken off prices. That is what the lawyer representing the Texas cattle growers told the Senate Agriculture Committee this week. A senator asked what he wanted in place of price control. He said he wanted the law of supply and demand.

That is a polite way of asking for a profiteer's market. Bernard Baruch has said a lot about that. With the Government, the war, as the big customer for everything, you cannot have normal operation of supply and demand as a price regulator. Demand is abnormal because of the war. Of course everybody knows that. This is only a demand for collecting all that the traffic will bear under these abnormal conditions.

The figures show what is being done now to hold down meat prices as against what happened in the last war when prices were uncontrolled, as the cattlemen's lawyer advocates now.

Here are the Bureau of Labor statistics retail price increases for the war years July 1914-18 and the corresponding price increases in the 4 years of this war. In percentages the figures are as follows:

PERCENTAGE INCREASE	1914-18	1939-43
Round steak	65.2	14.3
Rib roast	59.3	16.6
Chuck roast	72.2	29.3
Pork chops	70.0	23.0
Bacon	90.9	38.8
Sliced ham	75.2	13.4

Please look back over those figures and see how much better the housewife has been protected against rising prices this time.

Ordinary meat prices went up 70 per cent in many cases in the last war. This time the increases run from 15 per cent and the highest quoted is 38 per cent.

With the scarcity of meat available to consumers, you can well imagine what prices would be charged if we went back to supply and demand as the cattlemen want.

They are not doing so badly either. In the last war the price of live cattle went up 58 per cent, but this time they are getting 89 per cent more than at the start of the war. Hog prices went up 102 per cent in the last war and this time they are up 150 per cent.

The cattlemen are not the only ones who are down here with a blackjack. The labor crowd is running wild, demanding resignations from the War Labor Board, hammering Congress to overrule Economic Stabilization Director Vinson and grant a larger wage increase than he authorized. Ickes is asking higher coal prices than O.P.A. recommends because of the increased wages given to John Lewis.

It is a sickening thing to see happening in wartime, this greedy raid all around. American men are dying all around the world and Washington is engulfed in an obscene grab for the Almighty Dollar.

These pressure groups are running wild. Washington is being terrorized and every politician is fleeing for his life to fall in with the demand to break up price control and allow the cost of living to bounce up as high as the war shortages will carry it.

We are in serious danger. The greatest danger is that men in Washington are not standing up to it. We are not proving ourselves worthy of the men at the front if we give way now at home to an orgy of profiteering with everybody grabbing for rich white meat from the carcass of this war for security and peace.

Prewar

7/14/34

GENERAL HUGH S. JOHNSON, speaking at Waterloo, Iowa, denounced Adolf Hitler's recent "bloody purge" of the Nazi ranks as follows:

"A few days ago, in Germany, events occurred which shocked the world. I don't know how they may have affected you, but they made me sick—not figuratively, but physically and very actively sick. The idea that adult responsible men can be taken from their homes—stood up against a wall—backs to the rifles—and shot to death—is beyond expression. I have seen something of that sort among semicivilized people or savages half-drunk on sotol and marajuana—but that such a thing should happen in a country of some supposed culture passes comprehension."

7/15/34

There are broad aspects of the general situation in Germany which have potential importance in the United States. Internal chaos in Germany would be expected to retard economic recovery throughout Europe and to have a certain depressing effect in the United States. It would certainly delay the hope of major revival in American export trade. It would tend to prolong the necessity of restricting of American agriculture to a domestic consumption. The world has grown so small that a breakdown in one spot spreads its evil effects in ever-widening circles outside.

4/20/34

The United States has become the chief source of scrap iron for Japan which is obliged, through lack of natural resources, to import material for its large steel industry. Exports have risen sharply in the last two years. There are no data here to indicate how much of this is going into war materials.

For the moment the Administration takes the position that private industry is free to sell its goods wherever it finds customers.

11/35

How wholeheartedly American sentiment favored going into the European war in 1917 will always be debatable. Certainly the 1916 election showed there was tremendous sentiment against such participation. But events overcame such isolationist desire as there was, and we went in. And the moment it was over we snapped back more firmly than ever to our desire to keep out of other people's wars. This feeling was intensified by the long and futile attempt to collect the war debts.

Such international action as we took thereafter was always predicated on this strong isolationist feeling. Our enthusiasm for the Kellogg peace pact was a negative thing. The desire to prevent wars, which might involve us again, found its expression in a pious pledge by all nations that they would never resort to war as an instrument of policy. We have seen this pledge broken by Japan and by Italy. These affairs have only increased our isolationist inclination.

That the United States could go into the League of Nations and participate fully seems completely out of the question. That it can remain doggedly aloof, maintain its neutral trading "rights," and carry on commerce with a nation declared the aggressor seems equally difficult.

Such a course probably would subject this country's trade to interferences that would be irritating if nothing more. It would certainly subject the American government to a loss of prestige and to ill will among the great powers which would in the long run prove harmful. It would label us as an irresponsible people, and perhaps for many years to come would seriously affect our standing in the world. Most serious of all, it might prove an encouragement to some other nation to take a reckless course and thus bring new dangers upon the world.

11/12/37

During 20 years of political reporting in America I have observed all sorts of national politicians in action, but I never have encountered anything as puzzling as the worship of the German people for Hitler.

Soon after I arrived here in Berlin I saw Hitler in action before an audience of 20,000.

Nazi political theatricals are unmatched in America. We have nothing like the impressive entrance of the color guard advancing through a lane of black shirts, followed by lines of brown shirts marching in to fill the side aisles. Finally the stage is set. There is a period of breathless silence. The rear doors are flung open and with the whole audience standing with arms extended in the Nazi salute, Hitler, a man of slightly less than medium height, wearing a raincoat, strides down the center aisle.

Hundreds, with arms still outstretched in salute, scramble toward the aisle to see him more closely. He returns the salute by flipping his arm upward very quickly, looking straight ahead, poker-faced, as if in a trance.

He mounts the platform and faces the audience. It strikes the foreigner as an anticlimax because as Hitler stands there after this impressive military build-up, with no flicker of a smile on his face, there is some hint of comic appearance—undoubtedly arising in American minds because his mustache suggests Charlie Chaplin.

Hitler begins to speak. His voice has no arresting quality, none of the smooth resonance of Roosevelt's nor the sharply penetrating huskiness of Al Smith—the two most effective political speakers I have ever heard. But soon his tempo increases until his words are pouring out in torrents, his neck cords bulging. Interrupted by applause, he twists his neck and rolls his eyes upward while waiting to resume.

I have observed countless audiences and never have I seen more intense or more sustained attention. Not a head turns away. Laughs and applause burst forth from all parts of the hall with the bursting impact which comes only from spontaneity, not from claque leaders. I have never seen an audience more a unit. There were only two persons in the hall—Hitler and the audience—completely meshed in their mutual responsiveness. As he left, the crowd again surged to the center aisle to be near him.

I hear of underground grumbling, but I believe Hitler has the fanatical devotion of a large majority of the German people. The others are forced into acquiescence but they are the minority. I am told that in rural Germany children pray to Hitler at night. He is the German god, a brooding, fanatical figure, who becomes more incredible as you read his *Mein Kampf.*

His secret must include his obvious sincerity, his fanatical devotion to Germany. Also he has by military and diplomatic aggressiveness restored the pride of the German people. Then he has put everyone back to work, literally. It may be unsound work, armaments, work camps, or what, but everyone is working. Factory chimneys pour out smoke even on Sundays, as I saw around Essen. This may be at suicidal cost, but the machinery is turning. Theatricals, propaganda, and compulsion are not enough to account for the enthusiasm for Hitler. He is the miracle man to the German people.

Although no one questions that he could carry a truly free election overwhelmingly, he is open in his contempt for democracy. He says bluntly that he must have unquestioning obedience. He gets it. Most of it is offered gladly, the rest forced by the iron hand. This phenomenon seems natural to an ignorant people but not to the intelligent, advanced German nation. Yet there it is.

As an American, believing in democracy, I see these things with one reaction. No human being is wise enough to deserve to hold millions of his fellow men in his absolute power, without their right to question or change.

In Germany as in Russia, whole peoples have been thrown back into the age of despotism. They have lost all semblance of control over their own destinies. The only thing to be said in favor of these systems is that physically an attempt is being made by these dictators to improve the conditions of life. Modern dictators have that in their favor as against the old despots.

In return they rob their subjects of the right to think, deprive them of the opportunity to think. Newspapers, books, magazines, education are all shaped to permit these people to know only what the dictator wants them to know, to hold only the opinions he wants them to hold. No man deserves to have such power. But they have it.

And the strangest thing of all is that if you put it to a vote, in either Russia or Germany, the people would not change it.

Well, they can have it. All of it.

11/8/37

Labor under the Nazi regime has been rather thoroughly enslaved, but the government seeks to soften the rigors of the system with its "Joy Through Work" campaign. This is a skillful propaganda activity which provides workingmen with low-priced holiday trips, morale-building activities, and a good deal of talk about the "beauty of labor."

As part of this general campaign workingmen are encouraged to make their surroundings as attractive as possible. Accordingly, in one factory which I visited, employees recently had obtained permission from the management to convert an unused plot within the factory grounds into a flower garden. Each employee donated one hour of his own time to making flower beds—that is, each employee except one, who said he had other use for his spare time. Promptly a Nazi party official, to whom the incident had been reported, took his working card or "labor passport" away from him. His discharge from his job was automatic and he will be unable to obtain another job, as employers are forbidden to hire anyone without a government working card. This suggests the severity of the discipline.

Often it was said in defense of slavery in the South that the Negro was cared for by his master and was always sure of food and shelter. Much the same may be said for labor under the Nazi regime. Also you can say the same for workers in Communist Russia. The standard of living is higher than that which American slaves had to endure, but there is little more freedom. The workman in Russia and Germany pays a price for his subsistence. The price is the virtually complete surrender of his freedom. The difference is that in Russia they promise to give him back his freedom someday and in Germany they don't.

Under both regimes at present the workman is the economic slave of a dictator. He is as much subject to the supreme will at the top as if he were living under Ivan the Terrible. He does get better food and clothing perhaps. But what the Communists call the slaves of capitalism are as free as air compared with robots of fascism and Communism. Over here and in Moscow they say that capitalism gives the workman the freedom to walk the streets in search of a job. Here they guarantee him a job—in fact, if he has nothing better, they compel him to work on the road gangs or at some other form of forced labor. You can take your choice.

In Russia the individual works for the state and is as bound to it as if he were in the army. In Germany he technically works for a private employer, but in designated industries he is forbidden to change his employment without permission of the government labor office. Under this procedure the worker is virtually bound to his job, a situation probably without precedent in the modern capitalistic state.

People are told—both employees and their bosses—what they have to do. The government calls it "the obligation to produce," and the obligation is whatever the government says it is, regardless of the wishes and plans of the individual manufacturer, farmer, or workman. For instance, employers in essential industries may not increase their personnel by more than ten men within a three-month period without government permission.

Nazi policy is that the interest of capital and labor alike must be submerged in the state. Trades unions and employers' associations have been merged into a single "Labor Front." Employees, with the approval of the party, elect a plant spokesman. In one plant which I visited he was a minor clerical employee. He negotiates with the management regarding minor plant matters, such as sanitary facilities. Soon after the Nazi regime came in the old-line labor leaders surrendered without a struggle; many were thrown into prison; and labor was taken over and knit into the state as completely as the army, for all practical purposes.

Every youth is conscripted for six months' duty in labor camps prior to two years' army service. Soon every girl also will be conscripted for six months' labor-camp duty. All classes must serve. They all do manual work. There is a democratizing benefit to this and a physical benefit which is not without its worth. But the period is used for intensive "political education." In effect, while building youthful bodies, the regime warps their minds so that—it hopes—they will forever afterward know only Nazi philosophy.

Physically, labor is perhaps better off under the regime than it could have been without rigid control, considering the acute shortage of raw materials. But the price paid is permanent distortion of the mind so that always what Hitler says is right and above question. They think that is a necessary price.

But I hear that in some other countries people manage to keep from starving while retaining some of that freedom of thought and action which, to Americans anyway, is one of the great privileges of civilization.

11/5/37

I unlearned a good deal about Fascist Germany by talking with an employer. He manufactures for general retail sale and is not producing for either rearmament or export, and therefore does not have the special privileges which those two classes enjoy. So he can be regarded as typical of the ordinary manufacturer in Germany, a capitalist trying to get along.

He wouldn't say it himself, but the first thing that was apparent was that Fascist Germany is no more run for the special benefit of the employer than Soviet Russia is for the special benefit of the worker. Under both systems the individual exists for the state, not the state for the individual. In both countries labor, management, and property are under control and dictation by the state. What Stalin or Hitler says goes all down the line, even to the price the butcher charges for a slice of pork. Hence the wisecrack, current underground here, that the chief difference between Russia and Germany is that Russia has colder weather.

In Russia all means of production—factories, farms, and the stores which distribute the products—are owned by the state. In Germany the title is left in the hands of the private owner, but that is about all he retains. He has little control over his property. He must operate it at the direction of the state. The government fixes the wages he pays, the cost of his raw materials, his prices, in many instances the amount he can produce. It tells him whether he may enlarge his factory or not, and whether he may discharge his employees. It drastically limits his profits. In fact it controls everything, including the squeal, because if he objects he is likely to find himself out on the sidewalk if not worse. Criticism is practically treason.

Because the supply of many manufacturing materials is extremely limited in Germany the government rations out much of it, giving first preference to manufacture for export—because of the acute need of obtaining foreign exchange—and the next preference to armament manufacture. After that, what is oddly called "free industry" can scramble for the remainder.

Perhaps my manufacturing friend wants 10 tons of sheet steel. He knows that the supplier of steel will have many more orders than he can fill and will favor the customer who can provide him with some scrap metal in exchange. So before going out to buy sheet steel, my friend tries to obtain 10 tons of scrap metal with which to sweeten the deal.

The junkman, therefore, is important in Germany. Citizens are required to save metal tooth-paste tubes. School children have holidays so they can collect bones for glue factories and horse chestnuts for vegetable oil. For a time the government solved every man's problem of disposing of used razor blades by collecting them. But this laudable activity later was abandoned. Handling the blades was too troublesome.

This manufacturer was ordered by the government to cease using copper for certain parts of his product. Instead of zinc-coated metal he was obliged to use a plastic, like bakelite, in parts where government experts decided the substitution could be made. In dozens of respects his operations are regulated by decrees which come rolling out of the Nazi government offices without warning or argument. He can't fire workmen. If he finds an employee inefficient he takes it up with the government. He can't hire a workman who does not have a government "labor passport" or work card. Having fixed the price of his product, he can't increase it without government consent and then only after a showing that his production costs have risen more than 20 per cent.

If the government decides his product isn't needed and is therefore taking raw materials from some more essential activity, he must close down. And he can't shut up his plant unless the government approves. Dividends over 6 per cent must be paid in government bonds—practically a confiscation of his profits above 6 per cent. Furthermore, corporation profits are taxed roughly 30 per cent, plus special levies to finance export subsidies, and the usual property taxes. Personal income taxes are graduated up to 50 per cent.

So the businessman under fascism escapes with his shirt but little more, unless he happens to be favored as a producer of rearmament material, in which case the government is apt to be generous in the prices it pays so that he can count upon a fair slice of velvet.

And the whole process of business activity is so difficult, so cluttered with red tape, government permits, decrees, and bureaucracy that there is much lost motion and heavy overhead expense.

Dictatorship is not as efficient as private capitalism in the ordinary operating processes. Its advantage is that the government can control the industrial machine for special purposes, and in cases of shortages can still get what it wants. But if any businessman in America thinks he is having a hard time and longs for a fascist dictator, he is crazy. He would have no strike problem, but in place of that he would have a dozen problems that are worse.

11/3/37

The Soviet Union is observing its twentieth anniversary this week and shortly will hold its first general elections under the new democratic constitution. These two events are significant, one as to the past, the other as to the future.

In 20 years the Soviet regime has taken a country that was in ruins and one which had never really undertaken to develop its tremendous natural resources, a country which was as needlessly wretched as any on earth, and has put it on the path toward industrial greatness.

This pioneering task has been carried on under almost inconceivable difficulties. Not only was there no going plant to begin with, but the wreckage of a most backward civilization has had to be cleared away and that task is far from completed.

For instance, the Soviet regime has inherited from the past an ignorant, untrained people unbelievably clumsy in craftsmanship, cursed with slovenly habits of work and with a tradition of terrorism, secret police, stupid bureaucracy, and an almost complete absence of the tools of modern industrial life. The Soviet Union has to build its national house, teach its people up through childhood an entirely new set of habits, and all the while keep its rifle in hand—as did our own pioneers in the Indian country—against attack from without.

In that gigantic undertaking Soviet leaders have shown great courage, astounding determination, resourcefulness, and persistence which lead me to think that in the end they will succeed. There is a national will at work which is as determined as was our own in our early days. The Soviet Union is learning as it goes along and its efforts often are wasteful and ineffective, as were many of our own. But as in our case, it has the cushion of great natural resources, which compensates for many human failures. No matter how many failures they experience here, they still have food, coal, iron, cotton, and wool, so that they can get through somehow.

As an industrial nation Russia still is in a primitive stage. I believe its industrial maturity is yet a considerable distance in the future. At least it must wait until the oncoming generation has been thoroughly trained in workmanship. And it must wait until the technique of administration has been more fully mastered. Perhaps many changes in forms of control will have to be made. It is a question still whether such a vast, complicated industrial civilization as is possible here can be operated by one central nervous system concentrated in a few hands. One virtue of capitalism is that it is to a large degree self-motivating and self-controlling. The Soviet system operates down to the last minor individual unit from a central control tower and it is questionable whether any small group can manage such a vast mechanism successfully.

Although the new constitution is a quite democratic document, carrying guarantees of personal liberty similar to ours, it is likely to remain a theoretical instrument for a long time to come. The dictatorship is all powerful and absolute and shows no signs of relaxing. The regime simply brushes aside the constitution by saying it was not intended that it should be used as a screen for opponents of the regime. Democracy as contemplated under the constitution undoubtedly is many years away at best.

Russia has nothing to gain by war and I am convinced will go to great lengths to avoid it. War would be disastrous. Russia has nothing to gain by conquest. She has all she wants. But she is a rich prize and is fearful of attack and therefore has concentrated on defense, which is far in advance of the national development otherwise. She is able now apparently to protect herself against any probable enemy.

In my opinion the future of the Soviet Union will not be determined for some time, not until the oncoming generation now being trained has its chance to show what it can do. Stalin's hope is based on youth. It is being given every possible training for industrial life.

If this growing generation can, through education, escape the curse of old national habits, if it can learn the use of modern tools, learn modern administrative technique, find ways of functioning without resort to demoralizing espionage and terrorism, we are likely to see here in years to come one of the great civilizations of the world.

The Soviet regime has changed almost everything except human nature. The test is whether it can change that. If it can, then it can do anything. If not—then a monumental tragedy must be in store.

3/17/38

Such are the depths to which standards have sunk that because Chamberlain has a decent and humanitarian reluctance to subject his people to the mass murder of modern warfare if he can find any other way out, he is branded as a weakling. Because he does not itch to send English youths to their death and to expose England to devastation, he is viewed with contempt by Hitler, Mussolini, and their worshipers. Because the English people have not been abased and have not been mentally warped into unquestioning obedience of a reckless fanatic, they are pictured as soft.

Hitler, on the other hand, is having his triumphs now. The man who pulls his gun on no provocation, who incites his followers to outrages upon feeble victims whose only crime was to have been born of a race which Hitler happens personally to despise, is hailed as the strong man. Hitler is the hero of what has been so aptly termed the brutalitarian state.

Added to Hitler's laurels now are the agonizing suicides in Vienna, part of his liberation of Austria. A former vice-chancellor kills his wife and their nineteen-year-old son and then shoots himself, preferring death to the kind of liberation he was doomed to receive from the Nazis. An industrialist's daughter kills her father and shoots herself. A professor of medicine at Innsbruck and his daughter commit suicide, as do a prominent Vienna dermatologist and his wife.

Those desperate escapes from the persecution of the Nazis are the fruit of Hitler's liberation of Austria. They are the fruit of his own agitation. He asks for it in his book *Mein Kampf,* which is the Bible of the Nazis. He describes how he developed his hatred of Jews: "From being a feeble world-citizen I became a fanatical anti-Semite. . . . Thus did I now believe that I must act in the sense of the Almighty Creator; by defending myself against the Jews, I am fighting for the Lord's work."

This book revels in brutal contempt for weaker peoples, for minorities, for democracy, and glorifies the absolute dictator. "In small things and great," Hitler says, "the movement stands for the principle of unquestioned authority of the leader, combined with the fullest responsibility. . . . The greatness of any active organization which is the embodiment of an idea lies in the spirit of religious fanaticism and intolerance in which it attacks all others, being fanatically convinced that it alone is right."

Hitler calls himself a fanatic. No one will dispute him.

Such is the hero of the moment. Not only of his own subjects. But of some Americans. Surprisingly I have received numbers of letters defending and lauding Hitler. A businessman in Alabama writes me that he has read "with amazement your column where you abuse Adolf Hitler so unjustly."

And a reader in Pittsburgh floors me with this:

"I am an American but still I am 100 per cent for him [Hitler]. He has the blessing of God in Heaven or else he couldn't perform miracles like he is doing. No one out of work in Germany. All babies healthy because Hitler sees to it. No ugly girls. Very few young people wear glasses. Very few have false teeth. Hitler looks after them. . . . I wish we had a man in this country that had the power of God to do the same thing."

But perhaps the footnote to this man's letter tells the story. He says, "I am an American, down and out, wife, four small children, live on unemployment insurance. Willing to work but there ain't no jobs because every Democratic politician has two to four jobs for himself. . . . God bless Hitler."

That letter is from Pittsburgh, U.S.A. When democratic capitalism doesn't take care of people, they are apt to welcome anything else that does. Liberty becomes less important than bread.

10/31/38

This country has not even begun to grasp the domestic significance of the defense program which has been made imperative by Germany's sudden domination of Europe and the breakdown of Great Britain as the unofficial but very real policeman of the world.

With Munich a new world was born. In that Caesarean operation, a huge chunk of world power changed hands. It passed from the democratic bloc led by Britain to the authoritarian bloc led by Germany. This epochal shift of power has suddenly left the United

States standing alone and unprotected in the world game of power politics. In a word, Britain has been our first line of defense. Britain has been a protector of the Monroe Doctrine. Britain, almost as much as the United States, has stood firmly for the status quo on the Western Hemisphere. Now she is no longer able to serve forcefully in that role. Britain dares not use her fleet now against the wish of Hitler, for fear he will blow the British Isles out of the water from the air. We are now on our own in protecting the Western Hemisphere.

That fundamental transfer of the seat of power, from London to Berlin, necessitates internal changes in our affairs which will be so important as to make our present political issues, and the partisan bickering over New Deal measures, seem like trivial nursery babble.

Last week the utilities industry agreed to embark upon a gigantic expansion program. The expansion will take place, not entirely as private enterprise desires, but in sections where the Government says it is necessary for national defense. War industry needs adequate power and it is the War Department, together with Federal Power Commission experts, who are telling the utility people where enlarged facilities are needed. The R.F.C. will help finance the undertakings. Similarly, in many other ways our industrial machinery will have to be shaped, not alone as private enterprise would wish, but as national-defense needs require.

New ideas of national defense have come out of the Munich affair. Adequate defense is now seen to mean infinitely more than merely adding battleships, cruisers, destroyers, airplanes, coast-defense guns, and such equipment to our store of defense material. Germany has taught us that static defense is inadequate. We need dynamic defense. That means that our defense preparation must be considered as a going concern, as a producing organization able to provide adequate expansion and replacement. The rate of production of war material is as important as the quantity on hand. Preparedness must from now on be judged not only by the size of our inventory, but by the rate of production.

Not only did Germany have more planes than England and France. Her airplane factories were capable of turning out replacement planes far more rapidly than the other two powers. France and Britain had an air force that was practically static. French labor troubles had slowed down the production rate. Germany had an air force that was dynamic because behind it was a highly geared, mass-production aviation industry.

This point, the importance of a dynamic preparedness machine, means internal industrial defense, integrated, working in closest collaboration with the Government, and protected against labor breakdowns. It means raw-material supplies must be protected.

Our problem is how to achieve this without going into fascism. Hitler integrated his machine by establishing an authoritarian government. Democracies have been unable to match him in preparation, even with their infinitely greater resources, because they lacked the efficient industrial integration.

We have the lesson of Britain and France. It still is up to us to demonstrate that democracy can work and protect itself. What Hitler achieves by compulsion, we must achieve by voluntary methods, using our own common sense and self-restraint, and by rising in a spirit of national unity. The test proved too severe for democracy in France and England. The ability of democracy to survive in this world of modern desperadoes is now put to the test—right here in America.

11/3/38

Weigh these headlines:

"Japan proclaims domination of all eastern Asia."

"Germany and Italy decide controversy between Czechoslovakia and Hungary; Britain not consulted."

"Chamberlain acknowledges German domination of Central and Southeastern Europe."

"Secretary Hull warns totalitarian nations there'll be no compromise in trade policies of U.S."

There, in four headlines from papers which have just reached my desk, is unfolding the new post-Munich world. In those developments is being written the new role which the United States must play no matter whether the Democrats or the Republicans elect that senator in Kansas. No matter who is in the White House during the next few years, be it Roosevelt, Senator Barkley, Tom Dewey, Bruce Barton, or one of those Martians imported by Orson Welles, his lines are being written for him now, to be trumpeted out of the horn of time.

Japan dominating the East. Germany dominating Europe. Britain, under whose protection we have been so secure throughout our whole national history, now struggling to keep afloat, no longer the arbiter of Europe, no longer the policeman of the world, no longer able to stand as the first line of defense for our Monroe Doctrine. That is the new world.

From the birth of this nation, we have lived in a world ruled by Great Britain. Now she is only a fourth hand in a game run by Germany, Italy, and Japan. France has her hands full trying to escape from complete collapse.

So, for the first time in these 162 years of American independence, we are definitely on our own, with no Mother England to guide us.

Secretary Hull made plain in his foreign-trade speech in New York this week that, despite England's capitulation, we will go ahead on a policy of no compromise with autarchy. Chamberlain of necessity must follow a compromise policy. We choose to stand our ground—alone if we have to.

This is not a simple undertaking. It will require not only much more military preparedness, and not only a static quantitative preparedness, figured in numbers of ships, but a dynamic preparedness, measured as a going, producing plant. All of that will require internal industrial and economic readjustments.

In addition this new world forces on us increased diplomatic defense and diplomatic preparedness. That demands more secure relations and loyalties with Latin American countries. It requires watchfulness against diplomatic maneuvers that might be to our disadvantage.

Suppose Britain, to keep the vital African colonies which Germany wants back, suggests instead giving to Germany some of her holdings in the Western Hemisphere—British Honduras, on the Central American mainland, or some of the Caribbean island possessions. Hitler might like to have a submarine or aviation base in there. That's just a hint of the complications which may develop during the trading among the European powers and which will be of enormous importance to us. There's where our diplomatic preparedness will come in.

11/22/38

The German ambassador to Washington, Hans Dieckhoff, who has been called to Berlin to report to Chancellor Hitler on the "strange attitude" of the United States toward German handling of the Jews, is in a position, fortunately, to give his government a frank and accurate picture, if that is what is wanted.

While this move probably was primarily in retaliation for the calling home of our ambassador, Hugh Wilson, it is fortunate that Dieckhoff is going back, because whether a full report is asked for or not, German officials inevitably will gather some indication of how much the handling of the Jewish question has cost Germany in American good will.

Ambassador Dieckhoff knows America well. In the first place he is a career diplomat, and has been in the German diplomatic service for nearly 30 years, so that by training he is an experienced judge of opinion and currents of feeling. It has been his business to detect them and report them. Furthermore he is a pleasant and charming person, who has enjoyed many years of popularity in Washington.

Dieckhoff long antedates the Hitler regime, of course, and he spent five years here, in the middle twenties, as counsellor of embassy when American feeling was friendly toward Germany. That was not long after the war, but even so American sentiment had swung around toward Germany. Dieckhoff was here under Baron Maltzan, who was the second German postwar ambassador to the United States and who enjoyed enormous popularity. He was something of a social lion in Washington and the German Embassy was a brilliant center of activity.

From those years, during which Dieckhoff enjoyed the friendship of a wide range of American figures, he knows that the United

States was among the first of Germany's wartime enemies to forgive and to extend a helping hand. While some of Germany's other former enemies were still grinding her under heel, the United States was extending not only sympathy but large financial help. Millions of dollars were lent to Germany to help her get back on her feet.

When the French marched into the Ruhr, the United States made no effort to conceal its disapproval of such tactics. Over a long period, the United States took the position that the best interests of the world lay in bringing Germany back into friendship with other nations and in helping the New Germany democracy to recover.

In time this attitude was adopted by some other nations, especially by Britain. In spite of our policy of political isolation, we joined in revising reparations downward and, through the Dawes- and Young-plan loans, helped finance Germany.

Ambassador Dieckhoff, of his personal experience, knows that the United States, in the decade after the war, was a genuine friend of the new German democracy. It was not until some time after Hitler assumed power that our coolness developed.

That was during the time of Ambassador Hans Luther, predecessor of Dieckhoff as ambassador. Luther, although not a Nazi, was loyal to his government and was much distressed at growing signs of American feeling against the Hitler regime. I recall a luncheon conversation in which he asked why Americans were unsympathetic toward Germany and why we would not recognize that Germany had to turn to controlled economy in order to survive. I said that as a newspaper reporter it appeared to me that we didn't care much what type of internal political government Germany chose to adopt but that Americans distrusted the Hitler regime because they could not understand the persecution of the Jews, and that unfavorable American opinion would not disappear while this persecution continued. It was as evident then as it is now that Americans will be satisfied with no explanations. We used to feel the same way about the Turks when they persecuted the Armenians, and most of us didn't know any Armenians at all.

To a German this attitude may or may not make any sense, but it is a big fact in the way of Hitler being accepted as a leader that anybody wants to do business with.

Ambassador Dieckhoff is too understanding and too informed an observer of the United States not to know this. Hitler could learn a lot from him.

4/22/39

Incidents overnight turn sentiment upside down. To steer a country through such a complicated period as this, a President must have something more in mind than the momentary applause of the country. To employ no more substantial criterion than that is to invite suicide—political and national.

In shaping foreign policy, a statesman must try to visualize what his country, 50 years hence, will have wanted done. In foreign policy a statesman tries to make the grade in the post-mortem. He can be out of line with popular opinion on the first reaction. What he wants is to be vindicated when the nation makes its second guess, after the thing is done.

To think of the immediate situation in terms of whether Roosevelt is trying to get us into war or trying to keep us out is to miss the issue that confronts the United States. We have two primary concerns in the game of world power.

One is the imperative protection of the Western Hemisphere. That is sacred to our national interest and there will be no whittling compromise whatever.

The other concern is the interest which we have in the preservation of British sea power. It polices most of the world for us. Roosevelt thinks of what kind of world it would be for us if British sea power were transferred by force into the hands of a German-Italian-Japanese fleet. How would it be for the Japanese to control Singapore and to control the rubber and tin from the East Indies which are essential to our economy?

I suspect that questions like that—rather than who is going to be elected in 1940—are in Roosevelt's mind as he tries to figure out how we can give breaks to the British and French without having our own tails caught in the wringer.

6/22/39

We have ducked and squirmed and looked the other way, but the hour of decision is drawing close. Are we going to stay in the Far East or are we going to pull out? Are we going to hold the Philippines or leave? Are we ready to see Japan take complete control in the western Pacific?

That is the question which we cannot escape answering much longer.

Just now the news wires bring in bulletins stating that Japan has captured the last important Chinese seaport. Japan now controls the whole Chinese coast. Britain has been reduced to the humiliating position of having to beg Japan not to strip British citizens and subject them to personal indignities at Tientsin. Japan appears to have decided that now is the time to throw the Occidental out of the Orient.

The next step is the rich archipelago—including the Dutch East Indies, with their oil, rubber, and tin, the chief source of quinine and other less well-known but important commodities, which are very necessary to us. We have had access to them through the protection of the British fleet.

Obviously Great Britain—harassed by threats of a new crisis in Europe—is in no position alone to interpose real resistance to the Japanese march which is now gaining momentum. In this area of rich raw materials which Japan is heading for are the Philippines. That is the definite, tangible, visible chip which we have in the grim game in the Far East.

We might as well face the situation cold. These are our alternatives:

First, we can say that Japan is determined to dominate the Orient and the adjacent raw-material supplies, as we dominate the Western Hemisphere and as Hitler dominates the continent of Europe. That means, in time, that we shall have to obtain rubber for our automobile industry and tin for industrial purposes at the pleasure of Japan. That means that we shall be able to sell goods in Eastern Asia subject to Japanese conditions and against the preferential conditions which Japan will impose in favor of her own nationals.

It means that the politicians in the Philippines will turn to Tokyo to make the best terms of surrender they can. The Philippines are to us what Czechoslovakia was to Chamberlain.

If we are going to take that course, then we can forget at once about the Far East and this present crisis there and begin putting our own economic affairs in shape for the drastic readjustment that would be certain to come. We should better begin developing the rubber industry in Brazil, begin devising practical substitutes for tin. We should better pull our Navy back to the Pearl Harbor line and dig in behind it to make the Western Hemisphere essentially a self-contained economy.

Or (the second alternative) we can take a chance on making a stand, take a chance on the British being able to put up some resistance on their own, apply the strongest threats of pressure on Japan, threaten to cut off cotton—which would be a blow to our South—to cut off munitions and industrial exports to Japan—which would be a blow to our industry in the North—and get our Navy in position to meet any retaliation that might result from such a course.

Neither of these choices is easy. Both are loaded with risk and economic hardship to certain large groups of our population, and in the second alternative of resistance there is the risk of naval warfare, which no one can contemplate lightly.

Yet suppose we continue to drift, to wait and hope. That is what Britain did. Japan, as did Hitler, will continue to press on. We shall be subjected to constant pushing around, to making futile rear-guard protests, to making belated concessions that bring us humiliation but no real relief. And in the end we should be squeezed out of the Philippines and the whole Far East as completely as if we threw the towel into the ring now.

The time when we can interpose to check this process is almost over. A little bit longer and Japan will have advanced beyond the point where she can be turned back.

I do not mean to be alarmist, nor to indulge in jingo flag waving. I am only trying, as an American citizen, with children growing up, to think through to some of the implications which this crisis in the Far East holds for the future of this nation. We are living in a dangerous world and we might as well be getting the lay of the land now, before the power of decision is taken out of our hands.

12/29/38

Maybe Hitler's technique works on some peoples but if there is one thing that does not make friends and influence people in the United States, it is Nazi propaganda. It succeeds only in biting itself.

Americans just don't understand the Nazi tactics. When German newspaper correspondents at Lima were not invited to a certain cocktail party, they complained to their government. Two weeks ago the German correspondents in London were invited to the Foreign Press Association dinner at which Prime Minister Chamberlain was the speaker and guest of honor. But having heard confidentially that he might criticize some Nazi press methods, twenty-five German newspapermen and ten German officials including the German ambassador in London boycotted the dinner without warning, leaving Chamberlain to face gaping chairs around the room. Such hobnailed tactics leave most Americans cold.

Now Germany is trying to sell its anti-Semitic campaign by comparing it to the "Jim Crow" regulations in our Southern states.

Actually the policy of our Government and the pressure is directed toward improving the condition of the Negro race and has been ever since the Civil War, whereas the policy of Hitler's regime and all of its pressure is directed at driving the Jews back into a status more cruel than that from which the United States rescued the Negroes 75 years ago. Only a few days ago the Supreme Court ordered the University of Missouri to provide a Negro law student with the same educational facilities that it grants to white students.

Where our public policy is to combat race hatred, public policy in Germany is to inflame it. In racial tolerance, the Nazis and the United States face in opposite directions.

The most hopeless of all enterprises of the Hitler regime is its attempt to propagandize its ideas in the United States. It is hopeless because in America Nazi ideas are self-defeating, so alien and repugnant are they to Americans. The most effective answer to German propaganda is to let it speak for itself. That is exactly what is done in a book just issued, which consists of reprints of German regulations and admonitions to Americans of German origin.

For instance, a passage taken from the yearbook of the German-American Volksbund, addressed to persons of German blood in America, says, "Germany considers it as a service to the nation if you greet the rebirth of the German folk, the glorious folk movement of National Socialism, with understanding; when you openly accept the German language, German custom, and manner. . . . We stand here as the heralds of the Third Reich, as preachers of the German world viewpoint of National Socialism which has displayed before the eyes of the world the incomparable German miracle, the miracle of National Socialism."

Hitler is even making Mussolini's brand of fascism more repugnant, for he has introduced virulent anti-Semitism into Italy.

From a professor of Italian language and literature at Smith College have just come the details of a tragic incident in Italy, where news of the suicide of a prominent publisher, Dr. A. F. Formiggini, was suppressed because Italian papers may no longer print obituary notices of Jews. He was the publisher of the Italian *Who's Who,* but was ordered to suppress names of all Italians regarded with disfavor by the regime. His books and publications were taken from circulation and he was removed as head of an Italian cultural society which he had founded. On Dec. 1, he leaped from a tower and in his pockets were found biting notes condemning the racial brutality of the regime.

Such is the progress of the "incomparable German miracle, the miracle of National Socialism," which it is hoped in Germany will find friendly root in America.

7/19/39

For us neutrality can be only a state of mind. It can be nothing more. If we embargo arms to all belligerents, we may think we are acting in a way that is neutral, that neither aids nor injures either side. But that is not the fact. If we embargo shipments we give

Germany tremendous additional leverage by leaving her opponents infinitely weaker. If we sell, we strengthen Britain.

So whether we sell or do not sell, whether we keep the embargo or repeal it, either way we exert an effect upon the relative strength of the opposing groups of powers—possibly a decisive effect, but in any case a considerable one.

Thus it is impossible to hide behind the word "neutrality." If we were a small, inconsequential nation, then we could be "neutral." What we did would have little effect. We are victims, so to speak, of our enormous resources. They exert their force in world politics whether we want them to or not. We are helpless in the matter. We can only say where this force will be directed. And if we say we won't direct it anywhere, it still is directed automatically in favor of Germany.

Secretary Hull, in his recent statement which was transmitted to Congress by President Roosevelt, says, "Those of us who support the recommendations formulated for elimination of the embargo are convinced that the arms embargo plays into the hands of those nations which have taken the lead in building up their fighting power."

Translated into plain language, he is saying that the arms embargo helps Germany and Italy.

9/22/39

Returning to international law means returning to international anarchy. International law isn't something enacted and put into a statute book like a domestic law and enforced by a court. The word law is misleading. So-called international law is a phrase to cover the accumulation of international usages and interpretations of them by scholars. These amount in the last analysis to whatever nations have been able to get away with.

In wartime "international law" means nothing. Each nation conducts itself as it thinks is necessary to win. During the First World War we were screaming daily about violations of international law by both the British and the Germans. It is no law common to sovereign states. There is no tribunal to enforce the usages. You observe "international law" when it fits in with your game and forget it when it does not.

We would be on more realistic ground if the phrase were dropped. It sounds nice and orderly to the ear, but it is only a trap that drags nations in these times into futile note writing and legalistic arguments. Talk of "returning to international law" only confuses our task, which is to keep out of the line of fire if possible.

4/10/40

All Washington moves, in these hours, under a sense of sober humility, in the presence of events which confound the faith and ethics of the Christian world. One thinks of democracy, of the decent way of life so laboriously cultivated through the ages, and sees it now hanging on the cross. And one wonders what is to come after this Calvary.

Who knows any answers in these times? On an afternoon like this, when the sky is so warm and bright here, and dripping with death in Europe, words coming out of a typewriter seem but trivial bits of futile impertinence.

Without in any sense minimizing the feeling of outrage that exists here over Hitler's latest desperate stroke, German occupation of Norway, it does not appear to have created any new reason for our entering the war. This stroke has been expected for a long time.

Two things seem mainly to be called for: First, intensified preparedness. Second, continuation of our efforts to speed military planes to the Allies.

Talk of additional defense appropriations already has begun in Congress. It is likely that the Army and Navy will be given a green light.

There is much doubt as to the efficiency of our national defense. So much so that it would be highly desirable to have a thorough inquiry—preferably by a composite board of qualified civilians, congressional leaders, and former military men, meeting in secret so that ruthless scrutiny would be possible.

Additional attention is being given to accumulation of supplies of rubber and tin, two vital raw materials which must be imported from the Far East. Woeful neglect has left us with only small stocks on hand, sufficient for only a few weeks.

Most critical at the moment is the grave Allied weakness in the air. German bombing power, so our authorities say, is four times that of England and France combined. That is the hard fact of the situation. That explains Churchill's statement that the Allies are condemned for some time to come to a great deal of suffering and danger.

The British and French have poorly prepared themselves in the air. They are paying dearly now, as they did in Norway. German plane production is 3,000 a month, and is set for 6,000 a month in September. British and French together produce about 1,200, although their capacity is greater. They are not even using our aircraft facilities to full advantage.

By going into the war, we could do little more for them than we are doing. They have shown an inefficiency that has been appalling to those who have observed it closehand. That has dampened some enthusiasm here and a feeling exists that there is not much more we could do to help when the Allies are not operating more effectively themselves. Recently a strong tendency is showing itself along the line that we had best watch our own interests in the Western Hemisphere and be prepared to safeguard them against whatever may come.

I have written the foregoing in direct words, which may seem harsher than they are meant to be. Perhaps on this particular day they were better left unsaid.

6/13/40

Talk of the desirability of a deal with Japan is spreading through the Middle West, stimulated by *The Chicago Tribune* and followed up by other oracles. The idea is that to prevent the totalitarian powers from ganging up on us, we should detach Japan and make an ally of her. Then, if it became necessary to face Germany, we should have Japan a loyal friend at our back.

If we are taken in by that argument, we shall have learned nothing from the disastrous experience of Britain. It amounts to a proposal for appeasement. The proposition is the product of fear.

Because we are afraid, we should try to appease Japan. How? By selling out now. By turning adrift to the tender mercies of the yellow race Australia, New Zealand, the Philippines, the Dutch East Indies, and all way stations.

In order to buy Japan's friendship and support, we should put the seal of our approval upon such a betrayal. We should scuttle on every international ideal. For our treachery we should gain nothing but a Munich, to last until the day when Japan wanted something else that had not been included in the bargain. Then Japan would take whatever it was that she wanted and pay no more heed to her deal with us than she paid to her treaty pledges when she went into Manchukuo, into China proper, or when she fortified the mandate islands in the Pacific.

If Japan is determined to extend her domination in the Far East, at least let it not be done with our approval, as part of a deal with us. Let us not be a party to it in a craven act that would instantly be a tip-off to the totalitarian powers that we had lost our nerve as completely as the British lost theirs in the early thirties, when Japan went into Manchukuo, or as the French lost theirs when they permitted Hitler to reoccupy the Rhineland.

Don't think that a deal with Japan would not be recognized as a tip-off to all Latin America, a tip-off that the third great democracy also was on the run. Are we to invite every Latin American country to begin saying of us, as the little nations of Europe did of Britain, that they cannot depend upon us? Are we to give them that encouragement to rush into deals with Hitler as the new rising force that is to replace the United States as the protector of the Western Hemisphere?

Of course, the idea of a deal with Japan is stated in neat, seemingly safe terms. So was Munich. Yet Munich turned the balance fatally against the Allies. Everything since has been inevitable sequel.

This is world revolution, not only war for conquest. It is a revolution to overthrow capitalist democracy everywhere, to overthrow the system set up through British leadership and to supplant the British domination and pattern with German domination and pattern.

Britain achieved a world-wide empire, shaped to the mechanics which best suited her. Germany aspired to replace that world domination with mechanics of her own. Italy and Japan are her left and right hands. The Old Bolsheviks had an idea of world revolution, but they couldn't put it over. Hitler has a similar idea and he is on the way toward putting it over where the Communist world-wide revolution failed.

Note Mussolini's significant phrases in his declaration of war, "Black shirts of the revolution . . . we take the field against the plutocratic and reactionary democracies. . . . This gigantic conflict is only a phase of the logical development of our revolution. . . . It is a conflict between two ages, two ideas . . . an event of import for the centuries . . . proletarian, fascist Italy."

This is not old-style nineteenth-century imperialism any more than was the unsuccessful Communist try at a world revolution. Britain has been mistress of the world, why not Germany? Why not destruction of the old capitalist democratic governments? Once it sounded like ballyhoo. But Germany is sacrificing thousands of her lives to achieve it, and the great stakes are almost within her grasp.

When France and England have been crushed, only the United States and our system on the Western Hemisphere, plus what we may take over from the British Empire, will be left standing in the way.

In this situation we can trust nobody but ourselves. We can trust only our own force. We want none of the false sense of security that a deal with Japan would give us, a deal that might prove as treacherous as Munich. Japan is playing the same game as the other crowd and we should be foolish to deceive ourselves. We must make busy being the strong neighbor in the Western Hemisphere. No neighbor now is a good neighbor unless he is strong. We need guns, not treaties.

8/26/40

Our danger never has been that we couldn't do the job. It always has been that we were slow in waking up to what had to be done. Now again, that is our chief danger. We can do it when, and only when, we believe that it really must be done. Our trouble now is that we still do not really believe that we are in danger.

2/4/41

This might be called the "confession of an isolationist." I am prompted to take stock by a Pittsburgh reader with a good memory who writes in to chide me with an accusation that might apply to many of us in America today.

He says, "During the last 16 months you have written several sound and convincing articles against American involvement abroad. To judge from more recent writings, you have switched to the support of those who believe in throwing the resources of this nation again into the never-ending European madness." He asks this pertinent question, "What essential change has occurred in the world situation since the fall of 1939 which justifies a change in the attitude of the American people?"

The gentleman is correct. I have switched, almost completely around. The evidence is written into many columns under this signature.

Returning from Europe in November, 1937, I was a stronger isolationist even than before: "Europe is . . . grimly preparing for suicide. . . . The next war, instead of making the world safe for democracy, is likely only to make it safe for revolution. . . . The most useful crusade that the United States could engage in would be to protect itself thoroughly and to make secure on the Western Hemisphere a mode of life based on orderly freedom."

The same a year later, on the eve of Munich.

October, 1938, after Munich: "This Government does not feel reassured by the settlement. It is disturbed. High officials of this Government have the conviction that they should not stop hammering for a more orderly world, but that all efforts should be redoubled."

Oct. 26, 1938: "We shall have to think in terms of a two-ocean navy. . . . It is a new world—Germany dominant on the continent; France almost an international cipher; the British fleet paralyzed at least for the time being by German power to blow the British Isles out of the water; Japan in control of the whole Chinese coast and Britain there reduced to impotency."

Oct. 27, 1938: "A new spirit of national unity is called for. . . . Our industrial plant must be integrated and closely dovetailed with war needs and a considerable amount of Government dictation and subsidy will be necessary. . . . Something very fundamental has occurred in the world and it is bound to have its effects upon us."

Oct. 31, 1938: "With Munich a new world was born. . . . A huge chunk of power changed hands. . . . This has suddenly left the United States standing alone and unprotected in the world game of power politics. . . . Britain has been our first line of defense. . . . Britain has been a protector of the Monroe Doctrine, has stood firmly for the status quo on the Western Hemisphere. Now she is no longer able to serve forcefully in that role. . . . We are now on our own in protecting the Western Hemisphere. . . . It means internal industrial defense. . . . The ability of democracy to survive in this world of modern desperadoes is now put to the test—right here in America."

Nov. 3, 1938: "Britain, under whose protection we have been so secure throughout our whole national history, now is struggling to keep afloat, no longer the arbiter of Europe, no longer the policeman of the world, no longer able to stand as the first line of defense for our Monroe Doctrine. That is the new world."

I could go on quoting from later columns written in 1939, 1940, and this year, but the point of view evolves out of the change as noted in the foregoing excerpts. Munich revealed that Hitler had blown off the lid of a world that was set up to our own national advantage. The conquests of Scandinavia, Holland, Belgium, and France, and the attempt now to complete the job by conquering England, only sharpen the picture disclosed at Munich, where Hitler turned up holding the ace cards which we had thought were in the hands of our friends.

Yes, I have switched. I try to learn from events. Events are not consistent; therefore, why should I be consistent? Some people, once they adopt an idea, bury it in the ground and go on the rest of their lives defending it, without ever reexamining it to see whether time and the elements have caused it to decay into a worthless handful of dust. In that way you can be always consistent—and often wrong.

3/17/41

We are all now being carried in the hands of destiny, as everyone who heard President Roosevelt Saturday night must realize.

A newspaper correspondent listens to many speeches, writes about them, and then gladly forgets them. They rarely live on with him after the next edition. Only once or twice in a lifetime—twice in my case—does a newspaperman hear something which vibrates beyond the language of words, which breaks through his occupational insulation and digs its way into his bones.

Once I reported the Scopes evolution trial at Dayton, Tenn. A young high-school science teacher was on trial, charged with explaining to his students Darwin's theory of evolution. The hot, moist country courtroom reeked with ignorance and bigotry. A second-string attorney, Dudley Field Malone, rose in an unscheduled address to the jury. He could restrain himself no longer and lashed out in a plea for the freedom of the mind. I suddenly found myself applauding, as was the entire press section. I don't recall now a word he said, but even as I write today the quiver of the moment is back, years later. It was, I suppose, the response to a voice that was willing and able to speak up, to brush at the cobwebs of the soul, and say when they needed saying the things in which I believed.

Again, on a night in June, 1936, I was at Franklin Field, Philadelphia, where President Roosevelt accepted his second-term nomination. We were under the sky, a hundred thousand people. The Philadelphia Symphony Orchestra set the mood by playing the vigorous, triumphal final movement of Tschaikowsky's Fifth Symphony, a heroic and exultant thing of conquering fire. President Roosevelt spoke more truly than he knew. He said this generation of Americans had a rendezvous with destiny.

Now it is here.

We knew it was here when we listened to him Saturday night. At Franklin Field, nearly five years ago, he had said that in this world of ours, in other lands, there are some people who, in times past, have lived and fought for freedom, and seem to have grown too weary to carry on the fight. They have, he said, sold their heritage of freedom for the illusion of a living. They have yielded their democracy. Our success in America, and only that, can stir their ancient hope.

He didn't know about France then. He didn't know that the time would come when England alone, and a few pitiful allies entirely dependent upon England, would be left standing out in the weary struggle. But he knew that somehow or other the rendezvous had been decreed.

Now, in the spring of 1941, the date has arrived.

Mr. Roosevelt's address to the White House Correspondents Association was the acknowledgment that America intends to keep that rendezvous. There is no turning back. Everyone who was in the room when Mr. Roosevelt spoke must have heard the leaf of history turning. Twenty years of isolationism gone. We sought a life as in *Lost Horizon,* where we could shut out the ugly world, but we found we could not stay there. We have come out again.

So the "total victory" speech of March 15, I suppose, becomes with me a third of those occasions. It was strange. It was a war speech without war, a fighting speech without the troops, such a speech as a President might make after war had been declared. Yet, at the next table to me was the place of one of the members of the White House Correspondents Association, my old friend Kurt Sell, correspondent of the German official news agency. He telephoned the entire text of the speech to Berlin and then came to the dinner. He is a gentleman and quietly left a few moments before Mr. Roosevelt spoke. Many Army and Navy officers were among the guests. The only uniforms present were worn by members of the band.

The night will be remembered. A strange rendezvous. We see the grave face at the speakers' stand. We hear the voice. . . . This is an all-out effort. Nothing short of an all-out effort will win. . . . All of our aid. . . . From now on that aid will be increased—and yet again increased—until total victory has been won.

Total victory. Fateful words.

4/5/41

Although relations between the United States and the Axis are growing worse daily, there is every indication of strong public reluctance against going more deeply into the war, and I think the reason for that is that none of us can bring himself to demand that fellow Americans risk their lives to carry out a national policy. I can't sit at a typewriter and ask that some younger fellow go out and offer to sacrifice his life. That undoubtedly is true of most people. It is the secret of our national dilemma.

I am getting into this deep and chilly water because I think the time has come for us to be brutally frank with ourselves. We have reached the point where we must decide whether to risk lives or not. That is the stark crux of the convoy question.

Our people are overwhelmingly supporting material aid to Britain. But by all polls that have been taken, they are with equal decisiveness opposed to going into active war, or even into the convoying of ships, which everyone recognizes would almost certainly lead to shooting war. I believe the reason for that is a reluctance to ask for the sacrifice of lives. No other explanation seems to fit.

Other possible reasons can be eliminated.

We are not determined to be neutral. We are the opposite. The outstanding fact of the whole situation is a strong popular desire that Germany be defeated.

Neither do we object to sacrificing American property to help England win the war. We have voted the $7,000,000,000 lend-lease bill as evidence of that. Much of the money will never come back. We didn't get paid for the last war and we know we won't be paid in full for this one. We are willing to shovel out virtually without limit to help defeat Hitler.

Third, we don't object to helping kill Germans. We are struggling desperately to send as many bombers to England as possible, not to take sight-seeing cruises but to shower bombs on German industrial cities.

Fourth, we don't object to becoming involved in this war because it will disrupt our economy. We are rationing aluminum, fixing prices, giving the President enormous discretionary powers, threatening to take over industrial plants tied up by strikes, and Congress is even agitating for enactment of antistrike legislation against labor—all to the end of increasing war production for use against Germany. Beyond that we have adopted conscription and are sending our young men into Army camps, forcing them to interrupt their education or their careers. No, we are perfectly willing to turn our economy upside down to help England win the war. We are willingly taking much heavier taxation in order to do all of this.

Thus, all of those reasons that might be advanced against our going into the war already have been set aside as having no weight against the desirability of crushing Hitler. I can think of no others except the one concerning American lives. We have, in face of all that we have done, retained the neutrality restrictions on merchant shipping so that American commercial ships cannot go into the war zone where they might be sunk. We still prohibit American citizens from traveling on passenger ships of belligerent nations because they might be lost. Whenever human life comes into the question, we suddenly pull up in a dead stop.

In the last war, events such as the loss of American lives in submarine sinkings provided their own call to which the country responded. This time we have insulated ourselves against such loss of life. Unless Berlin begins a series of outrages against American citizens in Germany, there is remote prospect of incidents that might stir the American people.

It seems to me that the Administration has reached the point where it must do one of two things. It must either recognize that our aid to Britain will go no further, except as to quantity of materials, or else it must directly call for the risk of some loss of life. I think we have got down to the bedrock question.

4/7/41

We say these are Hitler's crucial days—that this is the year in which it will be decided whether he is to be victor or vanquished.

But already he is among the doomed. Not even military victory can save him, because the oppressor never wins an enduring victory. His triumph rests on the sullen backs of resentful victims, and at most he may only fend off the day when they shake themselves free again.

The only men whose victories have lived have been the liberators, who brought to their own people relief from oppressors, relief from the weakness of division, and gave them the strength of a united nation. The Alexanders, the Caesars, the Napoleons who reached out for other peoples created structures that quickly crumbled. A leader may free his people and they will make his victory a living thing. But when he conquers other peoples, they will sooner or later undo his victory. During this Holy Week millions will pray, though they feel the breath of Hitler on their bowed heads, for strength to live until they can drive him away. The history of Europe is the story of conquerors who planted their yoke only to have it thrown off. Time runs against the conqueror and with the conquered.

Will Holland ever become reconciled to Nazi rule, any more than Poland through the years accepted willingly the rule of the czars? Will Belgium? Will Frenchmen forever live in dumb submission to the Teuton?

They will not. Force will keep them down for a while. But always there must be force, and more force. England herself knows all about that, and over the years has been compelled to ease the yoke until we see Eire sitting by coolly neutral while England is in a deathly struggle. Advanced peoples, capable of self-government as are all of these victims of Hitler, never submit permanently to alien rule.

That is why Hitler cannot win. It is why his conquests cannot stand. No matter how much military might he is able to muster at the moment, when it relaxes, as it must relax in time, the subject peoples will rebound. Always Hitler's rule must be against this pressure of resistance. He can never be free of it.

This instinct for freedom among peoples who have once enjoyed it has the same spiritual vitality that made the great liberating religion of Christ live through campaigns of extermination. Repression only makes the spirit stronger. No matter how dark the days, nor how long, the spirit grows and prepares for the day of liberation. Against it Hitler will be as futile in the long run as Herod and the Roman authorities were. Hitler is in a war with the human spirit and it is a war that no man can win.

It is important that we keep this always in mind. Because the presence of this spirit, silently waging war on Hitler day and night, never sleeping, never tiring, is one of the mighty elements in this war. It has kept England from defeat. It will keep Hitler from victory. It should be counted always as part of the strength at work as the battle goes on.

Victory is not won solely by matching gun against gun. In this war every gun pointed at Hitler carries a second unseen barrel which is firing ceaselessly. The human spirit can multiply fire power. It can make itself almost immune to the hardships of war. It can snatch victory out of the jaws of death.

This is Britain's ally and it has already proved to be a mightier ally than France was with its boasted army.

Against this ally, Hitler may win battles. He can never win the war.

4/28/41

Many letters come in to me from mothers who don't want their sons to go to war. Sometimes letters come in from young men who ask why their lives should be taken in hand by the Government.

One can sympathize with the thousands of personal tragedies that are involved, with thwarted hopes and ambitions, and separations from families. Upon many people will fall a heavy burden of personal sacrifice.

But with those who must sacrifice only dollars, I can feel no sympathy whatever. When anybody begins to complain about taxes, that is a sure sign he has enough income to be rated as a lucky man and the tears that splatter upon his income-tax check leave me as cold as a fish. In other words, I don't think it ought to be any harder to draft a dollar than to draft a man.

And they can talk about profits being the wages of capital and about how nobody will work at defense unless he can wring a two-yacht profit out of the operation. But I think that is hooey, too. If the men who are smart enough to be in business and who have the ability to run a business don't see anything more in this situation than a chance to grab profits, then Hitler has already conquered America and it remains only for him to choose the time when he shall make his triumphal entry.

5/27/41

We say good-by now to the land we have known. Like lovers about to be separated by a long journey, we sit in this hour of mellow twilight, thinking fondly of the past, wondering. Words seem almost an intrusion.

What tomorrow will bring we do not know. We only know that this golden day is slipping inevitably from us, clutch at it as we will. We have had our troubles. Sometimes we were poorly clothed and poorly fed. But always tomorrow was full of promise. Hardship would diminish. Happiness would grow. Progress was the fixed law of life. We never doubted it, even when the going was rough.

As I write this, President Roosevelt is preparing his fireside talk. From England comes the call for help, a desperate call for more and more and more. Most of the men now looking over Mr. Roosevelt's shoulder as he writes want him to answer that call. Germany's naval chief warns us that already we are engaged in warlike actions with our naval patrol. He warns us to go no further. Laval, that dark stooge of Berlin, warns us to stay out. Japan, sensing that we may go in, begins to wriggle to find some way of escaping the Axis bargain to go in if we do. I don't know what Mr. Roosevelt has decided to say. But we are moving toward war, not away from it. The only uncertainty is how much faster we shall move from now on.

Whether we go to war or not, we shall act more and more as if we were going to war. Our lives will all be affected by this. Our ways will change drastically, whether or not a drop of blood is lost.

Habits must be changed. Peacetime ways have to be sacrificed. For years, dozens of materials will be almost completely monopolized by war needs and there will be little left for civilian purposes. Even senators and congressmen in some instances may have to give up their automobiles and move to small living quarters, for taxes are going to rip sharply into the lives of every family above the very lowest level of living. For this year and next, we have set aside 40 billion dollars for war production. More may be added to that. Already we are planning to spend far more than we spent in the last war. Labor, still living in a dreamworld of constantly rising wages and constantly shorter hours, is going to wake up very soon with a terrific shock.

I mention only the more pleasant aspects of the future and pass over the heavy hearts, the separated families, the young careers that will have to wait, those inward wounds which are more numerous than the wounds of the battlefield.

Regimented people. Regimented trade. The waste of war. The millions of days of human labor to make the guns, the shells, the planes, the tanks, and the ships. The huge plants useful only to manufacture weapons of slaughter. That's our future. It will be the same whether we go into the war or not.

It's been a grand life in America. We have had to work hard. But usually there was good reward. We have had poverty, but also the hope that if the individual man threw in enough struggle and labor he could find his place. Man has gained steadily in security and dignity, in hours of leisure, in those things that made his family comfortable and gave lift to his spirit. Under his feet, however rough the road, he felt the firm security of a nation fundamentally strong, safe from any enemy, able to live at peace by wishing to. In every one of us lived the promise of America.

Now we see the distant fire rolling toward us. It is not being put out. It still is some distance away, but the evil wind blows it toward us.

So ends our reverie in the twilight, over the dear, dead days.

7/18/41

This Government has tried to appease Japan. It has incurred strong public criticism in so doing. For sentiment in the United States is much more belligerent with regard to Japan than with regard to the European war.

For months the Government has been pounded for allowing oil and other supplies to go to Japan. The Government has sought to appease Japan in the face of this public criticism at home for plain reasons of strategy—and not for any love of what Japan was doing.

Tokyo apparently is strongly tempted to pull the trigger during the next few days.

Japan should not delude herself that the United States is too busy in the Atlantic to give attention to the Pacific if Tokyo embarks upon new aggression there that threatens American interests. Japan must know that the American flag still is in the Philippines and that we are prepared to defend it. Japan must know that vital raw materials are located in the East Indies and that we could not afford to stand idly by and see them cut off. Japan must know that what we have done in the Atlantic has always been done with one eye on the dangers in the Pacific, and that we have not made any transfers out of the Pacific that would prevent us from protecting our interests.

Japan must know that for months not only ourselves but the British have been reinforcing every stronghold in the far Pacific.

She must know that any gains she makes now at the expense of the United States would be only temporary and that after the Battle of the Atlantic is won, she would be up against the crushing superiority of the two leading naval powers of the world. And the Battle of the Atlantic is being won slowly but steadily and behind that is growing by rapid leaps now the building of a second American Navy and the greatest air force that was ever created—one that will far pass Germany's. Japan, being a maritime power, dependent upon use of the sea, cannot afford to fight the two leading naval powers.

Lastly, Japan should not misjudge American reluctance to fight. For years the Navy has been trained with Japan as the potential enemy. The western part of the United States always has been hostile toward Japan. Recently a pacifist speaker, addressing a non-interventionist audience in a West Coast city, was asked if the United States should fight if Germany attacked us. The speaker said no. The audience applauded. The speaker was then asked if the United States should fight if Japan attacked us. Again the speaker said no. This time the audience, instead of applauding, was deadly silent. Senator Hiram Johnson of California may deplore every step the Administration makes in the European war. But if there is trouble with Japan, you know where Senator Johnson and every other Western senator and representative will stand.

7/6/41

This is my last broadcast from London. As I look back over these 2 weeks of broadcasts it seems to me that I have failed to tell you much. I have talked about conditions, about things, about questions. And I have failed to tell you about what really counts in England —the people. I should have been telling you about Father Groser, the Anglican priest who lives with the East End people in their shelters which he has built under the railroad tracks. A thin, gentle man with a young face and snow-white hair and understanding eyes.

The other night we walked around his shelters, through the recreation room where fifty youngsters up to about sixteen were playing checkers and other table games in the dim light. I stopped at his little canteen where they can get hot coffee. He has gas, electricity, and coal so that no matter what the blitz knocks out he can provide hot coffee.

Senator Tobey, so I read in the dispatches from America, is afraid that if he came over here he might be invited to tea and that his convictions could not stand up under such blandishment. How those cockney dock hands who form Father Groser's shelter council would roar over that one. He has about a dozen dockers who help him police the shelters. We looked in on the Red Cross first-aid station which has just been opened for the winter. They discovered there was no telephone and called a council meeting to see if they could obtain one.

At another shelter the young warden, also a dock hand, was working on Lady Limerick, one of the Red Cross leaders here, to get them additional space for a recreation room. I have been down in the East End several times in the shelters and pubs. These cockneys are in their glory now in the midst of the bomb ruins. Long unappreciated in the rigid class system which has prevailed in England and which has given them so little, these little people, stunted, lucky to have an extra shirt, are now buddies of upper-class people from the West End who have helped them organize and equip their shelters. The cockneys have had to stand up to these terrible blitzes just as the West End aristocrats have had to stand up to them. Every cockney knows that under his shabby clothing, under his unshaven face, behind his squinting eyes, he is able to take the same punishment—harder punishment, than those he used to consider his betters. The West Enders know now that the cockneys, who have nothing to lose except their England which has treated them so poorly, are ready to fight to the end. From top to bottom, and especially at the bottom, they stand immovable against Hitler.

I was in an East End pub, down by the docks, a historic pub mentioned in Pepys' Diary; it is known as the Prospect of Whitby. Most of the tenements around it have been demolished. I found a wedding party having a big Saturday night. The bridegroom was home on four days' leave. The bride works in a garment factory. Her father is a dock hand. Senator Tobey's idea of England is having tea with some whisky manufacturer who because of campaign contributions to the party is now known as Lord somebody. Well, these cockneys, jumping up and down in a pub on Saturday night and singing "Roll Out the Barrel" are England too. So is the lame woman who lives at the Shoreditch firehouse and goes out in the blitz to pull victims out of the ruins. So is the frail wife of a naval officer who for two years—except when she had to take three months' sick leave because of tuberculosis—lives at Fire Brigade Headquarters to supervise the army of volunteer fire women. She could live at her house in the country and have the servants bring breakfast in bed. England is the clerks who spend one or two nights a week on top of buildings watching for fires and engaged in work that during a blitz is more dangerous than being on a night bomber. England is the shipyard and factory workers who, on the morning after a blitz, go back to work. It is all of these people as well as the ones you read about in the newspapers that make England.

There is Lord Beaverbrook, working furiously in his open-air balcony office overlooking the Thames Embankment. There is Arthur Greenwood, one of the labor ministers, becoming so excited as he talks about what must be done after the war that he lights his cork-tipped cigarette on the wrong end. There is Lord Woolton, the department-store merchant, who is trying to feed England and getting nothing but complaints for his pains. There is the Minister of Home Security, Herbert Morrison, dreaming about a new London to be built. There is Ernest Bevin, who always talks with a cigarette in his lips, figuring how to spread England's man power out more thinly over the vast work to be done. There is Miss Ellen Wilkinson, the tiny, red-headed fireball, a Member of Parliament and of the Home Security Ministry, needling everybody into more effective effort. Over it all is that eighteenth-century squire, referred to by everyone from Cabinet ministers down to the boys in the shelters of Stepney as Winston, holding it all together, driving it along, inspiring the whole nation with his rugged eloquence and his unbreakable spirit.

These are what count in England. Not the ruins of the city which in moonlight take on a strange whiteness against the dome of St. Paul's and look like the bleached bones of some ancient civilization. Not the gaping holes you see all over London. Not the Guildhall potted by bombs. Not the shambles that the Germans have made in Plymouth, Coventry, and Hull. These are not England. England is a living people—a people that has never been more alive than now —a people fighting for its existence. Fighting to save the kind of freedom that we enjoy in the United States; living for the day when children will once more play in Kensington Gardens and when the little statue of Peter Pan there will no longer be festooned with cobwebs.

Senator Tobey attaches too much importance to a cup of British tea which is really quite a trifling incident in one's life here now. There are more important things in life here today, and Senator Tobey might be a wiser man if he were a little more familiar with them. But they won't come out of a teacup.

Well, I have had three rich weeks in England—days packed with kindness on the part of a hard-pressed people and days packed with glimpses of a spirit which I hope shall never perish from the earth. I carry back to America many memories.

11/26/41

The State Department has been following a generous policy toward Japan, Vichy, France, and pro-Nazi Spain. This has been described by critics in and out of the Administration as appeasement.

The policy roughly has been to cultivate these pro-Axis governments, to do them favors, to treat them generously, hoping to win them from the Axis or induce them to slow down on collaboration with the Axis and play our game as much as possible. It has been a policy of doing favors in the hope of having the favors reciprocated. For a long time we sent oil and other materials to Japan, and we began to shut down only after new aggression by Japan. We have sent oil, food, and other supplies into Vichy's North African colonies and into Spain until the last few days. And now we have had to stop it because we found it was getting us nowhere.

This policy had been decidedly unpopular with some sections of American opinion. Some within the Government have considered it futile, if not actually harmful to American interests.

Secretary Hull and Under Secretary Welles are men of high ability, seasoned judgment, and long experience in international relations. My own inclination has been to give them the benefit of the doubt in this policy, as they knew much more about the facts with which they were dealing than I could possibly know. In these matters one must take a good deal on faith and wait for the results. In this case the results have not justified the policy. On that basis the policy must be put down as having been a mistaken one.

The proof of the failure is written in the events themselves. In spite of our easy policy, Japan continued her aggression and was moving steadily further south until we were compelled as a measure of punishment to tighten the blockade. Japan took advantage of the easy policy as long as she could and then became abusive when we refused to continue it. She showed no disposition to reciprocate while we were allowing supplies to go to her, and only became more ugly when the spigot was turned off. The policy didn't do anything except supply Japan with materials which were essential to her war effort.

The argument was that by supplying these materials we would be encouraging the peaceful elements in Japan and would be denying the Japanese militarists an excuse for action. We have learned that when the militarists in Japan want an excuse they find it regardless of what our policy might be.

We supplied oil and other materials to French North Africa in the hope of cultivating the favor of General Weygand. The object was to wean him from Vichy in the hope that eventually he would break and throw his North African section of the French empire to the Allied side. That was a policy built on one fragile fact, the presence of Weygand in North Africa. When the Germans decided the time had come, they pulled the chain and overnight General Weygand was washed down the drain and we were left without our potential friend. We then cut off exports to French North Africa. It is said we gained time. We gained only so much time as Hitler cared to allow and no more. In addition we supplied a large quantity of materials to a territory which is now in Hitler's grasp.

We have known all along that Spain was playing ball with Hitler. But we thought to check this by allowing oil to go to Spain. There is some suspicion that this oil was in excess of Spanish needs and has found its way into Axis hands. We don't know much about what has actually happened to it. So within the last few days we have revoked export licenses for oil to Spain.

Reluctantly, and after long delay, the State Department has acquiesced in the view which many groups have had for a long time that it is a waste of time to try to play ball with Axis and pro-Axis countries. It has become clear that such efforts mean only one thing. We are used by the other side. We have learned our lesson so far as Vichy is concerned. It remains to be seen whether we have learned it with regard to Japan. The test will be whether we relax the economic squeeze which has been applied during the last few months for anything short of an improbable reversal of Japanese policy.

11/28/41

Some tangible token of good faith is necessary from Japan before the United States can go any further in trying to work out a peace in the Pacific.

The United States is entitled to feel it has not been fairly dealt with when it discovers that during the last few days, while peace talks were going on here, Japan has been unloading thousands of troops, and equipment for them, in Indo-China.

There can be no purpose in this other than further aggression. Japan already is in control of the area and is under no threat from land forces. The occupation of French Indo-China in the first place was arranged through Hitler's pressure on Vichy at Japan's request. That, like the invasion of China, violates the basic principles of nonaggression to which the United States is committed. But even while the broader settlement was under discussion, Japan moved secretly to mobilize further in this advanced southern area of Asia, looking toward the Burma Road and the rich island sources of raw materials below Singapore.

This Government has given every indication that it does not want war in the Pacific. If the need for sending our supplies to Europe and Africa did not make it obvious that we wanted to avoid a war in the Pacific, our own actions would in themselves make it clear. We continued, long after many in this country and some even within the Government objected, to send materials to Japan which enabled her to continue her war effort in China.

We have welcomed every opportunity to talk peace with Japan. When Japan sent Admiral Nomura here as ambassador, Secretary Hull began a series of conversations which have continued since last March.

When Japan decided to send a second negotiator a few weeks ago, he was accepted as an emissary searching for a formula of settlement, and not merely as an agent to check on Nomura's size-up of the situation in the United States—which may have been the real purpose of the trip, rather than making peace.

During all this the Japanese Premier and Foreign Minister made blustering statements and laid down conditions of settlement, such as being allowed a free hand in China, which could not possibly be accepted by the United States. Still we chose to ignore those statements, even though they seemed aimed at sabotaging the discussions. Now finally the word comes in from Indo-China that the Japanese are being heavily reinforced and are evidently preparing to take the offensive within the very near future.

This makes a mockery of peace talk. It would make us appear like innocent saps to go on talking peace, looking hard the other way so as not to notice the Japanese troops marching. How can we with any confidence discuss a permanent arrangement that would rest upon the good faith of Japan when this kind of business occurs during the negotiations?

For 10 years Japan has been inching along, brandishing the sword at home and the promise of an olive branch abroad, waging a kind of conquest short of war. If she is ever to show by actions rather than words that she wants a settlement in the Pacific, now is the time.

Hints have been dropped during the negotiations that Japan would not hesitate to throw the Axis over if she obtained a favorable settlement. Even the question of withdrawing from Indo-China has been discussed, with some signs that the Japanese might consider it. We have made it clear in the discussion that throwing China open to all on a basis of economic equality would still give Japan a natural trade advantage because of her proximity and because Japan can produce many goods more cheaply than any other country.

But the promises involved in a settlement on such terms require confidence that they will be carried out. Japan has not given the slightest indication of good faith in this respect by any action. The actions within the last few days have been in the contrary direction.

It takes both sides to make peace, and it is time for the other side to show some action that indicates desire in that direction. Unless it is forthcoming, the chances are that relations will progressively break down and at some point lead to war.

12/2/41

Those who are trying to figure out the prospects in the Far East would do well to ignore the detailed footwork that is going on now.

Visits of the Japanese to the State Department are now superficial incidents. One day the talks with Secretary Hull are off and the next day they are on. One day the Japanese Premier points his gun and the next day Tokyo wants to talk some more. That kind of news is almost meaningless now. The crisis towers ominously above such maneuvers.

The key fact is that after eight months of talking, during which Secretary Hull has tried every possible avenue of reaching a workable adjustment with Japan, it looks hopeless. Our people here see no cause for optimism. The two governments are so far apart that the two positions are considered irreconcilable.

As he left the State Department, Japanese Ambassador Nomura said there must be wise statesmanship to save the situation. Indeed it will take wise statesmanship to save this situation. The tragedy is that the necessary wisdom does not appear to exist in Tokyo.

No information here indicates the slightest intention on the part of Japan to halt the program of further conquest. Although the displeasure of this Government was made clear several days ago, Japan continues to mobilize for the expected attack on Thailand.

It is the considered view here that the United States could not stand idly by in event of such an attack. That is the situation.

Such an attack will challenge the United States to defend its interests on three grounds:

First, there is the direct menace to the Philippines in this encircling movement. Sooner or later Japan would find it necessary to reduce the Philippines, which lie on the flank of the present southward push.

Second, the next move by Japan would menace our sources of defense raw materials in the East Indies.

Third, it would menace our aid to China, and if successful would force capitulation by the Chinese.

More broadly, the Japanese government appears determined to push the white man out of the Far East. It would mean that, if Japan were successful, no American ship could sail out on the Pacific with any certainty of being able to complete its voyage except at the discretion of Japan. If this move of Japan's succeeds, it means the United States is stopped at Hawaii. From there on out, we must ask Tokyo for favors. We should have to ask Tokyo to allow us to have rubber and tin and tungsten, so we could continue our production of war materials.

By all the indications at hand, Japan has set out to make herself master of the Orient. The Japanese may work out some milder translation of Premier Tojo's speech over the week end in which he said the influence of the United States and Britain must be purged from the Orient. But no softened translation can erase the fact that this is the studied policy of Tokyo. It is an attempt to set up a closed world covering roughly half of the population of the earth, and to use this control in cooperation with Germany. The issue now is whether that area is to remain open to other nations on a basis of equality.

Japan is playing for a little more time. That is all that the visits of the Japanese representatives to the State Department mean now. They can result in no relaxation of our preparations. War may be delayed. There is but the faintest hope now that it can be avoided, because there is nothing whatever to indicate that Japan will cease, so long as she remains undefeated, to work toward the end of fencing off the other side of the Pacific.

War

12/8/41

AMERICANS can be proud today. We can be proud that we tried to the bitter end to avoid war.

In the face of advancing savagery the Government of the United States continued to labor for peace. We tried to throw our moral weight against aggression and for the protection of all nations and for equal opportunity. We can be proud that we continued to do this until Japan struck.

Twelve hours before Japanese planes appeared over Honolulu, President Roosevelt appealed personally to the Emperor of Japan to join him in a peaceful adjustment. Even as the news of the attack was flashed to Washington, Secretary Hull was talking with the two Japanese representatives in his office. We were shot at while still in the act of seeking peace.

A strong nation can take pride in that, and in the record of patience and fair dealing. We can be proud of President Roosevelt and Secretary Hull, and of their cool and steady loyalty to those basic principles that must, after the last drop of blood has been spilled, rise again to guide nations. Our efforts failed. But we can be proud that those efforts were made, and that no American gun fired before we were attacked. Only today have we put on the uniform of war.

Japan has made our decision for us. This nation hates war so deeply, is so convinced of its futility as a method of adjusting differences, that we could not take the initiative. Within the last few days I have heard diplomats who have participated in some of the Far Eastern discussions express doubt that the United States would go to war even if Thailand were attacked by Japan. It would have been easy for Japan to avoid war with the United States.

But now all of our doubts, all of our reluctance, all of our hesitations, have been swept away from us. Practically every leading isolationist already has been heard from. Their answer to the attack on Honolulu is that we must fight. Wheeler and Taft, and McNary, leader of the Senate Republicans, have taken their stand with the Government. Japan has united this country for us. Congress will very soon register the unity of this nation.

This is suicide for Japan. A desperate, fourth-rate nation, the spoiled little gangster of the Orient will have to be exterminated as a power. Japan has asked for it and now she will get it.

Japan could have joined the United States and Britain as one of the three controlling sea powers of the globe. Her geography and economic situation made that her logical course. Japan can live only by sea trade. But she has chosen to war with the two other sea powers. She preferred to take her chances with armed force just as Germany has done. Japan chose to live by the sword and she will die by the sword. Japan will be blasted, bombed, burned, starved. Her people will suffer ghastly tortures. A nation which has possibilities of becoming one of the rulers of the world will be reduced to a pitiful huddling people on a poor little group of islands.

The modern world can no longer tolerate the anarchy of conquest by force. The two nations most addicted to this barbarism are Germany and Japan. They must be disarmed. Force must be hereafter kept in the hands of nations that will use it to bring about a peaceful world.

We shall come out of this war with fighting strength the like of which has never been seen. We shall have plenty of it for our protection. I hope we shall use it also in cooperation with other nations so that no power again can commit such an assault against the peace as Japan has just been guilty of.

This war must be fought until Japanese military strength is exterminated.

But more than that must come out of it. Our victory must be used to bring about a new era of benevolent force which will secure for all men and women and their children a new kind of peace in which the human race can progress toward that happier life which science and industry have made possible.

America can open that door.

12/30/41

Read it and weep. Marines on Wake Island fighting off the Japanese with only four planes, then with only two, and finally with only one plane. American soldiers in the Philippines defending bridges with rifles and hand grenades.

It won't be our men out there that will lose the Philippines. If the islands are lost they will have been lost here, by our lagging war production.

For 18 months record-breaking automobile production has been using up precious chrome. Now chrome mines in the Philippines have been evacuated in the face of the Japanese advance. O.P.M. has just been compelled to order restricted use of chrome steel. For several years Germany and Japan have been buying up such supplies. For instance, they ran up their copper purchases from Latin American countries to several times normal. They were getting ready for war at any cost. Officials here who months ago were pleading that our Government do the same thing were considered impractical nuts and were brushed aside as panicmongers.

There is only one point in bringing this up. It is to emphasize that the confusion, divided authority, and hesitant state of mind that caused these failures still exist.

1/27/42

As I read the Roberts report on Pearl Harbor, I kept thinking that would be a hell of a way to run a newspaper.

I don't know anything about military affairs. But I have been around newspaper offices all my life. A newspaper office is organized to be ready for the unexpected. We hire an Army and Navy to protect us from the unexpected. But I never saw a newsroom that was as slack and sloppy as the Roberts report shows the Army and Navy at Hawaii to have been.

Go through any well-run newspaper office and you will find galleys of type, with headlines and art, all ready to be thrown into the paper at an instant's notice. Let a flash come through about the sudden death of any prominent figure and the paper will be ready to roll within a few minutes.

A newspaper office always goes on the assumption that the worst is about to happen the next minute. An incredible amount of planning, labor, and watchfulness goes into this side of a newspaper—much of it in vain. But it is necessary if you are not to be caught asleep when a big story breaks.

I remember when Carl Groat, now editor of *The Cincinnati Post,* was manager of the United Press bureau at Washington. After the Shenandoah dirigible disaster he sent a reporter to camp on a deathwatch at the Navy Department whenever a dirigible made a flight. The man-hours which reporters spend on deathwatches and on chasing down tips which do not materialize, the newsless days they put in hovering around prominent figures just so they will be on hand in case something happens, are all part of the routine of being prepared for the unexpected.

Around Scripps-Howard newspaper offices is the old story of the Oklahoma City hanging years ago. The sheriff was all ready. Most of the reporters in town were on hand. But one city editor sent a reporter out to watch the governor, who was opposed to capital punishment. Ten minutes before the hanging was to take place, the governor commuted the sentence. The newspaper which was on the job had its newsboys selling papers to the crowd waiting in the jail yard to see the hanging that had been called off.

Newspapers are prepared always for the unexpected. Hawaii seems to have operated on the conviction that the unexpected couldn't happen.

More than that, the Roberts report shows appalling lack of coordination between the Army and Navy. The Army thought the Navy was patrolling. The Navy thought the Army had its detection service operating. Neither bothered to check with the other—or maybe they were not on speaking terms.

In any newspaper office the first business of the managing editor is to see that his city editor and his telegraph editor clear with each other on space. If the city editor went on his own and the telegraph editor sent wire copy to the composing room to his heart's desire, you would have enough type set to fill three newspapers. If a big local story breaks, the telegraph editor's space is reduced. If a big telegraph story breaks, the city editor takes a cut in space. The two subordinate executives must work together.

I have always thought civilians should be extremely sparing in their advice about military affairs, which seem so simple and yet are so intricate. But the Roberts report shows two glaring situations which come down, in civilian language, to sloppy operation. First, the Army and Navy acted on the assumption that the unexpected would not happen, when they should have assumed the opposite. Second, the two services were totally uncoordinated, and neither knew what the other was doing—or, in this case, not doing. And the air force, so supremely important in the new warfare, apparently was regarded by both as a minor auxiliary.

2/18/42

Is it possible that the Army and Navy still haven't awakened to the primary place the airplane has taken in this war? The evidence would fill books. Pearl Harbor. Crete. The way the Germans used air protection to get their battleships through the Straits of Dover the other day. The cry of everybody in the Far East for planes. Cecil Brown reports from there that thirty Flying Fortresses six weeks ago might have changed the story. Dutch officials have begged our Government frantically for just a few planes—far less than a month's production. Harold Guard, the United Press correspondent, tells us how brave British troops had to lie in the mud at Singapore while Japanese planes machine-gunned them with not a defending plane in the area. Every dispatch from out there cries for planes. They are not asking for battleships. Battleships are no good without planes to protect them, as the British have finally discovered. I'm not competent to marshal all the evidence that exists.

At Pearl Harbor our people were looking for sabotage, for submarine attack, for naval attack, but they don't seem to have thought of the possibility of air attack—so the Roberts report tells us. Just a few days ago General Marshall said that pilot training would be added to the curriculum at West Point within a month. They apparently hadn't bothered with air much before, and had gone on turning out groundbound officers in the midst of a war in which air had become the key to most decisive actions.

Laymen can have only the vaguest ideas about such matters as these. We are obliged to give the benefit of the doubt to professionals. Yet there are times when the evidence seems so clear to the layman that he cannot repress astonishment at what appears to be stubborn resistance, or at least a habitbound inability to see the obvious.

It is like the British officers who say they didn't think it was possible for the Japanese to come down to Singapore through the back jungles. The British sat there at Singapore waiting for the Japanese to come in by water. When the perverse little devils did just the opposite, the British couldn't understand it.

For a long time the Army continued to reject aluminum sheets for airplanes because they were discolored. Only after plane manufacturers proved to them that the sheets were just as strong in spite of slight color blemish would the Army change its specifications.

It's that kind of attitude that shakes the confidence of laymen in professionals who are supposed to know their business. Of course, always we remember what the Army did to Billy Mitchell. It makes you suspect that sometimes the brass hats learn too late.

2/19/43

I took time off this week to see some of the tools the Navy uses—its fighter planes, its torpedo planes, and especially its battleships. You get tired of words around here.

First of all, when you begin to climb around these tools of war, you realize that modern war is a gigantic industrial operation. Only a handful of large industrial nations can wage it. If a small country fights, it is only as a pawn with arms supplied by a big country.

Can you imagine a small country such as Uruguay building a battleship like the *Iowa,* which I climbed around in Brooklyn Navy Yard this week?

So far as we know, this is the biggest fighting machine ever produced. It has been 2½ years building thus far, and that is at rush pace that has cut the usual time by months. They used 45 tons of grease to slide her down the ways at the launching.

This is the first of our 45,000-ton battle monsters. We are air-minded, but we also know that when other nations have battleships we should have them too. We are building six of these of the *Iowa* type. I saw the *Missouri* partly finished at Brooklyn. The *New Jersey* was launched in December. The *Wisconsin* and *Illinois* are building at Philadelphia, and the *Kentucky* at Norfolk. Although the Navy has not released any official data regarding these ships, they are reportedly 880 feet long—which is 200 feet shorter than the old *Normandie*. They have 9½ acres of deck and platform space. Climbing up to the top of the control tower is like climbing halfway to the top of the Washington Monument. Only a nation with large industrial facilities could build half a dozen of these titans at one time.

In construction the *Iowa* has been modified time and again to take advantage of lessons learned in the Pacific fighting. Nine of the 16-inch guns and twenty of the 5-inch guns give her the top heavyweight wallop. She bristles all over with Bofors and Oerlikon antiaircraft guns. I remember about 10 years ago going on the shakedown cruise of the *Arizona,* which was sunk at Pearl Harbor. She had just been modernized to meet demands of air warfare as it was then known. The new *Iowa* bears little resemblance to that modernized job of 10 years ago.

Two of these 45,000-tonners and a number of smaller ships are being built or overhauled in Brooklyn Navy Yard. That is a gigantic industrial community in itself, employing many thousand people, filled with high buildings, and cluttered with enormous swinging cranes.

You can't make 16-inch guns in a village blacksmith shop. The heavy armor-plated turrets, as big as a house and filled with complicated machinery, can't be made except in enormous steel works. The driving machinery, the shafts and turbines are the products of great industrial organizations.

It is the same on land. Only a big nation can make the artillery, the tanks, the motorized equipment that modern armies must have. The brave little Finns, the brave Norwegians, the brave Dutch, the brave little any people are just brave little people unless they can get the war tools in large quantity from some big nations.

War now can only be the business of a very few nations—ourselves, Great Britain, Russia, Germany, and Japan—because those are the only nations with the industrial strength to fight modern war.

8/29/42

Once upon a time I read about some men called Pharisees. They caught a young fellow named Jesus doing something on the Sabbath which they thought he should have put off until the next day. He said something about the Sabbath being made for man and not man for the Sabbath. There have always been scofflaws, and if we insist on trying to win this war with the kind of sloppy, inefficient control of raw materials that we are getting now, we will have to win it with the help of the scofflaws. Which are you going to do, build ships or win the war with court orders?

Now Old Man Kaiser turns up in the clutches of the courts.

Yes, they've got the old fellow. He was trying to build ships and was doing mighty damned well at it—turning them out faster than anybody else. He had to use a lot of steel. The Government could give him the contracts, but its control over steel supply was so loose and erratic that the Government couldn't ensure him steel.

So Old Man Kaiser's people—if the Government's charge is correct—got to buying steel on the black market. They paid a little more than the ceiling price in order to get the steel. The Government went after the black-market steel dealer. And they also got Old Man Kaiser for buying steel from him.

The indictment is not against Old Man Kaiser but against this arsenal of bureaucracy down here which has had so much lead in its feet that manufacturers either had to go to a black market or stop making war weapons. Old Man Kaiser would be damned if he would be shut down, so he went out and got steel wherever he could at whatever price he had to pay.

If I believed every derogatory word about Old Man Kaiser that one hears around here in Washington, which I don't, I would say it was too bad but don't stop him from building ships. He is building them faster than anybody else. He has just set a new record. If it is a stunt it's the kind of stunt we can watch without ever becoming tired of it. Well, the ships float and they carry cargo and they're in fact excellent ships. So if it is a stunt that's just dandy.

12/28/42

In the coming year American industry probably will produce more war goods than any nation ever produced before.

To do that, some very uneconomical expenditures must be made by our Federal Government. War industry does not run just on materials produced in this country. For instance, war industry must have tungsten. We get it in Portugal, Turkey, and Spain. Germans are in those places trying to get it too. The lucky neutrals have the belligerents bidding against each other. Price is no object either to us or to Germany. You want the material at whatever price. If we pay ten or twenty times the normal market price, what of it?

We have to have mica for radio equipment. We were so desperate for it at one time that the air force used its own planes to fly supplies back from India. That certainly was not economical, in dollars.

When W.P.B. tells the Board of Economic Warfare it must have 5,000,000 carats of industrial diamonds for stock-pile purposes, that means the industrial diamonds must be obtained, and it means that you can't go to South Africa or South America and be choosy about price. You take what you can get at the prices you have to pay.

We are trying to obtain natural rubber in the Western Hemisphere at prices and in ways that would normally be too expensive to bother with. But the synthetic production isn't coming along very fast. We won't be up anywhere near our requirements in 1943. So regardless of cost we are financing expeditions into the wild rubber jungles of Brazil and the growing of the cryptostegia plant in Haiti and other places. The rubber may cost us a dollar a pound but it is the quickest source of natural rubber. We need rubber, regardless of what it costs.

American correspondents visit American airfield in England. Left to right: Marquis Childs, Blair Bolles, Raymond Clapper, Col. A. Peterson, Charles Gratke, Major E. P. Roberts, Major Thor Smith.

Raymond Clapper looks over some American block busters at American airfield in England.

After the war is over investigating committees probably will go back over the deals that are being made now by the Board of Economic Warfare. Some politicians looking for a cheap way to get votes will be telling people how reckless the Government was with public money during the war. That was tried after the last war but Charles G. Dawes, later Vice-President, exposed the game by making the point that when you are trying to win a war you have no time to hunt for flyspecks.

Jesse Jones has found to his prolonged embarrassment that it was a mistake to haggle over the price of rubber instead of getting the rubber here before the Japs cut off our sources. Would we care now what price Jones had paid to get more rubber?

You can't be economical in running a war. War is the most wasteful enterprise of the human species. The only test of war is, not how cheaply you can run it, but whether you win it. Any cost is cheap if you win.

We have built enormous war industries, many of which will be junk after the war. The Government is financing them. Willow Run is not Ford's. It belongs to the Defense Plant Corporation. The big Detroit tank arsenal is not Chrysler's. It is the Government's, built and operated by Chrysler for the Government. All around those plants are signs reminding employees that they are working with Government property. Those plants and dozens of others represent enormous waste of public dollars, unless you believe that any cost is justified to win the war.

So when you look back on industry's miracle of war production, and look ahead to the greater volume that is still to come, just tuck away somewhere back in your mind the thought that it could not have been done without Government extravagance, without a wild shelling out of hard American dollars, on plants and on scarce materials that had to be bought in all corners of the world.

7/1/42

Getting ready to send out a troop convoy is like trying to empty a dozen mail-order warehouses at one time.

All around the terminal are huge supply dumps and vehicle

parks. I saw about an acre of one type of material ready to be hauled overseas. Large fields were packed with rows of trench diggers, bulldozers, ambulances, sterilizing trucks, air-corps repair shops on wheels, and gasoline trucks. These are rolled up and swung aboard the transports by great cranes.

The terminal buildings themselves all connect with the head house along the dock. The Services of Supply has its own switching engines, and switching crews were kept busy shunting freight cars up into the terminal warehouses. There were cases of string beans, condensed milk, sauerkraut, canned fruit, canned meat, beans, ketchup, and other articles hauled out to the ship. The S.O.S. uses small trucks called fork lifts which scoop up dozens of cases at a time and roll them out to the ship. One of these little scooters can do the work of several large gangs of handlers.

The complete secrecy around such an operation gives one a somewhat mysterious feeling. Some of the soldiers in this particular expedition had speculated every locality on the globe as a possible destination.

Incidentally the soldiers go aboard without any bands or cheering crowds. The whole scene is very matter-of-fact, much as it would be on any dock where a freighter was loading.

In looking over the merchandise which is to go out with the troops one realizes what infinite detail has gone into the planning. Some of the troops going aboard carried handsaws. On the docks were stacks of prefabricated houses. There were bundles of garden tools such as hoes, rakes, and spades, for raising vegetables for the commissary.

The actual loading must be planned with the nature of the expedition in mind. The most efficient way to load is to put the heavy material at the bottom of the ship. But if it is an expedition which may have to go into action as it lands, then the loading must be changed so that fighting equipment and ammunition are up on deck where the troops can get at them quickly.

Some idea of the quantity of foodstuffs which must be taken may be gained from the fact that several thousand men must be fed over a period of perhaps several weeks. It would be like stocking an enormous restaurant for a long siege. Because the number of troops aboard far exceeds the ordinary number of passengers, it is necessary to make special arrangements for feeding. In a particular transport rows of stand-up tables may be set up for cafeteria service. The men eat standing up. Only two meals a day can be served and the mess hall operates almost around the clock, feeding the troops in relays.

On another transport I saw the hospital arrangements. The main hospital is equipped with battery operating lights so that operations can be performed even if the ship's lighting system goes out. Other emergency operating equipment was stowed in various parts of the ship so that it could be put into use within one minute's time should the main operating room become unusable.

3/11/43

Can't we get across the idea in America that you don't have to love Communism to be in favor of helping Russia? Why do some of our people try to sell aid to Russia on the questionable argument that Communism is changing in Russia, that Russia is going capitalist, that there is freedom of religion in Russia, and in short that Russian Communism is practically just the same as the American way?

Our people don't believe that kind of propaganda. They don't like Communism and resent any propaganda effort abroad or at home to sell it to them with sugar-coating.

Why can't our Government somehow, Elmer Davis with his 4,000 employees and a good many millions of dollars, get across to the American people that it isn't a matter of perfuming Communism at all—but a matter of helping an ally that is fighting to smash the same enemy that we are fighting?

Churchill and Stalin don't get along. Uncle Joe is quite bitter toward Churchill.

Yet the relations between Great Britain and Russia are very much better than ours with Russia. The reason is that, thanks to Churchill, the British people are on a realistic and not a sentimental basis toward Russia.

In less than 24 hours after Germany attacked Russia in June of 1941, Churchill told his people what the score was. Churchill said he had fought Communism for 25 years and took back nothing that he had said. He said Nazism was indistinguishable from the worst features of Communism. But Churchill said he would help anybody that was fighting the Nazis.

Why not stand on that?

6/1/43

STOCKHOLM. It is impossible for anybody in the warring world to imagine the placid life here in the long summer sunlight of Sweden. Here it is difficult to realize that in the world outside there is the taut agony of the war of nerves. There are no nerves here, especially now when everyone is outdoors living in the sun.

In Sweden you get to wondering what the meaning of life really is. In America we strive intensely; the whole atmosphere is one of competition, of struggle to improve one's station in life and standard of living. Here there is a high standard of living, and on the whole the people lead a life that normally fulfills the average desires quite adequately. Yet there seems to be a kind of static contentment about it that I should think would pall on Americans accustomed to a more intense struggle. Americans keep raising their sights. While we have often deplored this as trying "to keep up with the Joneses," it may be the yeast of life that any nation, like any individual, should have.

To the eye nothing could be more inviting than the life that Swedes live now in these long summer days. The whole nation moves out into the sun. People eat in the sun in outdoor cafés. On a Sunday afternoon, or at lunch time during the week, you see young people and old people sitting on the steps of the State Theater or of the Art Museum, or on benches around the downtown parks, all with their faces turned up into the sun. This very day thousands of families are moving out into the country. Because of the long dark winters, Sweden makes the most of summer, with such emphasis on vacations that for a few weeks business almost comes to a standstill.

The many lakes, rivers, and inlets of the Baltic provide ideal vacation spots. But foreigners are excluded from some areas, for military reasons. The Government has posted in the Grand Hotel a list of summer places to which foreigners are permitted to go.

I have talked to many people in Sweden about Germany, and not one of them has expressed admiration for German efficiency or made any of the comments usually expected from pro-Nazis. On the contrary, they universally comment on the brutality and terrorism of the Nazis.

People here make a sharp distinction between the old Germany, to which they felt close, and Nazi Germany, which they abhor because of its inhuman treatment of conquered peoples.

This inhumanity is brought home to the Swedes because they are in such close and constant contact with occupied Norway. Many Norwegians escape across the border to this country, and they tell their friends here what has happened under German rule.

But the special horrors of the Nazi order are reserved for Poland. Knowledge of conditions in Poland helps to explain why the Nazis could never become permanent masters of Europe. It is impossible to make people accept such conditions, or to win the confidence of other peoples in the presence of such conditions. That is the big political mistake of the Nazis, which would have ruined them even if they had won military success, which also is now beyond their reach.

The Germans give the Poles worse treatment than anybody else except the Jews. They are cleaning the last of the Jews out of the Warsaw ghetto, which had a population of 400,000 when the war started and was down to 35,000 this spring. They have been removing the Jews at a rate of 3,000 a day, using machine guns when the slightest resistance is shown. The Nazis are renovating the ghetto quarters, and the Poles fear they are to be herded into the ghetto to replace the Jews, thus clearing better sections of Warsaw for the Germans.

Labor and management in Sweden are going along placidly, with no strikes for 10 years in most industries, and with labor accepting the formula of adjustment that gives it only half of the increase in the cost-of-living index. In contrast to the turbulent labor relations in America, labor here is docile, and accepts the judgment of union leaders, who seem to work on good terms with management. Augustus Lindberg, head of the Labor Federation, is very much like William Green in personality and outlook.

I do not mean to imply that there is no initiative on the part of industry here, as there has been a fast advance in production of wartime substitutes of many kinds. Also, Swedish businessmen not only think about postwar problems and possibilities but are working on them.

But life as a whole in Sweden seems far more placid, without the striving we know in America. This raises the question whether a nation is happier when contented or when driving in a hard struggle. In America we know that men often are least happy when they have made their pile and retire to "enjoy life." Possibly the same thing may apply to whole peoples as well as to individuals.

7/19/43

Most of today I have spent in the nose of a B-17 Flying Fortress which went to Rome and back.

This has been a rather long day, beginning out on the bomber station when we were called at 5:15 this morning. It was still dark —and quite chilly. We washed up in the colonel's tent and had a quick breakfast of wheat cakes and coffee. Then at 6:30 crews going on the bombing mission met in a briefing tent. That was when the crews were told they would go to Rome today. I wish you could have been there in the large tent full of American fliers.

At 8:05 we take off, with no more excitement than attends an 8 A.M. plane's departure from La Guardia airport. We circle around while other planes are taking off and as easily as birds do it, we suddenly are all in formation moving majestically over the North African mountains out to the sea. One of the crew says, "They'll be surprised. They don't think we dare to bomb the Eternal City."

I went up into the control cabin and talked with the pilots. Our pilot, Major Whitmore, has a snapshot of his wife and two-year-old baby pasted on the instrument panel. It was taken in Palm Beach,

Fla. He says it helps a lot to have them smiling at him. Right now everything is quiet. The automatic pilot does the work and there is little to do for the moment. You would be surprised how much dull time there is on a trip like this one to Rome. You just fly along mile after mile over water. You know this is a historic event, the first bombing of Rome, and that modern bombs make ruins in a flash where it takes nature centuries. We had been warned that we might run into considerable flak. But that is all some time off and you don't worry about it now. The run was 600 miles to the target—a total trip of seven hours.

At 10:10 we put on our parachutes. Now the first feeling of excitement appears. We have just started to climb. We adjust our oxygen masks and will wear them for the next 2 hours.

We should pick up our initial point—that is the beginning of the home stretch to the target—in about an hour, the navigator says. You sit down on the parachute and find it makes a good seat and you relax again. The weather is still perfect. Nobody can talk much now with the masks on but the crew members talk with a throat microphone that fits around the neck.

The bombardier is studying his charts closely now. He must be able to recognize instantly the pin-point aiming point as it comes up into his bomb sight. If he misses, then it has all been in vain.

Within a few minutes the first wave will be over Rome. You wonder what a shock that will be—in broad daylight—just before noon. It is warm in our nose compartment, in spite of the altitude.

You think how wonderful these boys are—doing this job the way they do, and good-natured, not surly, not militarists. Most of them don't think of themselves as military men and are waiting to get back to civilian life, yet they love this being around airplanes. At 11:05 our bombardier begins adjusting his bomb sight in earnest. He is notified what his ground speed over the target will be. We are still climbing hard to get up around 25,000 feet. The coast of Italy shows up very clearly now. We see Lake Bracciano. We reached the coast of Italy at the appointed time and place. We went in so as to come down on Rome from the north. The bombardier turned around and held up his thumb and forefinger in a circle to indicate a perfect landfall.

The bomb doors were opened and you could hear the rush of air which that caused. The bombardier was now shouting to the interphone guiding the pilot over the target. Out through the right window I could see the Vatican and St. Peter's clearly—and very wide of our path. We could not have hit them except by turning and going over that way. The railroad yards of San Lorenzo were coming up fast now. At 11:39 we dropped our bombs and the bombardier gave the traditional call—Bombs away.

We could see flak ahead—a barrage of it. But it was breaking well ahead of us. The ship rocked slightly but nothing hit us. Part of the flak was breaking below us. But two enemy fighters roared past us—and all of our Fortress guns threw a barrage of 50-calibre machine-gun fire after the fighters but they got away. They made no effort to attack. None of the flak hit. By 11:45 we were heading out to sea. The whole thing lasted only about fifteen minutes and the critical part of it only five minutes.

7/24/43

NORTH AFRICAN AIR FIELD. Just to keep the editors happy I am doing this potboiler sitting in the shade of one wing of our plane with my typewriter on a 5-gallon galvanized can, and Clapper's rear on a 2-gallon can which is beginning to sag in the middle.

You look out for yourself out in the field here, as all readers of Ernie Pyle know. He is widely known all over North Africa as the best camper among the correspondents. A tenderfoot like myself takes what the Army issues and becomes loaded down like one of John Steinbeck's Okies in *The Grapes of Wrath.*

We carry our own rations, for instance, as there is no certainty of finding mess in Sicily. I am carrying a carton containing three cans of salmon, four cans of meat and vegetables, two cans of ration sausages which are like weak hot dogs, five cartons of hardtack, and several packages of rations which are allegedly complete meals in a small box 3 by 6 by 2 inches. The whole meal occupies about the space of an ordinary three-decker sandwich at your drugstore fountain.

Each of us is eating and working under the plane wing. I find I have a breakfast box by mistake. The package reads U.S. Army Field Ration Breakfast Unit. Here is what the best fed Army in the world is given in a breakfast field-ration kit: one 2-ounce fruit bar which I will now open and eat. Pause. It seems to be ground, dried prunes of which one bite is more than sufficient. Next I find a small round can of veal and pork loaf—ingredients: cooked veal and pork, milk, cracker meal, salt, onions, eggs, and sugar and spice and everything nice—and sodium nitrate.

This I spread on seven biscuits, Nabisco size. Pause. It eats right well but I prefer the dinner-ration main course which is American rat cheese—I had that for lunch in the Flying Fortress coming back from Rome. Over under the other wing I see Artist George Biddle of the Army Art Unit cleaning his mess kit with a handful of grass. He is not working and hence is able to finish eating first. He is a brother of the Attorney General and is the third Biddle I have encountered this trip beginning with that great friend of everybody, Tony, in London. George Biddle is going around sketching the war which should make quite a sketch when it's all done.

I have some powdered coffee which I dissolve in the mess cup with cold water from my canteen. We get three lumps of sugar—thanks—all of which I use over here. Cool coffee for lunch is not bad, sitting here in the shade with a cool breeze blowing as if I were on the Washington Hotel roof.

I now find the ration includes three Chelsea cigarettes, which I will give away, one stick of Spearmint gum which I will chew. Just as I feared—the oil can has collapsed under the added weight of lunch and I will finish this quickly, sitting on the ground.

If you want me to tell you more I am carrying a typewriter, dispatch case for copy paper, maps, notebooks, a bag containing my mess kit, flashlight, towel, pajamas, toilet kit, toilet paper, which is most important, an extra fountain pen, ink, canteen, sunglasses, barracks bag containing rations, helmet, extra shirt, trousers, socks. You don't wear much underwear and that a long time here.

I also carry a bedding roll containing a cot, three blankets, and mosquito netting. On the hoof I weigh about 300 pounds. I wear an Army shirt, trousers, field cap, leggings, and good ole GI shoes which are the most comfortable footwear ever made. That's one job the Army has done to perfection—they've got a shoe that you can wear in peace.

Well, we must be going now and thanks to Uncle Sam for a nourishing lunch.

7/17/43

ALLIED COMMAND POST, North Africa. During a big historic event such as the invasion of Sicily it might be supposed that the commanding general would be clanking his weight around. After all this is a great moment in history because the Allies at last are carrying the war to Europe.

Furthermore, this is a gigantic operation with 3,000 ships involved and it might be expected that the commanding general would be jumping all over the place issuing orders right and left.

But General Eisenhower returned from the beaches of Sicily looking as if he had just come from a ball game which broke right for the home team. He was more like a big industrial executive who, on the day when the plant is breaking production records, will show visitors around the mill as if he had nothing else to do.

The fact is, Eisenhower's main work was done weeks and months ago. When the time came for the move to Sicily everything that he could do about the invasion had already been done and the rest was in the hands of others. Two weeks before the attack I saw him one afternoon and he talked for nearly two hours, with his time seemingly completely clear as probably it was because at that late date all plans were made.

The harbor outside his window was crowded with transports and with troops assembling for loading. If Eisenhower, weeks before, had overlooked something it was too late now. He was like the coach who had done all he could for the team and had to sit, waiting to see what happened.

Eisenhower went over to the beaches, not to direct operations, but to welcome the Canadians who were in action under him for the first time, also to call on various American generals conducting operations, to get a look at the end product of his months of hard work on infinite details and, finally, to give his aide, Naval Commander Harry Butcher, an opportunity to take two rolls of snapshots for their scrapbooks.

At this stage, General Eisenhower was watching chiefly for deficiencies in planning which can be corrected for future actions, noting messages that come in reporting the capture of new places, hearing reports of subordinates, attending to complaints. He hates the standard communiqué phrase "according to plan" but yet that's about the way it has been going thus far.

So instead of seeing a dust-covered, motorized version of General Grant at Shiloh, you see Eisenhower in neat shirt sleeves, with just one dudish touch—he wears a regulation army necktie, whereas everyone else in this area keeps his shirt collar open, even generals at dinner.

Air-force men, up to and including General Tooey Spaatz, keep their sleeves rolled up which you won't find authorized in the regulations. Except for that necktie touch, Eisenhower is informal, very much Kansas folks, although he's had occasion before this to make it clear who's boss.

Eisenhower doesn't seem to be a person who runs war by intuition. From what an outsider can observe it seems as if the Allied invasion was the result of slide-rule planning, more like a big engineering job than fiction-story war. Yet as it comes out there has been nothing more spectacular in history than this gigantic armada landing a mechanized army on the ancient shores of Sicily.

8/2/43

In a couple of hours of wandering around the ghostlike ruins of Palermo's harbor one gathers further convincing evidence of the irresistible force of air power when thrown in with determination and volume.

For throughout the entire semicircle of the harbor there is complete destruction. Twisted hulls and sunken ships are scattered everywhere. Several ships were blown out of the water and left lying on the docks. In two places, at least, fairly large ships are lying thus in pairs, flat on their sides up on the piers, as if some giant hand had scooped them up out of the water and dropped them there to dry, like dead fish.

The waterfront is lined with five- and six-story houses, not one of which is now habitable. Many are completely demolished. Others, for a space of three or four blocks back, will need to be completely rebuilt, because although the walls are still standing they have been wrenched and cracked beyond repair. The City Hall, an impressive structure where a lieutenant colonel of the AMGOT has taken over as administrator of civilian affairs, will need fundamental reconstruction before it is sound again.

One important point about this is that all the damage was done in the face of the most effective antiaircraft defense in Sicily. The Germans had excellent flak defense. We lost planes, but they put the place out of business.

Three of us wandered over the empty docks. Not a soul was there except a couple of American military guards at the gates, and two old men sitting in the shade of a shattered building looking out blankly at the devastation. We heard occasional rifle fire, as if snipers were busy, although we never had any other evidence of such activity or of a hostile attitude. Otherwise there was only deathly silence.

At least 150,000 people have fled from Palermo, which has a normal population of 400,000. No wonder the Italians welcomed the Americans with cheers, tossing lemons and even watermelons—one of which hit a correspondent and exploded like a bomb. The people of Palermo have everything to gain by the American occupation, which has ended the terrifying bombing.

An ironic footnote on our walk through the ghostly water front is that across all the street openings coming into the harbor area were new stone barriers with firing slits so that Palermo could be better defended against attack from the sea. The barricades were all intact, like low thresholds over which air power could walk in.

8/12/43

Air war is terrifying and brutal. That is one of the best things about it. At last we have the means of making cities uninhabitable, spreading a blight over ports, industrial areas, airfields, and—yes, why not be frank about it?—population areas. I have seen many blocks rendered uninhabitable around port areas in Africa and Sicily. At last war is being made so horrible for the civilian population that perhaps its ultimate stupidity will become clear.

For too long war has been a plaything of ambitious men, for too long it has been a convenient means by which politicians and dictators have resolved unemployment and other economic troubles, stifled opposition, and grasped more power. For too long have such aggressive men been able to plunge other countries into unwanted wars—and of all the people who have a just complaint on this score Americans are the first.

Perhaps the mutual destructiveness of war as it is now being waged will goad the world to drive politicians and statesmen out of the historic habit of resorting to this insanity as the handiest panacea for their headaches. When the Nazis begin to cry that some of our people are brutal ogres, killing their people, perhaps we are beginning to be really effective. That is the best tip to us to lay it on heavier than ever, to bring in planes, crews, bombs, and send them out in ever larger force, still deeper into the vitals of Germany.

For years the German people have been making war on the rest of the Western world, in other people's territory, and now they are getting a dose of it that has long been needed.

What I like about our side is the cool, calculating way we are going at this. Nothing is more touching than to see Air Chief Marshal Harris in his home, with the beautiful and young Lady Harris, and with their two-year-old daughter on his knee. Also there is nothing more terrifying than to be on the other end of that pair of blue eyes when they are turned on photographs of German targets. Nobody enjoys a vacation with his family at the beach more than Lieutenant General Carl Spaatz, the ranking American air officer in Africa. You should have seen one ecstatic young air general getting in the mail a snapshot of his four-year-old daughter and delaying his conference on the next raid until he had showed it to everybody and told everybody about her. In their personal relations these bombing chiefs may be reasonable, kind, shy, and have no more brutal impulses than a country parson. But their job is using this new weapon of mass destruction, and they are rightly making it as deadly and destructive as possible.

11/26/43

We can regret that it is necessary to bomb Berlin to partial destruction. But more appropriately we can thank God that the R.A.F. is able to do the job.

We can feel sorry for the families in Berlin, and especially for the children who are lost. They might have grown up to make Germany a better member of the family of nations.

But we can more appropriately regret the loss of brave R.A.F. fliers on these missions, and the losses of American fliers in other missions that are pounding Germany to defeat.

We need have no bad conscience about giving Berlin something like what Hitler gave to Rotterdam and Warsaw and countless other localities.

If you heard the radio première of Noel Coward's ironical song, "Let's Don't Be Beastly to the Germans," you know what I mean.

Germany must be defeated so convincingly this time that the German people will cease to glorify war as a means of national salvation. They have to learn it the hard way. With air attack the war, fortunately, is being carried right into the heart of Germany and the old trick of quitting before the enemy invades is not working this time.

I have talked with a person who has been in Germany in the last few months. After some of the heavy bombing, Berlin became a somewhat deserted city. People by the thousands crowded the trains in a panic evacuation. Many of the government offices moved away. At that time there had been little damage in the heart of the city, in the area around the Adlon Hotel. Only a few windows were out. But outlying industrial areas were badly hit and factories showed the effects of it.

Persons who saw working shifts change at these factories found that a large portion of the workmen were drafted labor from the occupied countries. Each wore a large identification badge on his lapel indicating his nationality. Many were Poles.

Conversation was much more independent than previously. Mussolini had fallen and there were street comments that if it could happen in Italy there was hope it might happen in Germany. Sources in which I have confidence size up home-front morale as being extremely low. The people are spiritless and overcome with a sense of hopelessness.

Still, these same sources think the Germans will continue to fight until well into next summer, and in personal betting prefer August as the month of the surrender.

Questions are raised as to whether our unconditional-surrender war aim should not be explained. Should we give the Germans some idea of what kind of a peace they might expect? The Nazi propaganda holds the German people in the war by telling them that the suffering of war is nothing to what the punishment will be after the surrender. They are saying more Germans will die in a month at the hands of outraged conquered peoples than would die in battle in a similar period.

They drive that point home by citing our unconditional-surrender slogan.

Our side has been considering the policy to be applied after Germany surrenders. Possibly very shortly some attempt will be made to get across to the German people that they can escape continuation of this savage air attack by ending the war. Otherwise land invasion is certain to follow the pulverizing blows from the air.

There won't be much conscience about it either. What Hitler has done has been too horrible. More Allied deaths will only increase the severity of the retribution. Nobody will worry much about the bomb victims. When you're up there over the target, you are not thinking about the people down below but only of getting back home. It is impersonal. Nothing that air raids can do will be any more brutal than the slow torture, and mental anguish as well, which the Nazis have inflicted upon millions of people.

12/2/43

The Cairo terms of the Allies make it likely that we are in for a very long war in the Pacific. Japan undoubtedly will fight until helpless rather than to accept those terms. They mean her disappearance as a world power.

Japan would be reduced to the status of a small island country, stripped of all empire and therefore of all materials necessary for war industry. Japan would be back, territorially, as Commodore Perry found it. All acquisitions, beginning with Formosa, which was taken from the Chinese 50 years ago, would be stripped away.

These are pledges which the Allies have made to each other. As nearly as it is possible to do so, the Allies have pronounced a sentence of death on the Japanese empire and have decreed the international equivalent of solitary confinement on this malicious race which has indulged in every kind of international crime to advance its material ambitions.

But the sentence is easier pronounced than executed.

Geography is our great foe. Our Navy is far superior to Japan's now, and we are building at a rate which permits us to go into the heaviest kind of war of attrition with certainty of victory in the end. If we lose ship for ship with the Japs, they can't win, because one day their ships are all gone and we are still there.

But the Japanese show no signs of coming out to fight—for that very reason. They probably will pull their fleet back and back as necessary and keep it under cover of land-based aircraft. Much as our Navy would welcome a full-dress battle between the two fleets, it is not likely to occur—not at least until we have driven through to the very gates of the Japanese homeland.

In the air, we are building some 9,000 planes a month. Certainly when Germany is defeated, we can expect to have Japan completely outnumbered in the air. We can lose plane for plane and Japan is sure to be driven out of the air.

But we are a long way from where we can get our planes to hit at the vitals of Japan. We are fighting far out on the fringes of Japan.

To reach Japan from the Chinese side we must retake Burma and drive the Japanese out of most of China. To reach Japan from the south we must retake a whole series of strong defenses, because the Philippines, Malaya, and other Japanese holdings lie between us and the homeland of Japan. To attack Japan from the direction of Pearl Harbor we must get over vast expanses of ocean in which Japan holds the outposts, and on which Japanese planes are based.

From the direction of Alaska, long stretches of islands are in the way.

We are still a long way from Wake, and Wake is 2,000 miles from Japan. That is more than twice the practical bombing range of our heavy bombing fleets. The B-29 will stretch out the range somewhat. We must get very much closer than we are now before we go beyond the stage of stunt bombing of Japan.

We are trying to get closer airfields. That is what the so-called island hopping is all about. At great cost we have taken airfields a bit closer in the Gilberts. We will get airfields in other islands, probably at great cost also.

Many people will think the war is almost over when Germany surrenders. For us the dying will only have begun.

Postwar

11/11/43

ARMISTICE DAY 20 years ago was cloudy and raw in Washington, as it is now outside my window.

I have always remembered the story I covered that day for the United Press. The war had been over five years. Woodrow Wilson had become a broken old man, living in seclusion at his home on S Street and what he said that day has come true, it seems to me, although you may not agree.

One felt very sad for him. Remember the time, if you can. By then Harding had been President and had died. Coolidge was in office and was feeling rather pleased—as he said at the time—because rigid economy had brought our expenditures within our income, and he hoped as we all believed, that we were on the threshold of a new era.

Yes, one felt that the times had moved far beyond Wilson. Harding had said the League of Nations was dead. It had been a rather fanciful dream of a college professor who did not know his way around in the practical world.

Democratic politicians felt it was not good politics to be publicly associated any longer with the Wilson dream. The following summer there was to be a strange scene in the Democratic National Convention in Madison Square Garden.

I remember that scene, too—Newton Baker, faithful to Wilson, standing before that convention of cynical trimmers, tears on his face and in some eyes in the press section, pleading with the Democrats not to betray the spirit of Woodrow Wilson.

Pardon an old reporter's memories. I wander too much.

That Armistice Sunday of 1923 was gray and the faithful followers of Wilson were a bedraggled crowd in the street in front of the house on S Street. They went there every Armistice Day and knelt down to pray in the street.

It always was a fairly good human-interest story. Nobody very prominent in the crowd, of course. Mostly fringe sentimentalists, cranks, and not very realistic people. Most of them were women, probably many of them mothers mourning for a son with a silent grief that would never pass. They were bound to grow misty over a broken idealist like Woodrow Wilson.

I think there was a minister in the crowd and, as I remember it, he said a prayer.

Then somebody went up and knocked on the door and in a few minutes Wilson came out on the stoop.

I have a photograph of him as he came out of the door and I stood about 10 feet away. He dragged himself through the door with some difficulty, for since his illness in the White House four years earlier he had not been able to move about freely. He leaned on a heavy cane. He had changed much since I had seen him last and especially since the day when he strode confidently down the center aisle of the Senate bringing the huge text of the Treaty of Versailles under his arm to ask for its ratification.

His hair was all white and hung in a fringe on his neck. But he wore his silk hat and a long cloak and pulled himself together for a dignified appearance.

Wilson lived only three months after that. The feeble man had difficulty in responding to the greeting of his admirers. After a few words of thanks he choked and apologized for his emotion.

Then for just a few seconds he fired up and spoke like an implacable prophet out of the Old Testament.

I looked up his words today in a yellowed copy of the World Almanac. They still vibrate and now I can hear them plainly:

"Just one word more. I cannot refrain from saying it: I am not one of those that have the least anxiety about the triumph of the principles I have stood for. I have seen fools resist Providence before and I have seen their destruction, as will come upon these again—utter destruction and contempt. That we shall prevail is as sure as that God reigns."

Those, I believe, are the last public words Woodrow Wilson ever spoke.

9/13/41

There is an opportunity for the United States to play a role in world history such as no nation has ever before played. We threw away a similar opportunity after the last war, and as a result got the kind of world we do not like—one that is now costing us over 50 billion dollars for armaments.

Through America's enormous strength, in cooperation with British sea power, which is still one of the great forces in the world, there exists a potential combination which can dominate the world and so shape it that there will not always be a menace requiring us to go into elaborate war preparations every few years.

Police the world? Well, it would be cheaper and easier to police the world than to have to go through these periodic frantic rearmament programs at fantastic expense and effort.

We have seen for the second time in our generation that, no matter how hard we try, we are unable to escape the heavy impact of major wars when they finally break out. After the last war our own depression was set off and aggravated by the chaotic conditions which brought collapse in Central Europe. We may wish to have nothing to do with Europe, but Europe affects us in our very vitals and there is no escaping it.

For a long time I was an isolationist. I wish it were possible for us to be isolated. We are so far ahead of every other country in our standard of living, our way of life is so infinitely more desirable, at least to my taste, that I would like nothing better than for us to be able to go our own way, paying no attention to the rest of the world and its endless wars.

But I can't see how it is possible. Experience is a stern master and we are learning the hard way. For 25 years we have been whipped around and up and down by the backwash from other lands. Since we can't escape it, we might as well try to do something about it.

The situation is thrust upon us. We might as well shape it to our ends rather than submit in futile lamentations and be encircled and squeezed down to the status of a second-rate power.

10/41

Peace must have its arsenal of strength no less than war. The mechanics offer only secondary difficulties. Once the will to do it is born the mechanics will appear. Give us the purpose. Give us faith to do it and it shall be done. The strength of America can be thrown into the balance for peace with such overwhelming force that it will always have sufficient allies to make itself irresistible.

What do we get out of it? Well, it is difficult to set a price on such a bargain as this. But as an American, I should be very proud to end my days believing that in generations to come, school children all over the globe would read in their books about the United States of America and what it did for the human race. They will read about Genghis Khan and Attila and the evil that Hitler has done to human beings. They will read also of Pasteur and Faraday and Edison and what they and others like them have done to liberate the race. I should like to have them read also of America as the nation that liberated the race from the most awful form of bondage that has inflicted it, the bondage of war. I should like to have them read of America as a nation which was fortunate enough to have great things given to it and which used them not only to build a civilization for its own people but also to benefit all humanity. I should like to have them know America as a nation that lived on as Lincoln would have wanted it to, a nation as tender as he and yet a nation that could be as hard as he in his fight against oppression. That wouldn't mean very much to any of us now living. Yet something tells me it would be the greatest bargain that America ever struck.

On the morning not long ago after I returned from England, I walked down in the woods by my house and sat down on my favorite rock. It is good to sit on a familiar rock. It is hard and firm and gives one a sense of security. My particular rock is like America. It is big and inert and does not know its own strength. There was not a sound of civilization except my dog, kicking through the leaves. Yes, he, my friends, is a work of civilization. The wolf has been taken out of this dog. He has been tamed to a peaceful life. What people have been unable to do for themselves they have done for dogs.

If Americans could only believe in America.

4/16/42

My feeling, after a month east of Suez, is that throughout Asia new forces are rising that will insist on control of their own destinies. The rise of Russia in one generation encourages these aspirations. Also, it is plain to all now that one nation in Asia, Japan, is able to defeat Western powers. These factors accentuate a long-developing ferment.

I have found many Americans in the Orient who are convinced that no victory can check this trend. They feel that we must prepare for a new deal in the Far East, regardless of the outcome of the war, and that so long as the United Nations appear to the Asiatics to be merely fighting to restore the status quo they will be denied the help of millions who are either indifferent as to who their masters are, or think they can use Japan to throw off one yoke without getting caught under a new and heavier one.

Even Americans, in some instances, wonder what purpose will be served if there is only to be a return to the status quo when the victory comes.

Those factors affect morale, and therefore become important along with military force in determining the outcome of the war in the East.

Furthermore, America itself is gradually assuming the appearance—to Eastern eyes—of fighting for imperialism. No matter how unjustified such feelings may be, the fact that they exist is the important thing needing attention. They do exist, and they are having a deteriorating effect on the Allied cause.

Insofar as America is assuming the responsibility for smashing the Japanese conquest, it properly becomes a matter for American concern that the victory shall be used to advance freedom, self-government, collective security, and equitable economic policies instead of restoring conditions which could only spur Asia to new efforts to throw off Western domination.

Revolutionary forces are loosening in Asia, independent of who wins, and there will be no end of trouble for the victors unless these forces are channeled into an effort by the United Nations as a group to bring about a new deal in this part of the world.

4/17/42

Before we can do justice to ourselves in Asia the United Nations must, I think, make a clear and convincing statement of why we are fighting there and what the shape of things will be after the victory.

Until that has been done, the vast masses of the people won't be throwing in their full weight. Japanese propaganda has been playing skillfully on the native hatred of Western imperialism. It is fantastic that the Japs should be regarded as liberators, yet we are letting them get away with it. Our propaganda job is yet to be done. But it can't be done until our own minds are clear as to what the war in Asia is all about, what the status of the native populations is to be after the war, whether to return to previous conditions or to move into a new state with more self-government.

A clear and effective statement of the United Nations' purposes would be convincing propaganda for the winning of confidence in Asia, which seems to me to be one of the most important weapons of the war in the East. Until we do that, we are as good as giving Japan extra divisions. It was so in Malaya and Burma, and it looks as if it might soon be so in India.

6/16/42

Some areas in Asia are not ready for self-government. Some sort of outside guidance for the peoples of these areas will be needed.

But in such cases, colonial policy should be determined and executed by the United Nations as a group, rather than by one imperialist nation. The aim here must be the same as in the areas which are capable of self-government. It must not be exploitation for outside profit. It must be development of each area in the way that will most benefit its own people. This means that whatever special resources—oil, rubber, tin, or rice—each area may possess must be available to all the world on equal terms.

We must not be diverted from our goal of a free Asia by the certainty that some of its peoples will not adopt political democracy. For one thing, the populations are not educated or trained in democratic methods. Secondly, their leaders may be unwilling to submit to the slow processes of democracy and prefer the short cuts of dictatorship to raise their standards of living.

8/29/42

India stands as a monument, a crumbling monument, to waste, inefficiency, shortsightedness. At the time I was there, India was far from being organized on a war basis. Even the facilities at hand were not being used to any real advantage. Ships were lying idle in ports for lack of repairs while some of the ship plants were working on minor Army contracts. Railroads were heavily overburdened, but there was no effective priority system to single out the most urgent shipments. India has the largest deposits of high-grade ore in the world, yet steel production is only a little more than a million tons a year. Steel must be brought in!

It isn't that industry cannot be developed in India. The Tata steel works are modern and efficiently run. They were built by American engineers with Indian capital. India has practically no chemical industry, although the raw materials are there. Textile mills are efficiently run. Native labor is skillful. It learns quickly because the native in India is exceedingly dexterous. True, he lacks ambition. Naturally. He has been undernourished for centuries, and been left a victim of malaria and other debilitating diseases. He has had little incentive to work, for, no matter how hard he labors, his reward is the barest subsistence. So he takes refuge in a fatalistic religion that bids him endure his lot with resignation and wait patiently to get his golden slippers in the next world.

Give him food, clean up the mosquitoes, and give him wages that will induce him to work, and you might see a difference. The

Tata steel works has efficient labor because it has an enlightened labor policy. Neither is it troubled by the natives fleeing from the danger of air raids in the way that many other employers have been deserted. Tata has given them shelters and made other provisions, and native workmen are staying on the job. At least, that was the case when I was there during the panic when the Japanese had a fleet up in the Bay of Bengal and were expected to land and come into Calcutta any day.

It isn't the fault of the British as such. The Dutch, the French, and the Belgians were much the same—and the Germans when they had a colonial empire. We have poured money into Puerto Rico and the Virgin Islands, but they are little better off, so we go into the same pot. The democracies have done wonders to develop their own countries, but they have failed with their possessions and are now paying a dear price for that lost opportunity.

In the Middle East the story is about the same. Only by the hardest kind of struggle have the Jews obtained an opportunity to do anything for themselves in Palestine. In Iran, conditions were so bad that the Germans found it easy to hire fifth columnists to stab the democracies in the back. Egypt is sullen in smoldering bitterness. Even though Egypt is an independent country theoretically, it has been treated rather cavalierly, and stands now with folded hands along the Nile while the United Nations fight the Axis invader.

Everywhere it is the same. British and Americans are there fighting. The natives are standing around, if not secretly playing the Axis game. Gandhi tells the British and Americans to get out of India. Nobody looks upon the British and ourselves as liberators. They look upon us as exploiters, intruders, and millstones. We are correct when we say that it would be worse for them if the Germans or the Japs got in; but the point is that they don't seem to think so and they don't help us. What matters is that all of these peoples throughout the back yard of the world are acting in a way to aid our enemies.

It is not that we should expect gratitude. That is not a common trait in any people. We expect any people to act for its own best interests as it sees them. All of these peoples act as if they thought their best interests would not be affected by defeat of the United Nations. The people of China are fighting. They are fighting for their own country. The guerrillas in the Philippines fought because they felt they were fighting for their own country. But it does not seem to occur to the Indians, the Egyptians, the Iranians, the people of Iraq that their countries are in danger. They seem to have no sense of owning their own countries, but rather a sense of being compelled to work there for an outside exploiter.

I am using hard words because it seems to me that this condition is a devastating commentary on the way the democratic countries have conducted themselves in the back yard of the world.

It is a condition that should shock us into searching our own soul again. For if we expect to exercise any influence in the world to come after this war, we must profit by the tragic lessons of the opportunity which we lost during the years now gone. A system which leaves India, after all these years, merely a big flabby pulp, when it has resources and labor supply sufficient to make it one of the big industrial nations, has not justified its existence. The contrast between Palestine, after a few years of self-development on its own, and the surrounding misery must mean something.

I am not seeking to heckle our Allies. We showed no greater foresight ourselves when we refused to work with the rest of the world after the last war, and when we took the lead in raising tariff walls at a time which required, in all common sense, that we hold down our tariffs. The only profit that can come out of thinking about these matters is new resolution to benefit by past mistakes.

If the democratic world is to survive after victory, it will have to be built on a broader base. Those back-yard areas must not be left to waste their possibilities on the desert air. The democratic nations are heavy industrial producers and must sell and trade around the world. Millions—the largest share of the world's population—live in those areas. Their rich natural resources give them the opportunity for industrial development that will make possible a higher standard of living there. We need to have a higher standard of living there. Not merely because our humanitarian impulses cry out for it. That is all very fine. But we need it for our own economic purposes. We need larger consuming markets. Only as the standard of living in those backward areas rises will our outlets for manufactured surpluses grow. People can buy only as they produce. Industrial production will make new customers.

We are prosperous only when world trade is thriving. The industrial capacity of the democratic nations has been greatly expanded by the war. It can continue after the war only if new markets of consumption are developed abroad. These markets cannot develop under the narrow kind of exploitation that has ruled in the past.

And if humanitarian and economic reasons are not enough, then there is one other reason. We need those countries as allies—as strong, powerful allies. The United Nations need India as a strong industrial production base. We shall have those countries on our side after the war is won if we give them opportunity to develop, to live in a society of nations that is working toward an increase of freedom and better living standards through greater production. If we do not create that kind of a setting for them, they will continue to be undependable, furnishing revenue for those who happen to be parties to the exploitation but giving little strength to the democratic world itself.

Democracy's house is only half built. In the back yard it is still only a primitive hut. We have been living in a house divided.

4/11/42

China dreams of becoming the dominant power in East Asia when the war has been won, but it appears that her leaders are not thinking in terms of any regional bloc. Some advisers close to Generalissimo Chiang Kai-shek believe that a dominant China must ally herself with the rest of the United Nations, not simply with an Asiatic bloc, after the war.

Chinese officials here scoff at Japan's concept of a "Greater East Asia co-prosperity sphere" as economically unsound. Japan and China are not complementary, economically, any more than North and South America are. Both Japan and China lack oil. Both lack sufficient iron. Both, on the other hand, are heavy producers of textiles.

Chinese leaders with whom I have talked in Chungking think that there must be a world-wide interlocking of trade, not simply an Asiatic trade bloc. They feel that ultimately all countries will have to return to Secretary Hull's policy of reciprocal trade. And regionalism would only hamper that.

Also, China knows that her industrial development will require financial and technical assistance from the Western world. So she is opposed to any plan which would tend to cut off that help.

Furthermore, leaders feel that while the crushing of Japan is the first essential, it must be followed by an economic arrangement that will enable Japan to live, economically, although demilitarized.

China, like all other nations, is dependent on the resources of the East Indies—rubber, tin, quinine. So she is insistent that the Indies be kept open. There appears to be no ambition to control the Indies, but rather a determination that those resources should be held in trust for all nations.

China's leaders are realists. They care little who has political control of the East Indies so long as the economic resources are open for distribution—perhaps for allocation all around under the guidance of some world organization.

Inside the framework China expects to pursue a strong nationalism alongside a strong internationalism. The family of nations, it is felt by leaders in Chungking, should not consist of some strong states and some weak ones; rather, they think, all should be strong, self-respecting, and heavy producers, while recognizing that the strength of all is increased by the free exchange of goods and materials all over the world.

This view contrasts sharply with the ideal of the Japanese and the Germans—one strong nation bleeding all its neighbors, reducing them to pitiful weakness as Japan has done to Korea.

That is the way China is looking through the present hard days to the new world that is to come afterward.

12/18/41

The heroism of the dead at Pearl Harbor demands not only the crushing of Japan. It also demands that we organize security so that such murderous regimes are choked before they become full grown. Force banded together, and management so that every nation can have its chance to live if it behaves itself, must go together.

We know now that this cannot be done by inducing nations merely to sign peace treaties. Almost every nation, and all of the Axis nations, signed the Kellogg-Briand Pact, thereby pledging themselves not to resort to war as an instrument of national policy. But it remained a scrap of paper. Organization, with military and economic power behind it, must be used from here on.

Every step in that direction is worth taking without waiting for a more complete plan to be adopted. If a compact can be made now, and I suspect that it not only can but will be made, the nations on our side will have the nucleus of the combined force and resources to manage the armistice transition through the twilight period into peace.

Such a step now will give added purpose to our cause. It will give hope beyond victory. Unless we do this, victory will only mark the rise of new apprehension and preparation for more war. If the sacrifices of this war are to be fully vindicated, victory must mean not the end of united effort but only the beginning, because the aim of victory is to have our kind of world—security from without in order to have freedom within. To have security from without, we must work with our friends across all oceans to retain management control, and to share it only as other nations will fit themselves into a peaceful scheme of things.

12/25/42

I note some sage words by one of the wise men of the East, a great scholar of China, Dr. Hu Shih, the former Chinese ambassador here. He says that science and technology have made the world a physical unity. But man's backwardness in political thinking and planning, he says, has failed miserably to consolidate this physically unified world into a political and moral world community.

That's an old theme but it never pointed at us with such accusing truth as it does today.

We make ourselves out to be just a lot of dopes—like the genius who wasn't strong enough to put his gifts to any use.

In organized world murder, men show magnificent courage, invention, and ability to work together. But not when you try to leave the murder out of it and try to organize civilization for living instead of killing. If your purpose is to live instead of kill, then everything is different. Men and governments become cowards. They are afraid to experiment, afraid to take any risk—and of course they thereby only increase the danger of which they are afraid. They lose the inventive touch in statecraft and public affairs. They have the greatest difficulty in working together at anything long enough to make progress. Nations and peoples can work together to kill much better than they can to live.

12/25/41

For a few brightly remembered hours at this season we all usually retreat from the daily struggle and forget the pressure of reality while we enjoy the warmer glow of happiness among our dear ones and friends.

That is denied to many on this Christmas. In this particular year of Our Lord we are all tempted, I suppose, to feel bitter despair among the mangled ruins of what might have been. Hate against those who have done it chokes up the spirit.

What place have any words of hope in print beside the news that appears in these pages? Perhaps none. Perhaps they will be howled down by the screaming, deadly events.

They say human nature doesn't change. Peace has been the dream of the ages. But only a dream. For two thousand years the Star has been shining, and nothing has come of it.

Or has something come of it? I wonder. Why should we give in? Why give in now when we may be pulling up the last long mile toward the top of the hill? At least it looks like the top up there.

True, people have been climbing for centuries and they are tired. But we are a long way up the hill now. It is worth while to press the journey still a little farther.

If human nature does not change, it does change its standards. That we know. Even in the short life of the United States we have seen these standards change.

When this republic was founded, we were throwing people in prison because they could not pay their debts. Men and women are still living who remember slavery—who remember when human beings were sold on the auction block like a bale of tobacco.

I have here on my desk now an old newspaper, *The Washington Gazette,* the issue of July 26, 1797. John Adams, the New England Puritan, was President. On the first page is this advertisement: "A Runaway in Custody. Was committed to my custody a bright Mulatto Girl, about sixteen or seventeen years old, who says she was bound to a baker in Alexandria. The owner is requested to take her away and pay charges as the law directs. (signed) Joseph Boone, Sheriff."

Maybe human nature hasn't changed. But something has changed since that slave advertisement was published in the capital of the United States of America.

Something has changed even since I have been a newspaperman in Washington, and that's not so long either. Something has changed since Herbert Hoover left the White House. Within the present Administration we have changed our standards.

When a man is thrown out of work, we now recognize it as an obligation to support him out of public funds. Employers are taxed to provide unemployment insurance. We no longer force such victims of economic conditions to beg on the streets or to depend upon the charity of some private citizen.

During the present Administration the nation has assumed a whole new set of responsibilities which formerly were not considered the obligation of society at all. Whether human nature has changed or not, our attitude and conduct toward fellow beings have changed and the result comes to the same thing.

If the human nature of employers has not changed, they are now compelled by law to deal with unions of their employees so that the individual workman is not left at a hopeless disadvantage against a huge corporation. The price of labor is no longer fixed by the length of the line at the hiring gate. It wasn't necessary to change human nature. We just changed our ideas of what was fair and just, and put those ideas into effect without waiting for human nature to change.

Likewise when this war is won, the victorious nations, without waiting for human nature to change, can, if they will it strongly enough, put into effect measures that will prevent butcher regimes from ever again becoming strong enough to massacre civilization.

5/27/42

And yet here's something that puzzles me. When you talk about the need of organizing this world so that nations can operate in their daily affairs without having everything upset every 20 years by a general war, people say it sounds good but it isn't practical.

I have a good many friends, and some of them tell me that on some days I seem very practical and realistic and on other days I seem visionary and a sucker for beautiful dreams.

Perhaps so. No man is a good judge of himself. Yet I'm inclined to be stubborn about this.

I have been reporting politics and public affairs for some years. I've seen many realists in action and many so-called theorists.

A couple of years ago Washington had up the question of whether steel capacity should be enlarged. New Deal economists were giving me arguments to show that even though steel plants were then not running to full capacity the war would require more than we had built at that time. But I found several practical steel men disagreeing. They showed me figures, explained the intricacies of the industry, and put up a convincing case as to why we had all of the steel capacity we would need.

Yet today we have not enough steel for the ships and tanks we could build. But it is too late to build more capacity. The theorists were right in their judgment.

You can say they were only guessing, were only letting their imaginations run riot, but time and again I have seen the hunches of the outsiders come nearer the mark than the detailed calculations of the insiders.

Last winter President Roosevelt's production goals were put down as fantastic by most people who knew the practical difficulties. They said it was good propaganda but of course utterly impossible. Yet we are going to meet those goals and pass them in some respects.

After some years as a reporter I am not inclined to be too much impressed with the argument that a thing is not practical. I have seen it work the other way too often. Isn't the best team in a business a pair of fellows, one yeasty, full of all kinds of wild ideas, crazy as hell, keeping everybody dizzy with his overworking imagination, and the other a less imaginative, methodical mind who shakes it all down and knows how to get it done?

Haven't we got some such problem in this job that the war is going to thrust at us? There will be endless difficulties when we try to figure out how this world can be run without jumping off the track and ripping up everybody's life. The State Department analyses of those difficulties probably cover acres of white paper. It would be easy to convince anybody that no scheme is practical, that no detail of a proposition is practical.

Yet which makes sense—to let it ride and go through this repeatedly, or to find a way to prevent it or make it less likely? Is there anything more practical in this world than an attempt to find some way of fixing things up so that 5 or 6 million American young men can go on about their lives, marry, establish themselves in business and professions and in useful jobs? The war is going to be won someday. Will we be ready to make that victory mean something practical? Or will we throw it away in another political argument?

This war is costing us a lot—in lives and every other way. The practical thing, it seems to me, is to begin planning to get something for it.

But when you start talking that way, then people say you're getting visionary and impractical.

12/17/42

It is becoming fairly certain that the peace this time will not be simply a document drawn up in a conference, signed with a flourish, and then embalmed in some palace of the nations.

We tried that kind of static peace the last time and it failed. The modern world just won't be poured into a rigid mold. It wouldn't stay poured into the Treaty of Versailles and it won't stay poured into anything we can work out this time.

More likely the peace this time will be a flowing, ever-changing condition, requiring constant discussion and adjustment among statesmen of various nations. Peace will be a process, a method, rather than a frozen mold. Even in the happiest of large families, nothing stays still. There are always some matters to be settled, and the peacemaking labors of the mother are never done. No more will the next peace ever be completed so that you can put it away and forget about it. The next peace will continue an active process in which the long-distance telephone and the airplane, which can bring principals together on a few days' notice, will replace the formal green-baize conference table that symbolizes the futile, static peace method of the past.

6/4/42

Like millions of other Americans, Governor Stassen of Minnesota is trying to think through to some way of preventing this war from being fought in vain.

I am harping too much on this theme, perhaps, and hereafter I hope to restrain myself from too-frequent twanging on the same string. But the low-down on the situation as I see it is this: The American people already have generated the momentum that will grow and win the war. The drive is there and the results are beginning to show. But I think there is danger that we shall be cheated out of the peace that should come from this war unless we are on guard.

This Administration is making a fight to ensure that we shall not fight this war in vain. What Vice-President Wallace and Secretary Welles are saying is not just surface talk. They are talking for a purpose. This Administration is making a fight to ensure that we are not in this war just to start the same old game over again, the same old game that will be followed by a grabbing contest and then another world war.

I believe the Administration needs the support of every American citizen in that determination. Without America in there pitching, this war would be lost. Without America in there pitching, the peace will be lost. I'm certain of it.

The Republican Governor of Minnesota puts out a plan for the purpose, as he says, of stimulating discussion. Governor Stassen proposes a world association of free people. Those participating would agree to meet certain minimum standards which would include freedom of worship; a fair system of internal justice with protection of the rights of the accused; granting to all literate persons the right to participate at reasonable intervals in the selection of their governmental leadership.

Nations would participate on a proportional basis which would give recognition to their individual resources, the number of their literate people, and their contribution to the expenses of the world association.

Governor Stassen says this world association might well take these definite steps:

1. Promptly establish temporary governments over each of the Axis nations, preferably utilizing citizens of the United Nations whose Axis ancestry goes back to the Axis nation involved. These temporary governments to serve until Axis peoples can establish proper governments of their own.

2. Establish an airways commission to control great international airports of the future which will be important in aerial commercial development after the war.

3. Establish an administrative body to take control of gateways to the seven seas.

4. Establish a commission whose prime task would be to increase the literacy of peoples of the world, recognizing that ability to read and write is the foundation of progress.

5. Establish a code of justice for relations between peoples of the world, and machinery for administration of the code.

6. Establish a trade commission to work out gradually increased world trade, seeking to prevent either stifling obstructions or heavy dumping of goods, both of which break down economic systems and cause world distress.

7. Establish a world legion as a world police force to enforce the administration of world justice and to make effective administration of airways and seaways. This police force must be supreme in the world.

3/3/43

An expert is someone who makes things sound complicated. Experts make the organization of victory seem so complicated that they discourage people into thinking that perhaps such a difficult task better not be attempted.

Of course the questions are complicated. Every question that comes before the Supreme Court is complicated. But the court itself is a simple, broadly inspired institution that anybody can understand. It exists to handle complicated borderline questions. Likewise it is precisely because postwar affairs are so complicated that we need an organization, such as a continuing conference of the United Nations, to deal with them.

The fact that the questions are difficult, with much to be said on both sides, is exactly the reason for having an international institution to handle them—not a reason against it. As President Eric Johnston of the U.S. Chamber of Commerce says, tomorrow's world will be an international world.

If you don't have something like a United Nations organization, you will have anarchy, with every nation trying to chisel out its own place just as Premier Sikorski of Poland is running from London here and back and bickering with Moscow, trying to muscle out a safe place for Poland after the war. Of course it is complicated, with the big powers intent on strategic frontiers regardless of the little fellows.

But are these issues to be fought out by propaganda and pressure and power politics under conditions of anarchy where international blackmail is a common weapon? Or is not the fact that these problems are complex, with much justice on both sides, a strong reason for trying to place them inside an organization with technical facilities and deliberative processes? Suppose Supreme Court cases were fought out in political campaigns instead of inside the courtroom?

We should remember that it was the issue of Poland's territory that set off this war.

You can't talk about abandoning force in this world. You can only offer an alternative to force, as the Shotwell Commission to Study the Organization of Peace says in its third report, just issued. Force, says this realistic and practical, but broad-visioned, report, is inescapable in human affairs. It cannot merely be abandoned. It must be controlled and used.

War has been used for exploitation and conquest. But it also has been used to maintain rights, to uphold principles on which civilization advances. War has been used as the last resort by which a nation could settle its disputes, defend its rights, or remedy its wrongs. These are necessary functions, for which provision must be made in any society—as the Shotwell Commission's report emphasized. No nation can give up its right to make war, no matter how stupid or costly this method may be, until a substitute has been provided which can serve these purposes.

An international police force is necessary to restrain aggressors. But that is not enough. We must have a method for settling disputes, for remedying an unjust situation and for changing an unsatisfactory status quo.

Where do you start? You start by calling the United Nations into continuing conference—not to set up those permanent institutions, but to do emergency work on a small scale as a provisional body now.

When the war ends, or as allied armies advance, the liberated territory will be in chaos, starving, with complete political and economic disorder. The United Nations are pledged to restore order in the world. That is where they must begin—as a super-duper Red

Cross. If the United Nations can't organize now to do this, they will never organize later to do anything.

Experts fill their brief cases full of reasons why nothing can be done. But if President Roosevelt said the word it would be done. No allied nation could stay out—not even Russia, which has signed the United Nations declaration like everybody else.

3/15/43

The change in the times is clearly marked by the initiative that the Senate is taking with regard to the United Nations.

The Senate is getting ready to give the President some advice. But unlike the advice the Senate gave Woodrow Wilson a quarter of a century ago, the Senate this time is going to tell President Roosevelt to take the lead in organizing the United Nations.

This resolution has been prepared in consultation with the Senate leaders of both parties. The significant thing about it is that it comes up out of the Senate indigenously. It is nonpolitical, non-Administration, non-White House, non-State Department. President Roosevelt heard about the resolution only recently. Senators had talked over several points with Sumner Welles at the State Department. He mentioned it to the President, who then sent for the sponsors.

But this is a Senate show and the senators intend to keep it such. The men behind this move for international collaboration are middle-of-the-road men, mainly younger men, in both parties. It is not a crackpot brain child. Nor is it the child of any of the propaganda groups working for world peace.

This resolution has evolved and grown gradually in the minds of plain American senators who think that world wars are too frequent and too costly in lives and treasure and that the United States ought to try to do something to prevent any more of them. The whole move springs out of that simple, grass-roots common sense. The point of a Senate expression now is that since everybody here and abroad remembers that the Senate once scuttled the League of Nations, the Senate ought to make it clear now just where it stands.

One young Republican Senator, Joseph H. Ball of Minnesota,

campaigned for reelection and won, in a supposedly isolationist state, on a platform which was quite similar to the goal of this resolution. Senator Carl A. Hatch of New Mexico, the Democratic author of the clean-politics law, is working with Senator Ball on this. In introducing the resolution they are joined by Senator Lister Hill of Alabama, one of the Democratic leaders, and Senator Harold H. Burton of Ohio, a Republican. Senator Barkley, the Democratic Leader, and Senator McNary, the Republican Leader, have been consulted and their advice has been followed.

3/29/43

Mutual advantage, not sentiment, is the only basis on which we can hope to maintain satisfactory relations with other nations. That is something we have to learn now because we are going to be mixed up with other nations for a long time.

American officials who have gone out to China overflowing with warm sentimental ideas, often have come back home disillusioned and cynical, if not embittered. Traffic between America and China is that way—starry-eyed going out, and fishy-eyed coming back.

I have been told, by old China hands, that this is a common occurrence and that if you wait long enough the patient will usually swing back into a middle ground. Gradually a normal outlook will develop, and it will be realistic, recognizing the merits as well as the faults, and above all recognizing the national advantages to us as against the liabilities that we must carry in order to enjoy the advantages.

There hasn't been nearly the same tendency to sentimentalize about Britain as about China. Apparently they have no tendency in Britain to sentimentalize about us. Which is the way it should be. There is no reason why every American should like every Englishman or vice versa, any more than that all Englishmen should like each other or all Americans should like each other. An alliance doesn't necessarily make two peoples friends.

One American Army officer sends back a story of a British Army officer questioning a German officer who had been taken prisoner. They had both been educated at the same university. So at the end of the questioning the British officer said to the German prisoner, "Now, just talking as we used to talk, what do you Germans really think of the Italians?"

To which the German officer replied: "I should say just about what the Russians think of the British and the Americans."

As we try to build out of this war, we have to recognize that although we have known and been fond of many Germans, the German state has been a menace to our peace and security and it must be disarmed and kept disarmed and perhaps divided. We have to recognize that Great Britain and Russia, on either side of Germany, are the two logical allies that we must depend upon to form the nucleus of nations that will join together to protect each other.

There isn't any sentiment in a mutual fire-insurance company. But it is worth belonging to.

4/6/43

We must realize that the whole world is a small room. And we are all locked in it together. There is no escape for any of us. We must reconcile ourselves to living in this room with all the other nations and all the other races.

We may like some of our fellow inhabitants more than others. Some we know are dangerous and we must take their knives from them. Others are weak and must be helped. But, like it or not, we can't get out. We can't get off the globe. We must figure out how to make the best of it.

We must recognize that after the victory there will be only four powers—America, Great Britain, Russia, China. That is not being inconsiderate of small nations. It is just facing facts.

Nothing can be right if these four nations are not reasonably satisfied. If they are satisfied, and together, then other problems will fall into place without endangering the world.

Our own requirements for defense after this war will be greater than before. The long-range bombing plane, if nothing else, changes our security problems. We know that it would be possible, if war should come, for an enemy to strike at us with fifty Pearl Harbors all at once.

8/20/43

We have a traditional fear of being outsmarted by the British, and of thinking they will use us. It should be the other way around. They need us, and they are always fearful that we will run out as we did after the last war. We have most of the gold in the world. We will finish the war with the largest shipping fleet in the world. Our air force will probably outsize the rest of the world put together.

We have the big stack of blue chips. If our politicians who are always afraid of the British putting something over would only recognize that we have the chips, then we could go ahead on a regular horse-trading basis with the British to the advantage of both of us. There need be no sentiment in this. No Irishman need lay his harp aside in shame. It is a business proposition for both sides, if nothing more.

You have to admit that Churchill is a tough old rooster and he can drive a hard bargain. Even Roosevelt may sometimes get buck fever as he goes into a big negotiation. But we have the chips to impress even Churchill if we play our hand well. Otherwise I am not at all concerned about Americans not being able to take care of themselves in negotiations with the British. After all, poker is the American national game.

10/14/43

I think that the peace settlement with Germany must stress one central consideration—how to prevent Germany from beginning another war. That comes above everything else. Germany has pulled the trigger that set off two wars in our time. She is the first menace.

Thus far our side has remained free to write our own ticket. We have said our only terms were unconditional surrender. This time we have made no promises about fourteen points, no promises to give Germany any consideration whatever. There is no question of betraying pledges so far as America and Britain are concerned because we have stood for only one thing—destruction of Hitler and

Nazism and Prussian militarism. That is the curse of this century and we want to end it.

I hope we will make one test of every proposition—does it tend to prevent Germany starting another war? Or will it help her prepare for another war? That is the test of whether American boys will have to fight a third world war caused by Germany. There will be other problems, but they must all be subordinate to that.

How do you prevent Germany from becoming a war threat again?

That is where the argument begins.

Inside our Government thinking is along the line of keeping Germany disarmed, especially in air and in larger mechanized weapons such as in tanks and antiaircraft. Some of our people here believe Germany must not be permitted to manufacture aircraft of any kind, nor give instruction in flying. It is proposed to use United Nations inspectors to prevent violations of such prohibitions, and to enforce them by quarantine and if necessary by military attack. We would need also to ensure that neutral nations did not become fronts for aviation manufacture and training on behalf of Germany.

This program proposes to destroy Germany's military strength but not her economic strength. To be sure, there are many ways in which peacetime industry can be easily converted to war use—as in chemicals, for instance. But, it is thought here that if Germany is prevented from having any air strength and any antiaircraft defense, and any large ground force in tanks or heavy artillery, the disarmament problem is taken care of. Any sizable production of such items could not be concealed, and without them a modern nation is impotent.

The only difficulty in this is in sustaining the will of the victor nations. This program would be in danger of breaking down not because of the Germans but because of Allied weakness and failure to enforce it, as we know from history.

Everything I have suggested here was provided for in the Treaty of Versailles.

Germany was disarmed on land, sea, and in the air. The left bank of the Rhine was demilitarized. But when Hitler reintroduced conscription, nothing happened. When he began building bombing planes, nothing happened. When he began building battleships and submarines, nothing happened. When he marched into the Rhineland—nothing happened. And then Hitler knew that the path was clear. The Allies did not have it in them to stop him.

You can make the most airtight plan in the world and if it is not enforced—as the Versailles disarmament was not—then some new German Hitler is going to try it again—I think about the time our present war babies are old enough for the draft boards.

Once more American history tells us the answer. Several years after this Government was organized, farmers in western Pennsylvania challenged Federal authority to collect excises and staged the whisky rebellion. They beat up the Federal revenue collectors. George Washington knew that if the young Federal Government was defied this time, it would be defied again and again. So he sent Federal troops into Pennsylvania against the rebels. That was that.

Whether we like it or not, Germany is the industrial heart of the continent of Europe. Before the last war Germany had been Britain's best customer. When Germany couldn't buy from England after the war, England suffered from depression and unemployment. A poverty-stricken Germany meant a poverty-stricken Europe. A busy Germany meant a prosperous Europe. In 1931, when it looked as if the whole German financial structure was about to collapse, the other powers, including the United States, went to Germany's financial assistance, not out of pity but out of sheer self-interest.

Germany also was a good customer of the United States and after this war we shall need all the foreign outlets we can get for the products of our expanded industrial plants. We must have a far larger national income than we ever had before to prevent a serious depression here in America.

We probably are not going to collect much out of Germany in the way of reparations or payments in kind. The last time that effort proved abortive.

After the last war, Germany was required to hand over many tons of coal and numbers of cattle to France. But when Germany began to make those payments in kind, they upset the coal and cattle markets in France. Would American farmers and cattle raisers be willing to see us obtain large shipments of wheat, potatoes, sugar beets, or meat from Germany after the war? Would the American oil industry allow us to receive large amounts of synthetic oil and gasoline from Germany? Would American industry stand idly by while cargoes of German cameras, or tractors, or Diesel engines were sent here from Germany as reparations payments?

After the war Germany may need capital—or credits to get on her feet again. But this time we must supervise the credits more carefully than we did before.

After the last war foreign credits were used by Germany to make reparations payments—at least the amount of credit which the Allies sent into Germany was about equal to the reparations Germany paid to the Allies. After reparations ceased, Germany used foreign credits to build up war industries.

The Allies will be serving their own best interests by working for an economically sound Germany—and a disarmed Germany.

On the political side, some thought is given here to splitting Germany up. No official attitude has been expressed. Opinion leans to some kind of breakup but without crystallizing as to how many states should be formed.

Considerable sentiment exists favoring separation of Prussia. A number of Germans are understood to favor that. Other plans call for three or four states and some even would go back to the large number of princely states which existed up until nearly a century ago. But I believe as we come closer to grips with the problem, there will be less disposition to break up Germany beyond her pre-Hitler boundaries, and to treat the 80 million people there rather as a whole unless they themselves wish to split up. We need fewer rather than more national boundaries in Europe. Certainly it is not desirable to Balkanize the heart of Europe. I put little faith in separation schemes.

Military occupation will not be necessary over a long period provided internal order is established promptly. We will need permanent disarmament inspection but I think there is harm rather than benefit in a military occupation beyond the time after the Germans have reorganized a stable order. In the long run Germany must govern herself.

But before we do anything, I hope we will grab Hitler and shoot him. We would have shot Mussolini if we had laid hands on him and it is too bad he got away. The deader those two are the better. And we do not need to stop with them. There also are a number of Nazi killers that need to be stood against the wall without trial just as soon as they are captured and identified. I hope the orders providing for that are in the hands of the Allied military. If there are no such orders, then I hope the Allied military will just shoot them in the time-honored way—"while trying to escape"—as we say.

8/17/43

No trial is needed. We know they are guilty. They forced war when Chamberlain was begging for peace. Don't allow international law to lay its palsied hand on this business. If the international-law experts get into this nothing will ever happen. Why make it complicated? If you try to exile them, you will have their henchmen trying to help them return from Elba. We should always be having to watch them to guard against escape plots. Shooting is so much simpler.

What good will it do?

First, it will rid us of the two men who pulled the trigger for this war. Hitler and Mussolini saw the British Prime Minister and the French Premier crawl to Munich begging for peace. Hitler and Mussolini wanted to use war as their method, and they made it war. There can be no argument about war guilt this time. It is right there on the heads of two brutal dictators.

Second, it will be wholesome to show for a change that murder by wholesale is just as intolerable to society as murder in individual cases. We have never been able to see this straight. We shot Dillinger, whose crimes were trivial misdemeanors compared with the crimes of Hitler and Mussolini. Hitler's predecessor, the Kaiser, lost his war, but he moved to Holland, got himself a buxom new wife, and lived out a comfortable old age as a haughty country squire surrounded by luxury and lackeys. Let some kid murder a fellow in a drunken fight and he is executed. When a dictator plans and carries out the murder of hundreds of thousands, he becomes a sacred cow, and you mustn't touch him.

Third, I don't want to see the real problems with which we must deal obscured by a long postwar controversy over what to do with the two head men. We know they will be on our hands. Let's decide now what to do with them and dispose of that business quickly. That will simplify also the task of punishing the lesser criminals. There will have to be a list of those—but you may be sure that nothing can be done about them unless the two head men are promptly shot. You can't punish the little fellows while allowing the top men to retire to a life of ease.

I am not in favor of a Carthaginian peace. I came home by air last week with a German prisoner, a young Luftwaffe lieutenant. He was a pleasant lad and became quite popular among the American Army officers on the plane. They made him a Short Snorter. I have his signature on my bill. I sat beside him in the plane and pointed out the buildings on the New York sky line. The last I saw of him was a rather touching picture. A young American major, coming home from many months in a combat area, went up to the German prisoner to say good-by. They shook hands, saluted, and parted as old friends might have done.

9/14/43

An international organization supported by force is what Secretary Hull says he must have.

But he did not indicate the method by which force would be provided.

Behind the Secretary's broad phrases is the Administration idea of continuing and enlarging the membership of the combined chiefs of staff.

Some have jumped to the conclusion that Secretary Hull has been hinting at an international police force. But that term does not quite fit what the Allied leaders have in mind.

They have discussed the idea of using force in terms of working through the combined chiefs of staff. That method has very broad implications indeed, but it does not need to sacrifice the national identity of military forces.

Of one thing we may be sure. The national defense establishments will remain national defense establishments. You will never find Winston Churchill taking down the Union Jack and placing the British Navy under an international flag. The British Navy may do the bidding of the combined chiefs of staff—but it will carry out the mission under its own flag. You will never find Uncle Joe Stalin changing his valiant Red Guard regiments into uniforms of an international infantry. American Army Air Forces will not take off their wings to put on the rainbow colors of an international police force. No such wrenching of existing national military establishments is contemplated.

Only the Americans and the British have joined in the combined chiefs of staff. Both Roosevelt and Churchill have indicated they favor continuing the arrangement after the war. Public reaction has been favorable.

Some in Allied councils have favored a formal international agreement by which the combined chiefs of staff would be continued for a definite period—say, of 5 or 10 years with provisions so that any party might give notice of cancellation, or even that the agreement might renew itself automatically in the absence of notice to withdraw.

Unquestionably those high in Allied councils would consider that Russia must be brought into the postwar combined chiefs of staff. Russia has not been a member because there has been no common fighting front with American and British forces. But after the war, both diplomatic and military considerations would make it desirable that Russia should be on the combined chiefs of staff. China's presence also would be desirable.

Objection would be raised by some against including any nations except those providing the bulk of the military forces. The staff organization would be concerned with making military decisions. Therefore its membership must be compact and confined to those who will provide the main forces. Otherwise the organization would degenerate into a debating society.

10/2/43

One thing we must insist upon in connection with commercial air traffic after the war and that is freedom for American air lines to operate anywhere—freedom of transit for planes of all nations.

The American proposal is not for complete freedom of the air, so-called, in the sense that commercial air lines could trade anywhere. The matter breaks down into two elements: first the matter of actual operation of planes, the right of transit, stops for gasoline and service; second, the pickup and discharge of passengers and freight.

As to operating freedom, we hope for a standard international practice, so that the commercial planes of any country have the right of transit through any other country. With the new long-range planes that will come into use after the war, that right of transit will be of enormous importance apart entirely from whether passengers and freight can be picked up and discharged en route.

For instance, if we wished to open a commercial air line from the United States to Moscow, whether Russia wanted to allow us to go in there and do business would be a matter of negotiation between Moscow and Washington. The Russians might insist upon reciprocal rights or some other concession. That would be the usual horse-trading deal between two governments. Then if an agreement were reached that an American air line could fly to Moscow with passengers and freight and bring back passengers and freight, the next business would be to arrange fueling stops en route.

Under prewar conditions, that meant a series of tedious negotiations, and often a refusal for one reason or another, to grant transit rights. What is hoped for now is an international convention, under a world United Nations organization, by which the granting of transit rights would be automatic on application.

Will small countries object to transit air traffic? Reciprocal arrangements are to their advantage. The Netherlands was one of the largest air-line operators before the war. Dutch lines would wish transit rights over American territory, rights to gas at American island fields in the Pacific, for instance. Her interlocking operation with British airfields would perhaps be even closer.

This plan, advanced some months ago by Chairman Pogue of the Civil Aeronautics Board, and endorsed by most of our air lines, is broad, gives wide latitude for private operation or any other kind, and enables each country to horse trade for commercial business. But fundamentally it keeps the air open for actual physical operation of planes which is the vital thing, the one big thing that the air age demands. It must not be lost in a tangle of commercial air competition. In India war supplies going up from Calcutta to Assam to be flown to China have to be loaded and unloaded several times because of changes in the railroad gauge. Australia has had the same ridiculous handicap of different railroad gauges because commercial competition started each company's railroad off on its own private gauge.

Our prewar commercial planes are midgets to what our postwar commercial planes will be. We probably will be selling them to many other nations—so that no monopoly on type of equipment is involved. The big point is that these huge planes have such range that they must be free to go anywhere—whether they are ours, British, Russian, Dutch, or Swedish.

To try to shackle air traffic by arbitrary regulations would be a crime against progress. Keep the planes free to fly. Then we can haggle at our leisure over what they shall carry, and at what rates, and from where to where.

11/2/43

The declaration of Moscow is a start from which a new age can come.

At the advanced age of seventy-two, Cordell Hull flies halfway around the world, severely taxing his limited physical reserves. And there, where most people thought it would be impossible for him to achieve much, he participates in one of the most inspiring events of the war. A door is opened, and we see outside not the distant clouds of a third world war, as so many had feared, but we see instead lying off to the horizon the green, peaceful fields of hope. Until now victory has been something that would serve only as a pause before more inescapable war. We had felt imprisoned in a room where there could be no peace, only more war. Now we can see out through the door that has been opened at Moscow the broad highway over which we can go forward together into better days.

At last we have the promise that our men far away are not dying in vain.

We have others to thank also. For the almost universal American approval of what has been done at Moscow we can thank those in the Republican Party whose strong leadership ever since early 1940 has prevented making these matters partisan questions. To Wendell Willkie, as much as to any man, must go credit. Having argued and exhorted, having dramatized the issue by his travels around the world, he finally goaded his party into declarations which support in principle what Cordell Hull has done at Moscow.

12/30/43

The attack on Pearl Harbor and the Japanese advance throughout the Pacific was the result of our folly in the preceding 20 years. What happened at Pearl Harbor, and in the Pacific in the following months, could have been prevented if we had only pursued a different foreign policy in the Pacific—a more realistic policy after the First World War.

On Christmas Eve, President Roosevelt spoke with scorn of those "cheerful idiots" in this country who believed that there would be no more war for us if everybody in America would only retire into his home and lock the front door behind him.

I don't know about the cheerful idiots—it was pretty much the whole country, wasn't it? I remember Cordell Hull in 1922 saying that at the Washington Arms Conference we gave the Pacific Ocean to Japan—but I don't recall hearing very many others talking like that.

The Japanese attack on Pearl Harbor was launched from the Marshall Islands. It could not have been based on Japan proper—

the distance was too great. The Japs used the Marshalls because they were up closer to the target.

And how did Japan get the Marshall Islands? The incredible answer is that we practically gave them to Japan. We allowed Japan to take them over after the last war.

At the beginning of the First World War, Japan held no islands between the Philippines and Hawaii. There were three groups of such islands—the Marianas, the Carolines, and the Marshalls—but they belonged to Germany.

They need not have belonged to Germany. They could have belonged to us. In 1898, the year of our war with Spain, these islands were under the Spanish flag as were the Philippines. As a result of our victory over Spain, we took over the Philippines—and also Guam in the Mariana group. But we did not take the others and we allowed Spain to keep them. Then Spain, being hard up, the very next year sold the Mariana and Caroline groups of islands to Germany for $4,500,000. For that bagatelle—less than the cost of a destroyer—Germany got these wonderful natural fortresses in the center of the Pacific, like Truk.

We could have bought them ourselves then with dollars. Now we buy them with lives. Germany obtained the Marshall Islands by an agreement with Great Britain in 1886 whereby Britain got the Gilbert Islands just to the south.

Early in the First World War Japan seized all of these German islands. She held them. We put in no claim for them. President Wilson insisted we were not fighting for territorial loot but for the overthrow of militarism. So Japan held the islands by default under a league mandate which was a polite cover for allowing her to retain those islands, without violating technically the principles of Wilson.

But we had a wrong concept about territorial loot. These islands are not to be considered as economically valuable like the oil-bearing Dutch East Indies, for instance. There would be no commercial proceeds from these Pacific islands. They are useful only for military purposes. We very properly adopt the principle that we do not seek territorial loot out of war. But we were wrong in classing those islands as loot. They were a necessity for our security but we evidently did not know it at the time. After this war we must not make that fatal mistake again. We must recognize many Pacific islands not as loot but as essential to our safety—as an actual financial liability but necessary for security, like battleships.

12/25/43

At the end of this war we shall be sick of it. We shall be so sick of war that we may do as we did before, become impatient and dive into forgetfulness and indifference. That will be the certain way to permit future trouble.

The lesson is clear. Grapple with the lion cub before he grows too strong—and risk having a little war to prevent a big war.

The Christlike virtues work only in a community where they are recognized by all. We were too Christlike as a nation. When some people protested sending scrap iron to Japan, others said that to stop such shipments would only aggravate the militarists, and that if we did not take any action that would annoy them, the peace-loving Japanese would win out. We were dupes. The peace-loving Japanese served only one useful purpose to Japan—they had the voices that would lull our suspicions and keep us asleep until they could strike.

At the Washington Arms Conference we placed our trust in Japanese good faith. The Japs placed their trust in fortifications and secret armament and extended them 3,000 miles out from Tokyo, as we are finding in the Marshalls now. We have never really yet accepted the fact that if Germany were able, she would throw her hooks around the Western Hemisphere. We didn't take it in although the strongest country in South America is run by a pro-Axis crowd which would have served as a ready-made tie-in if Hitler had been able to hold Africa.

Why must we never forget these grim facts? Because if we do we open the way to another war. We must place force out in front as a weapon to preserve peace, and not leave it, as heretofore, to be used as a weapon of evil aggressors. The policeman ought to have a gun. It is better that he should have the gun than that the gangster should have it.

This time we shall have the industrial and military strength among the victor powers sufficient to police the victory and restrain anyone who tries to break the peace.

But it won't be done unless you and I and all of us who add up to public opinion insist upon it. War can come by default again. Public opinion can prevent it. Nothing else can. Nobody can make that public opinion except you and all of us. And if we don't do it —that in itself creates a public opinion of indifference, which is what warmakers of the future want out of us.

Last Mission

12/30/43

IT LOOKS as if I'm getting away for another trip to write about the war.

Once you have been out as a war correspondent and have come home with your nose clean, it is fairly easy getting out again. The War Department gave me back my original war correspondent's credentials, the same little green card I've carried on two previous trips into war theaters.

It is one of the early ones issued, No. 90, and is dated Feb. 28, 1942, a short time after Pearl Harbor.

I got it when I went out across the new air-supply route that Pan American Airways was throwing across the heart of Africa to transport spare parts and light supplies and personnel to the Middle East, India, and China. That air line was an amazing demonstration of what could be done quickly by air. Yet it was a pathetic, weak little Allied life line. When you think back on it, we must not have realized then how near we were to losing the war.

We had to cross Africa by going in below Dakar, down around Liberia and Accra and Lagos. That route skirted the edge of Axis forces. Fort-Lamy, one of our stops in the heart of Africa, had been bombed a short time before we went through. At that very time we were developing a parallel line still further south in case the first route was cut by the Axis. Cairo and Calcutta were in danger and evacuation was going on.

Now all Africa is ours, and the Mediterranean is ours.

I think about all that when I look at this little green war correspondent's identification card that bears my photograph, fingerprints, and description. I carried it to Sweden and to England last spring, and now it has been given back to me for another trip out to the war.

That card and my passport are the two most important things I carry, far more important than money or traveler's checks. You can travel as a war correspondent without using money, but you can't travel without credentials.

The State Department always gives me back my old passport. It was first issued when I went to England in the summer of 1941. This passport has been with me as far east as Chungking, as far north as Lapland in Sweden and Iceland. It has crossed the equator several times, has crossed the Atlantic by air six times, has flown in all more than 100,000 miles. It has been over the Amazon and through the African desert. It has visited the Pyramids, flown over Jerusalem, traveled in dusty trains through India, and followed General Patton's Seventh Army across Sicily. It has more visas than General MacArthur has decorations.

As I recall it the passport didn't get to go on the bombing of Rome. You are supposed on such occasions to check all your papers on the ground, except a letter which certifies the bearer as a non-combatant and entitled to be treated as a lawful belligerent in event of capture by the enemy. Nobody told me to get one of those papers until I was ready to climb aboard, and then it was too late. But this time I am going out with the Navy, and they checked me in with one of those certificates all fingerprinted and entitling me to be kicked around by the Japs as a lawful belligerent.

This time I didn't have to take any shots. I showed the doctor at the naval dispensary my Army immunization register from previous trips. It certifies that I am adequately loaded against smallpox, typhoid, tetanus, yellow fever, and typhus. They don't have any shots to keep your feet from cracking between the toes. But a friend has slipped me a couple of boxes of the new deadly secret louse powder. It's lucky for some people I'm leaving immediately.

Martin Codel, who was in Africa for the Red Cross, has just sent me his khaki dispatch case, the same one I borrowed to take to Sicily. A dispatch case is the Army field substitute for a brief case. Next to a typewriter it is a war correspondent's most useful piece of equipment.

I have forgotten one or two things, but at this writing I don't know what they are. I hope to think of them before shoving off.

1/3/44

HONOLULU. Our New Year's Eve party aboard a Navy freight plane bound from San Francisco to Honolulu was a simple one.

Frank Mason, special assistant to Secretary of the Navy Knox, and I were the only hitchhikers aboard. We were tucked among mailbags and a cargo of war supplies.

It was just midnight in the East. Frank and I climbed to the top turret of our big seaplane and stood there looking out on the lights of San Francisco as they faded in the distance. After a silence, moved simultaneously by the same impulse we grasped each other by the hand and said:

"God bless our folks back home!"

Then we went below, where the crew had a New Year's Eve dinner prepared by the Chinese boy, who came from Hong Kong 3 years ago to join the Navy and learn English. Heavy slabs of warm pot roast were served in paper plates, along with peas, fresh tomato salad, coffee, and a box of cigars bought by the crew.

As we sat down, Navigator Hank Phillips proudly passed around bright paper caps and New Year's Eve noisemakers that he had bought during the afternoon at Alameda.

Hank is the comedian of the crew, and he made our mouths water by his pantomime of drinking New Year's toasts in champagne. Hank didn't say much about it, but he was thinking about the baby of which he expects to become the father shortly, back in Janesville, Wis. In fliers' lingo, Hank said the baby's "ETA"—estimated time of arrival—is Jan. 12. After that we felt safe, because he is determined to be back in San Francisco on the date of the baby's arrival.

It surprised me to learn that most of the officers and men of this squadron are married. They claim the honor of being "the most pregnant squadron in the Navy." Of some 200 officers, all except a dozen either are fathers or expect to be soon. So these men of

Captain Don Smith's naval air-transport organization are known as the Stork Squadron.

Out of thousands of flights, running at least one a day over the longest regular water jump in the world, they have never had a plane even forced down. At this point I knock on wood.

The men argue, the way everybody else does, about when the war will end. Each school of thought has its own slogan: "Back Alive in Forty-Five," "Out of This Fix in Forty-Six," "Oh Heaven in Forty-Seven," and "The Golden Gate in Forty-Eight." That's as far as they've worked out the schedule.

The men talk a great deal about their families, and about incidents of previous flights, but relatively little about the war as a whole. No wonder. They are busy running back and forth between San Francisco and points in the Pacific, and they have their own work to do. For amusement they play poker or listen to "Tokyo Rose," who is their chief laugh.

When Tokyo Rose coos in soft English, "Listen, honey, how do you like those 4-F's back home taking your girl?" fellows like Hank who are waiting for the stork think it's a good joke.

We have no hang-overs from our simple New Year's celebration, but as Captain Bishop said, "What a hell of a way to make a living!"

1/3/44

HONOLULU. Navy people are full of talk about their SeaBees, or Construction Battalions. Everybody has his own SeaBee story. All of them are suggestive of men with ingenuity, courage, and a cocky indifference to tradition.

In no time at all—for this whole business started after Pearl Harbor—the SeaBees have become a kind of pick-and-shovel Marine Corps, although they would resent that comparison. In fact the SeaBees say that when the marines land the SeaBees are on hand to greet them.

There is much humorous rivalry between the marines and the SeaBees. At one post the marines put up a sign, "SeaBees under fifty-five not admitted." The next day marines faced a sign which said: "Any Marine with four years' service can apply to be a junior SeaBee."

Navy construction work, such as the building of landing fields, docks, and shore defenses as at Wake and Midway, was done before Pearl Harbor largely by private contractors who hired their own working forces. Now most of that work is done by the enlisted men of the Construction Battalions. They are mostly volunteers recruited from various trades and construction gangs.

SeaBees have simplified progress reports that run this way: "Can Do." "Will Do." "Did." They have improved on the technique of digging fox holes. One day a SeaBee, during a bomber attack on an airfield at which he was working, got the idea of hiding in an empty oil drum. So he scooped out a hole for the drum and crawled into it, giving himself an excellent, quickly devised shelter, which has now become common whenever men can get the oil drums.

They are combat construction battalions. They are trained to handle antiaircraft guns and light arms, which they often must use while grading an air strip under enemy bombardment. On Tarawa, SeaBees began running bulldozers over the pock-marked air strip before the fighting was over, and at one point a live Jap came out of a hidden tunnel and began shooting.

The SeaBees go in with assault troops. That is how our planes were able to land on Tarawa within 78 hours of the assault. They were helping also at Salerno and in Sicily, but their big renown has come from their work in the Pacific and it is in this theater that they have established the legends that are already part of Navy lore.

1/6/44

Everybody has a lot of high strategy to talk. They used to say that the desert war in Africa was a tactician's dream and a quartermaster's nightmare. It's about that way in the Pacific. This is a giant chessboard and the game is for keeps. It has an excitement about it that you feel in talking with officers. So much of land war is dull, hard slogging, knocking out a battery here and then another one farther up the road, and getting ammunition and supplies up to the batteries, and pushing the infantry slowly along foot by foot over miles that last for months. There probably has been no greater hell anywhere than in some of these island campaigns, yet much of the war is in the big wide-swinging blows, quick and changing frequently, with constant appeal to the imagination.

Every officer I have seen out here is excited and alive, and it makes you feel very good. Just before I left San Francisco I saw an old friend, Captain Robert Barry, who was assistant public-relations officer in Washington until recently. He had a party for his shipmates, and I never saw a man who seemed to be loving his job and the men around him and who was set for adventure more eagerly than he is.

1/7/44

SOMEWHERE IN AUSTRALIA. Our Navy freight plane came down in Australia at twilight after covering 9,500 miles in three days and three nights of flying from Washington.

Short stopovers have given me a general view of our biggest war theater, where the fighting will be the hardest and the longest. I will work my way back more slowly, in order to get a closer look at the Pacific war.

I have already visited some of the bases and seen acres of supplies. Even the first quick glance shows that preparations for the Pacific war are far more advanced than I had realized. Certainly our forces in the Pacific are not being starved. On the contrary, there has been a long period of building up.

Life aboard an airplane for three nights and three days is not as hard as one might think. You sleep a lot, even though you sit up all night. The galley is going all the time, and coffee and fruit juice and sandwiches are always available. Members of the crew who are off duty play cribbage or poker.

The crew members make passengers feel important by getting their signatures on Short Snorter bills. They flash crude Fiji Island money, and currency of almost every other country on earth, on which they have collected the signatures of everyone from Eleanor Roosevelt to General Marshall.

My favorite autograph is that of Major General Ralph Smith, who signed mine: "Makin taken." He was there.

I asked one man what he and the others thought about things at home.

"We're not interested in politics," he said. "Just send us the stuff to fight with."

"What about the strikes?" I asked him.

"What we say," he replied, "is send the strikers here and let us go home."

That was when we were riding through a coconut grove at a place where the SeaBees and Army engineer battalions have made a vast model military base in just 1 year, with 300 miles of road and accommodations for many thousands of men.

1/8/44

SOMEWHERE IN AUSTRALIA. When I went ashore at one South Pacific island base, the first sign that greeted me as I left the dock was a poster nailed to a tall coconut tree. One picture on the poster showed a ferocious-looking Jap soldier, and underneath was the phrase, "He Causes One Casualty." Next was a picture of an equally ferocious mosquito, with the line, "He Causes Many Casualties."

The fight is a never-ending one. They spray all the ditches with Diesel oil three times a week. The job is done largely by men being disciplined for minor infractions of the regulations. Life is so rugged that there are few privileges that can be taken away from men, so they get their punishment in the form of this tedious malaria-control work.

One finds vast differences in among the various islands. The malaria trouble I described above is on a mountainous, heavily overgrown island where steam seems to breed mosquitoes and there must be a constant fight against the jungle. On the day before I visited another kind of island—a low coral bar, with no vegetation whatever except for a few palm trees and shrubs. The fine dust from the coral gets into everything, and together with the moisture from the ocean makes a fine gritty gum that leaves windows and windshields with an almost permanent film. Shoes and clothing rot quickly.

I went up the steel steps of an observation tower that is only a year old and it was already rusted as if from 50 years of exposure.

The coral-reef island is really less inviting for living than the jungle island, since the latter has been well cleared. The coral island is just a strip of white glare about 200 yards wide, and our men feel like stranded gooney birds—which were the only inhabitants before the Americans came in.

1/21/44

WITH THE MARINES AT CAPE GLOUCESTER, New Britain. When the showers come they bring a foul jungle smell with them. The air reeks of the slime which lies under the jungle growth all around the marines' positions, and through which they had to fight after their landing here.

There have been only three clear days here out of the last 19. One storm washed out most of the roads and changed the beds of streams by 50 to 100 feet, which meant that new log bridges were necessary. No marine veteran of Guadalcanal had seen such rain. The fox holes all have standing water.

The marines' favorite way to sleep is in a mosquito-netted hammock with a rubberized shelter hung over it. They hang these hammocks between trees and dig fox holes directly underneath so they can roll out and hole up in a hurry.

In spite of the primitive conditions here only four cases of war neurosis have had to be evacuated. The low rate is due to the influence of Guadalcanal veterans as cadres among the newer men.

1/24/44

SOMEWHERE IN NEW GUINEA. We were up at 4:30, and at dawn we took off in a B-25—the Mitchell medium bomber that is now being used over here for strafing.

We came down at a gigantic field that is being constructed in a swampy jungle in the Markham River valley at Nadzab, near Lae. Our paratroopers took the field from the Japs, who had had it for

2 years but had installed only a small landing strip and no shops or supply dumps. So we started from scratch.

Everything was flown in, including three sawmills which cut the jungle lumber which was used in the construction of dozens of buildings. There were as many as 400 cargo-plane arrivals at this field in one day. Construction engineers were brought in by air with this equipment, including baby bulldozers, 10 days behind the paratroopers.

Meantime our forces were developing an area of 200 square miles. Each outfit was assigned a piece of jungle and swamp and told to cut its way in and build quarters.

The first outfit in was led by Lieutenant Wally Hoffrichter, twenty-six, who drove me around. He is a former swimming coach at the Dallas Athletic Club and a widely known swimmer. His first home here was a native-built grass shack, 10 feet by 10. Three men bunked and made their offices there. They were bombed the first night and stayed up the rest of the night digging fox holes.

Wally is known as "Lord Mayor of Nadzab." His jeep is marked "Lord Mayor."

Now dozens of bulldozers, road scrapers, and dredges are at work building air strips. For the first two strips they have built 52 miles of taxi ways, which gives you some idea of the size of this jungle job. I saw nothing in Great Britain or Africa as big as this, or constructed under such difficult conditions—often involving the clearing of the densest jungle and toughest swamp.

1/25/44

SOMEWHERE IN NEW GUINEA. The Japs' equipment is meager all round. Their air strips are so short and primitive that we can't use them effectively until they have been completely rebuilt. Our use of jeeps and other mechanized equipment in the jungle is far beyond the Japs. It leaves no question of the outcome provided we are willing to stay with it long enough.

The policy in this area thus far has been to land where the Jap isn't, whittle down his supply lines, starve him out, push him into the sea, always avoiding a costly frontal attack. That is the operating principle of General Douglas MacArthur as well as Lieutenant General Walter Krueger, his top field commander.

2/3/44

SOMEWHERE IN NEW GUINEA. I hope it will give comfort to many parents, wives, and sweethearts at home to know that, bad as conditions are where the fighting must be done, the wounded and ill in New Guinea are in the more serious cases evacuated back to station hospitals which are the opposite of what I had imagined jungle conditions here to be.

I visited the 171st station hospital, near Port Moresby. It consists of a large group of tents out in an open valley, overlooking the sparkling waters of the Coral Sea and fringed around with hillsides of brilliant flame trees in luxurious blossom.

"Four days after we were given this real estate, which was covered with high kunai grass, we had 500 patients," said Lieutenant Colonel C. T. Wilkinson, formerly a physician at Wake Forest, N.C.

They had to bring in water from miles away. There were Jap air raids every night. Doctors did the carpentry work for the operating room, and nurses painted the interior. Sawed-off coconut-tree trunks were left standing as supports for the second floor. In 14 months they have handled 1,174 patients, including a considerable number of psychoneurosis cases, most of whom have returned to duty. Some of these are boys who have been spoiled by easy luxury at home and find it hard to adjust to Army life, some are suffering from plain homesickness, some from fear. Four psychiatrists work with the patients.

The big thing about the hospital is the bright, open, cheerful atmosphere. When one group of patients came in after a long stretch in the jungle at the front, under severe conditions, one of them said to a nurse, "Gosh! White sheets, and women!"

Bright flowers are planted in little gardens all around the hospital tents. Many of the boys are sent seeds from home. I saw zinnias in bloom, and marigolds, and poppies, and native poinsettias, and morning-glory vines over the nurses' tents. Everything possible is done to help the men forget the gruesome sights of the front.

Patients work a 5-acre garden. Colonel Wilkinson picked a 15-pound watermelon outside his tent the day before I was there. Palms provide shade over the tents.

I was walking along with Colonel Wilkinson when suddenly we came upon a big open ward tent full of kneeling men. I could see the back of a priest, in white vestments, at an altar, and suddenly I realized it was Sunday. You can't tell one day from another out here, because everything goes on just the same. The hospital has Catholic and Protestant services on Sundays, Jewish services on Fridays, Mormon services on Wednesdays.

The Red Cross helps instruct patients in manual therapy, using old airplane metal and other scraps. The patients have just made 200 screen-wire flytraps. They convert shell packing cases into sinks, and do other improvised work. But it is gardening that seems most of all to heal the soul.

They have a rolling Army kitchen which they say is the only one used by any hospital. It is in charge of one of the nurses, Lieutenant Clara Palau, of Northfield, Minn., who told me the food was always cold when it had to be carried on trays to wards as far as a quarter of a mile from the kitchen. So they wangled this mobile kitchen from the Australian Army, and now they bring piping hot food to every patient.

The hospital streets are named after nurses. There is a baseball field, and there are movies five nights a week.

They have just used the new drug penicillin for the first time. Tail Gunner Patrick Missita, Glens Falls, N.Y., had an internal abscess and they couldn't operate. Penicillin saved him. He told me he was leaving the next day to go back to his gunning.

The last thing I saw on leaving the mess hall was a large poster: "Buy War Bonds."

2/8/44

GUADALCANAL. Guadalcanal has become a kind of shrine for the Pacific war in the minds of the American people, as it was here we won the long jungle struggle with the Japs that stopped their advance and marked the beginning of our slow march toward Tokyo.

Nobody will ever live happily on this place. It is not unpleasant to the eye along the coast. Some spots in our military developments, which stretch for 30 or more miles along the north coast, are as neat and attractive as an outdoor summer colony, with little huts under neatly cleared coconut groves, and little white coral walks edged with stones or small tree trunks. But it is wet. The rain, or what a Californian might call the Guadalcanal mist, drips as it did on the stage for Somerset Maugham's play, *Rain.*

The high surf broke two barges loose and they washed up on our beach. The tents never dry out. Everything becomes as wet as the outside of a beer bottle on a warm day.

Your fox hole will be completely full of water unless you cover it with canvas—in which case it will be only half full—although that is not so important here as at Munda, where 2 nights before I was there twenty men were injured because they stayed in bed instead of diving for their wet fox holes.

And when friendly little lizards run up your screen-wire walls you pay no attention. It's the mosquitoes you must watch out for.

Here, as at Munda, among the most conspicuous things you see when approaching by air are the white crosses in the cemeteries. Our vast airfields tell you at once that enormous developments have taken place under American occupation.

That always impresses me—the size of what we do—just as any downtown American business section is on a physical scale unapproached in any other country. Anything we do, we do it big. Great piles of ammunition, rations, and every other article of war are to be found all over the Pacific up to our front lines. That is now true of Guadalcanal. This is not an ideal base, for there is no protected anchorage, but it was the only place available at the time.

2/4/44

ABOARD AN AIRCRAFT CARRIER, Somewhere in the Pacific. On the night before a battle everybody gets a big holiday dinner. For breakfast on the morning of a battle beefsteak is served.

Everybody aboard knows when the time of battle is approaching. You begin to count the days as "D minus 4," "D minus 3," meaning four days or three days before the action is to begin. Sometimes, instead of calling it "D Day," they call it "Dog Day." And for some time after a battle begins the days are known as "D plus 1 day," or "D plus 2 days," instead of by the days of the week or the month. The calendar is forgotten, and all time is counted as before or after the beginning of the battle.

A slow, almost imperceptible rise of tension takes place as D Day approaches. But it is nothing very marked. Men begin to think more about their steel helmets, and to place them where they can be picked up quickly. At night you begin to have your red waterproof flashlight always within reach, and always in your pocket when you are moving about the ship. Some men keep heavy leather gloves in their pockets, because these are good to put on if you have to slide down a rope going overboard.

You are always studying the location of ladders, hatches, and bulkheads, and making mental notes of little landmarks around the ship so that you can find your way in a hurry in the dark with only a dim red flash to guide you. It is surprising how different ship passageways seem when you try to find your way around them with the lights out, and when many of the openings are closed.

Some 3,000 men are aboard this ship, and when the call to battle stations is sounded they must get to their places within seconds, or minutes at the most. Some of them must go the whole length of the ship, which is as far as a golf ball is ordinarily driven. Men are rushing both up and down narrow ladders. Hatches are being slammed. There is intense activity everywhere, with the general-quarters gong clanging its unmistakable warning of approaching danger.

Formerly ships would throw huge quantities of things overboard before going into action—all the mattresses, bedding, and other inflammable material. Now, with the vast improvement in fireproofing materials, and with greater fireproof construction and fire-fighting equipment, seldom is anything thrown overboard. There is very little around to burn.

Before I left Washington, one of the survivors of the carrier *Wasp,* Lieutenant Commander William C. Chambliss, gave me a copy of his article, "Recipe for Survival," which has been issued by the Training Division of the Navy's Bureau of Aeronautics. I find that many of his suggestions are being commonly adopted aboard this carrier, such as waterproof flashlights, heavy gloves, a large steel knife in a scabbard hitched to the belt—which is useful, as Chambliss says, in cutting yourself clear of lines or other impediments with which you may become involved in the water, and also for discouraging sharks or for opening emergency-ration cans.

Those are the kind of normal little preparations everyone makes, although very little is said about it and the conversation seldom touches on the possibilities of action. The laughing and joking go on as usual at mess and around the ship, with boys scuffling on the flight deck and the hangar deck, or playing cards, or sleeping under the planes, during slack times.

You always snatch a nap if you can, because in a combat area you are up long before dawn and until late at night, and there is considerable tension, at least subconsciously.

During battle, when the men are held at their stations for long hours, mess attendants carry sandwiches and coffee to them frequently, also hot soup, lemonade, fruit cakes, and various small items they can put into their pockets and nibble at while beside their guns.

For several days before an action the pilots spend hours listening to briefing lectures concerning the impending battle. They are told what they need to know in order to carry out their part of the battle. Especially they are given lectures about the territory they are to bomb or strafe. They are told about the history of the locality, the characteristics of the natives, the estimated strength of the enemy, and they make a careful study of aerial photographs and maps to mark the location of enemy airfields and other installations that may be targets.

But there is not the high tension that you might expect. Sometimes, when a report of exceptionally heavy enemy strength is given, there will be raucous shouts of "Wow!" Once when the briefing showed our own forces to be far in excess of what the enemy would have, somebody shouted from the rear of the room, "Let's go on to Tokyo while we're at it!"

But mostly the pilots are slouched down in their chairs, their favorite position being with both feet up on top of the high back of the chair in front. They act much like a bored classroom taking in a lecture with as little effort as possible, instead of fighting men, some of whom will not come back from the missions under discussion.

You have a sense of living in a world apart from what you knew at home, and there is almost no talk of life back in the States now. You live only minute by minute through the routine that carries you smoothly, as if drifting down a river, toward the day of battle.

2/9/44

ABOARD AN AIRCRAFT CARRIER, Somewhere in the Pacific. After a couple of weeks with the Army and the marines in the jungles of South Pacific islands, I came aboard this big, new, and most modern airplane carrier last night. I feel like a country boy going to the city, as I shift from the mud and the dirt to come aboard this floating community of some 3,000 persons.

As far as personal living is concerned, it is like a big hotel with an airfield on the roof.

My Army gear, which had been knocked around through the mud with the marines at Cape Gloucester and Munda and Guadalcanal, suddenly looked filthy and out of place when I saw it in my cabin with its neatly made bed and white sheets, its fresh-painted walls—and its modern bathroom instead of those ladders out over the water that we were using a few days ago.

I feel like the country boy in *Oklahoma!* who sings my favorite song, "Everything's Up to Date in Kansas City." For here they have "gone about as far as they can go." You turn a knob over your bed and you hear the radio from San Francisco. But our colored mess attendant tells me confidentially that although it sounds as if the music is coming from San Francisco, "You know they take it down and play it on records right here on the ship. You ain't listenin' to San Francisco. You just thinks you is."

This boy's name is Charles, and from Charles I have learned about city life again. My one pair of shoes had worn through walking on the coral rock of the islands. Charles said he could have my shoes resoled at the ship's shoe shop. I asked how long it would take. He said, "Oh, they can have them back this afternoon."

This is not only city life, it's a darn sight better city life than you can get in most places at home right now.

Of course there isn't a man on this ship who wouldn't rather take life at home, but if you have to be away the Navy has it over the Army in many things. As one sailor said,

"Why should anybody want to live in the mud when he can live on a ship? Of course you might get hit, but you can also get hit in the Army, and it's better to have it happen in a place like this than out in a fox hole full of mud and water."

Every day the ship's canteen sells 80 gallons of ice cream to the sailors, and 24 gallons of Coca-Cola. On my first night aboard I had filet mignon, although that probably was very special. For lunch today we had hamburger and black-eyed peas—and two helpings.

They have seven barbers aboard. I got a much-needed haircut from a young fellow who learned barbering in a small town in Tennessee.

"I didn't want to do barbering in the Navy," he said. "I just wanted to be a sailor. But they caught up with me, and so I'm barbering again."

He works mostly on officers. "They don't like Navy GI haircuts," he said, "so I have to do it a little more fancy. They all want hair tonic. I only have one kind, but I've got their backs to the mirror so I just give them anything they ask for out of this one bottle. They can't tell the difference."

LAST MISSION

2/10/44

ABOARD AN AIRCRAFT CARRIER, Somewhere in the Pacific. To the men aboard a warship in a combat zone, religion becomes a far more important thing than you might suppose if you judge by civilian standards at home. You can get some idea of the reason why from the story of a flier who became afraid. I have his name, but I shall not use it now.

One of the chaplains was telling about it because it was a strange and puzzling experience. Chaplains have many unusual experiences with the men, because, as this one said, bluejackets are not as irreligious as they seem or want to appear.

This particular chaplain, a young man, has been with the Navy 7 years. Before that he was pastor of a Lutheran church at a West Coast port.

It was on Christmas Eve that the young man who was afraid, a radio gunner, came to the Protestant chaplain after communion and asked to see him privately. They were going to strike at Kavieng on Christmas morning, and this was the communion service the night before the dangerous mission.

We will just call this young man the unknown flier, for I suppose he was something like all of these men and like all the rest of us. Formerly he had been doing quiet patrol work in the Caribbean, and he asked for more active duty aboard a carrier. He was transferred to Norfolk for carrier training. There he met a girl and they were married, and some months later he came out here. Their baby is to be born this month, or it may have come into the world by now.

The young airman had been on five attacks during the softening up of Tarawa, on two against Nauru, and on the first very tough blow at Rabaul. So he had been through some of it.

On Christmas Eve the chaplain sat down with him. The boy said his baby was to be born soon and he was afraid to go up the next day. The chaplain asked if he had ever been scared before. He said he had, but never like this.

"I have been sick to my stomach," he said, "I am so scared."

The chaplain said he thought he could get the boy excused from the Christmas Day raid. The boy wouldn't hear of that.

"I am not yellow," he said. "I have to fly tomorrow. If I don't I will never fly again. I want you to help me."

The chaplain was silent for a moment before he went on.

"I tried to assure him of the Lord's care and that He would watch over him," he told me.

He said the boy was more afraid of being afraid than he was afraid of flying.

Early Christmas morning the planes went out. When they came back the young airman was dead in the rear cockpit. He was the only one hit among those who came back. There were only two small machine-gun bullet holes on the underside of the plane. Both these bullets hit him.

Because this carrier was operating under battle conditions no regular services could be held Christmas Day. All hands were at battle stations all day. But a few minutes were taken out to hold services for burial at sea.

Three of us were in the room talking, and it was a long time before we looked up at each other.

"I have heard of such things," said the chaplain at last. "But that was my first contact with it. It is one of those mysteries for which I can find no explanation. I don't suppose anyone has found an explanation."

I don't know exactly why I should feel the story of this young man so far down in my throat even now as I write it.

2/12/44

WITH THE PACIFIC FLEET, in the Marshall Islands. A few days before we went into the Battle of the Marshalls I attended Sunday services aboard one of the several big aircraft carriers in this huge fleet. The chaplain, the Reverend J. F. Dreith, took as his text the Sermon on the Mount.

Sitting among the bluejackets on the forecastle, I was gazing out at several battleships around our horizon as the chaplain read to us, from Matthew, about how the meek would inherit the earth. I wondered whether we had not confused meekness with weakness. To be meek and humble in spirit is not necessarily to be weak physically, although we have distorted the idea into that. Scorn of force became a national policy with us. We believed that if we renounced aggression, and disarmed—in other words, if we bowed in meekness and weakness before the world—it would encourage world peace and certainly would bring peace to America. But that policy did neither. It encouraged aggressors, and they finally attacked us.

We have discovered our error. The fleet in the midst of which I have been riding for some days seems to me to be the beginning of wisdom on our part. With the world as it is we must hold the islands out here which are useful for airfields. We must use them to protect ourselves.

I have seen island after island out here in the Pacific where except for some coconut trees and the British flag everything is the work of Americans—airfields, soldiers, great dumps of military supplies, docks, and ships.

Meek and humble in spirit, yes. Encouragement and help to other peoples, yes. The spirit of the Sermon on the Mount is the essence of democracy. But, like the Pilgrims at Plymouth, we must carry our muskets to church.

As I looked around the horizon during the services that Sunday it seemed to me that we were carrying some very large muskets with us.

2/14/44

ABOARD AN AIRCRAFT CARRIER, in the Marshall Islands. Every flier naturally thinks about what his chances are of coming back, and all of them would rather be shot down over Germany than over Japanese territory.

Commander Dixon, incidentally, is the pilot who after sinking a Japanese carrier sent the message back to the *Lexington,* "Scratch one flattop!" He won the Navy Cross. He said that if he had known

aymond Clapper bids ice-Admiral W. A. Fitch ɔod-bye in South Pacific hile Frank Mason, Spe-al Assistant to the Secre-ry of the Navy, looks on.

ficial U. S. Marine Corps Photo Staff Sgt. Edwin Hart

aymond Clapper in plane Munda shakes hands ith Major General Ralph Mitchell, Commander of arine Air Units in the lomons.

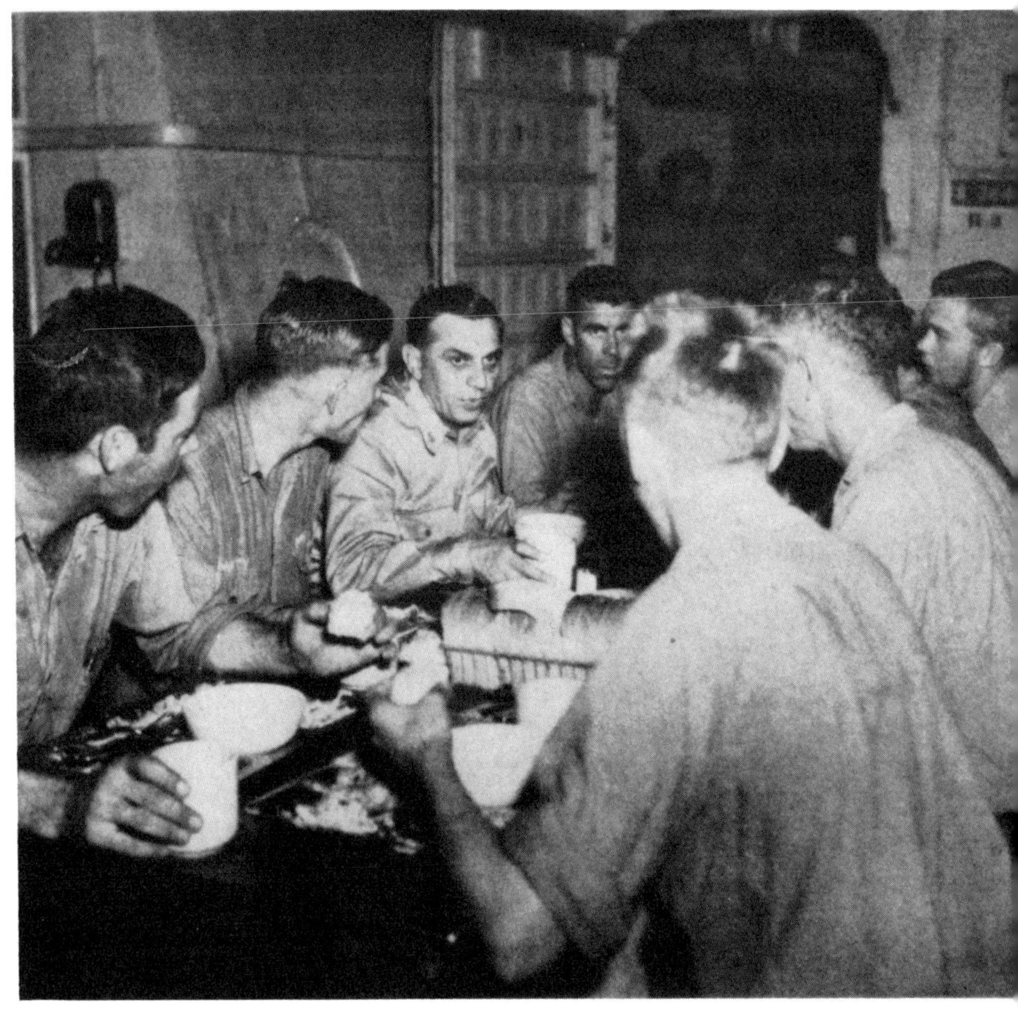

Photo by ship's photogra

Raymond Clapper (third from left) at ship's mess with crew members the night before his fatal accident. On back of photograph was this inscription, "We of the Bunker Hill are proud that he stood his last duty with us."

his remark would be printed in the newspapers he would have tried to think up something better.

From the flight deck of our carrier I have seen two of our planes crash in the water within sight of the ship. In each case a plane circled overhead while one of the escorting destroyers rushed up to save the men. Each time the men were hauled aboard a destroyer within 15 minutes.

One of our destroyers unexpectedly fell into the star role of our task force because of a rescue mission during the attack on Kwajalein. The Lieutenant Commander commanding our torpedo-plane squadron was in the midst of a dive on Kwajalein when word came over his radio that one of his planes was making a forced landing. He came out of his dive and called his flight officer to circle over the three men, who were in a rubber boat, while he obtained a destroyer. He radioed the carrier, and under orders of Admiral Sherman a destroyer was taken out of the escort and sent 90 miles away to rescue the crew.

Fighter cover was given the destroyer, and the pilot guided it to the rubber boat. The men were taken aboard after 3 or 4 hours in the water.

That is the kind of work destroyers must do—running errands. But this hard-working little destroyer had the break that night which every big ship in our task force was hoping to get.

On the way back to our task force, the destroyer overtook a small Japanese convoy of four ships—a tanker, a medium-sized cargo ship, and two smaller ones. He sank all four. Next morning he messaged Admiral Sherman, aboard the carrier, that he had sunk four ships. And he added, "Enjoyed picnic."

Admiral Sherman sent back congratulations to the destroyer's skipper, Lieutenant Commander D. T. Eller, and added, "When I sent you on a rescue I didn't know I was also going to give you monkey meat for a picnic."

Admiral Sherman is bitter over some of the Japanese incidents of brutality to his pilots. He says one Jap fighter pilot, out of ammunition, deliberately ran his propeller into one of our parachuting fliers.

LAST MISSION

2/16/44

ABOARD AN AIRCRAFT CARRIER, Somewhere in the Pacific. It was from some of the youngsters on the forward guns that I learned about the captain of this carrier, and incidentally something about the youngsters.

It was still dark. We had just put off the dawn patrol, and I had had someone point out to me the Southern Cross, which below the equator is to amateur astronomers what the Big Dipper is north of the equator. We were at general quarters, with all hands at battle stations. I had been on the flag bridge watching the operation, and then I went over to the forward gun platform to talk with these youngsters.

One of them, who has a wife and two children in Massachusetts, plays in the ship's band. He and a partner had a garage until the draft took their help, whereupon they closed up and our friend joined the Navy. With him was a blond youngster who also plays in the band. He grew up in New Jersey but has a wife and baby in Tennessee.

"How old is the baby?" I asked.

"Two months and three days," he said, which shows what kind of new father he is. He has never seen his baby. He studied music at the Juilliard School in New York, and like his buddy he stands by on the guns when the call for battle stations is sounded.

I didn't bring up the matter of the skipper. They did.

I was saying how glad I was to be aboard.

"We think we have the best skipper in the Navy," said one of the boys.

"His talks to us before we go into battle are wonderful," said the other. "You should have heard the talk he made to us when the ship was commissioned. He said this ship would take us right into Tokyo."

Some of these boys think it is the skill of the captain that has brought the carrier through six tough fights without a scratch.

"You should have seen the near misses dropping around us on the Rabaul strike!" one of them said. "They were coming down right close on one side and then on the other side, but the skipper just swung her around and we got through between them."

When I asked the captain about it, he said God was with the ship. He has had luck, and not the least of it is to have a friendly, straight-shooting personality to go with his skill. He does not go in for the bellowing, sadistic explosions affected by old-time sea dogs. He commands not only the confidence of the entire personnel but its affection, to a degree I have not observed elsewhere in this war, and which officers aboard say is exceptional.

Any number of bluejackets have volunteered to me some remark or other about the skipper of this happy ship. They say they will make any kind of fight for him.

2/17/44

ABOARD AN AIRCRAFT CARRIER, Somewhere in the Pacific. Few aside from professional Navy people can really know what is involved in being the skipper of a capital ship, especially of a new carrier such as this one.

A month after this ship was launched the captain set up offices ashore at the shipyard. From then until the middle of last year he and his staff worked at outfitting the ship. When the outfitting was finished they marched the crew aboard, and a month was spent in drilling, putting stores aboard, testing equipment. It took 1 week just to load the ammunition, with the crew working until midnight or 2 A.M., the captain said.

When the ship was transferred to the Pacific she was used on one run as a transport, and carried not only extra planes but 2,600 Navy personnel, which with the crew meant a total of more than 5,000 men aboard. It meant sleeping in passageways and on deck, and running the mess at double capacity.

This ship had its first action on Armistice Day at Rabaul. It was in action on Christmas Day and on New Year's Day. As one of the gun crew pointed out, "We hit on holidays."

I said the next holiday was Lincoln's Birthday. "We won't wait for that," the gunner said. "We'll make our own holidays."

The chaplain said a majority of the men on this ship had never been to sea before they set out last summer, and that an even larger proportion had never been aboard a carrier. He said few of those aboard were aware of the change that was taking place, as the green crew shook down into high efficiency, until they had their baptism of fire at Rabaul—when 150 Japanese planes, including many dreaded "Bettys," or low bombers, were fought off with heavy losses to the Japs, and not one man pulled away from his post during the engagement.

The skipper who has been the subject of these observations volunteered to me from all over the ship is not an impressive-looking man. He is lean, like most fliers, and very bald. He has humorous, blinking eyes, and a rather slow, drawling speech.

Perhaps a part of his success is due to his exceptional experience in this war with carriers. The captain was executive officer of a carrier operating in the Atlantic. Then he was given command of the first carrier to be converted from a cargo vessel. Then he was chief of staff to an air command, and most of this tour of duty was spent at sea. Under that particular command air cover was provided for the Casablanca phase of the North African invasion.

Thus at forty-seven, after 24 years of flying, he has had experience in this war on both big and small carriers and as a chief of staff.

He is prouder of this ship than of anything else that will ever come to him. Last summer he was able to anchor it in a river almost in front of his home.

"I couldn't help showing my ship off for the family," he said.

2/19/44

This is Raymond Clapper's last column. It was written aboard the carrier from which he flew to his death in the Battle of the Marshall Islands. The column was only about two-thirds completed; the second page of manuscript carried the slug "More."

WITH THE PACIFIC FLEET, in the Marshall Islands. Contrary to many predictions that I heard in Washington and in the Southwest Pacific, the invasion of the Marshalls did not prove to be another Tarawa. All concerned had one thought in mind in planning the Marshalls campaign—that there must be no repetition of Tarawa.

Nobody will admit officially that Tarawa fell short of what it should have been. But there were some faults in the plan of operations. For the Marshalls campaign, changes in planning were made to ensure that no matter how much delay the troops might encounter upon reaching shore, their cover would stay with them and hold the Japs in their holes.

Furthermore, the approach to the main objectives was planned on an entirely different basis for the Marshalls campaign. We not only made sure that the Japanese air power was knocked out before our landings began, but the landings themselves were planned differently.

We slipped around to one of the rear atolls where we were not expected. On the first day we occupied small undefended islands near the larger ones of Roi and Kwajalein. The purpose in occupying those was to set up artillery for heavy bombardment of our main targets.

And above all there was an enormous concentration of the Pacific fleet, with sufficient strength to have taken on any defense Japan wanted to attempt, including the use of her fleet.

The night before the battle began the captain of the happy carrier which I was aboard during the air attack talked to his entire ship about the battle that was about to begin. He said the Marshalls battle was well planned and carefully thought out, and that we started out with "a powerhouse of strength." He said this was the biggest task group ever assembled in the Pacific.

The men aboard all had complete confidence. There were no jitters. There was almost a holiday air, because they knew that what the captain said was true. For days we had traveled in the midst of a large number of battleships, cruisers, and other carriers. You could not look around the horizon without seeing the flat tops of carriers and the peaked-pagoda effect of the low-water silhouettes of our newest battleships.

After the first days of hammering at Kwajalein, as we swung out for our "strike" the next morning before dawn at Eniwetok, which is within bomber range of the great Jap base at Truk, one of our Navy fighter pilots, Lieutenant Robert A. Ogden, an Ohio State law graduate from Portsmouth, O., reflected the spirit on board when he announced, "Tomorrow night, 'East Lynne' at Eniwetok."

We are not bothering to clean out all the Japs from the Marshall Islands. It is more economical, and just as effective, to cut them off and let them "die on the vine," as the method is referred to out here. That is what General MacArthur is doing in New Guinea. It is a form of piecemeal blockade.

(more)

Here the dispatch ended.